China and the United States

China and the United States

Cooperation and Competition in Northeast Asia

Edited by Suisheng Zhao

palgrave
macmillan

CHINA AND THE UNITED STATES

First published in 2008 by PALGRAVE MACMILLAN® in the US—a division of St. Martin's Press LLC, 175 Fifth Avenue, New York, NY 10010.

Where this book is distributed in the UK, Europe and the rest of the world, this is by Palgrave Macmillan, a division of Macmillan Publishers Limited, registered in England, company number 785998, of Houndmills, Basingstoke, Hampshire RG21 6XS.

Palgrave Macmillan is the global academic imprint of the above companies and has companies and representatives throughout the world.

ISBN-13: 978-0-230-60848-1
ISBN-10: 0-230-60848-5

Library of Congress Cataloging-in-Publication Data

China and the United States : cooperation and competition in northeast Asia / edited by Suisheng Zhao.
p. cm.
Includes bibliographical references and index.
ISBN 0-230-60848-5
1. United States—Foreign relations--China. 2. China—Foreign relations—United States. 3. United States—Foreign economic relations—China. 4. China—Foreign economic relations—United States. 5. International cooperation—Case studies. 6. Competition—United States. 7. Competition—China. 8. East Asia—Politics and government. 9. East Asia—Economic conditions. I. Zhao, Suisheng, 1954–

E183.8.C5C4634 2008
327.73051—dc22 2008015073

A catalogue record of the book is available from the British Library.

Design by Scribe Inc.

First edition: November 2008

10 9 8 7 6 5 4 3 2 1

Printed in the United States of America.

To Yi, Lillian, Sandra, and Justinian

Contents

About the Editor and Contributors

The Editor

Suisheng Zhao is Professor and Executive Director of the Center for China–U.S. Cooperation and the Institute of U.S.–East Asia Cooperation at Graduate School of International Studies, University of Denver; founder and editor of the *Journal of Contemporary China*; a member of the Board of Governors of the U.S. Committee of the Council for Security Cooperation in the Asia Pacific (USCSCAP); a member of National Committee on U.S.–China Relations; a Research Associate at the Fairbanks Center for East Asian Research in Harvard University; and a *jianzhi* professor at Beijing University, Renmin University and Fudan University. A Campbell National Fellow at Hoover Institution of Stanford University, he was Associate Professor of Political Science/International Studies at Washington College in Maryland, and Associate Professor of Government/East Asian Politics at Colby College in Maine. He received a PhD degree in political science from the University of California, San Diego; a MA degree in Sociology from the University of Missouri; and a MA degree in economics from Peking University. He is the author and editor of nine books. His most recent books are *China-U.S. Relations Transformed: Perspectives and Strategic Interactions* (Routledge, 2008); *Debating Political Reform in China: Rule of Law versus Democratization* (M. E. Sharpe, 2006); *A Nation-State by Construction: Dynamics of Modern Chinese Nationalism* (Stanford University Press, 2004); *Chinese Foreign Policy: Pragmatism and Strategic Behavior* (M. E. Sharpe, 2003); *China and Democracy: Reconsidering the Prospects for a Democratic China* (Routledge, 2000); *Across the Taiwan Strait: Mainland China, Taiwan, and the Crisis of 1995–96* (Routledge, 1999). His articles have appeared in *Political Science Quarterly*, *The Wilson Quarterly*,

Washington Quarterly, *International Politik*, *The China Quarterly*, *World Affairs*, *Asian Survey*, *Asian Affairs*, *Journal of Democracy*, *Pacific Affairs*, *Communism and Post-Communism Studies*, *Problems of Post-Communism*, *Issues and Studies*, and elsewhere.

CONTRIBUTORS

Chien-min Chao is Professor and Director of Sun Yat-sen Graduate Institute of Social Sciences and Humanities at National Chengchi University. He has been a visiting distinguished professor at George Washington University, and visiting teaching professor at University of Wisconsin, Madison. He has won a variety of research and publication awards. He has written and edited eight books, including *Lee Teng-hui's Legacy: Democratic Consolidation and Foreign Relations* (M. E. Sharpe, 2002); *Rethinking the Chinese State: Strategies, Society, and Security* (Routledge, 2001); *The ROC on the Threshold of the 21st Century: A Paradigm Reexamined* (University of Maryland, 1999); *Cross-strait Relations and Taiwan's Foreign Policies* (Taipei, 2000); *An Analysis to Contemporary Chinese Politics* (Wunan, 1997); *Taiwan and Mainland China: Relations and Foreign Competition* (Yeh-yeh, 1992); *Authoritarian Politics* (Youshi, 1994). Dr. Chao has also produced over one hundred articles in academic journals such as *Asian Survey, China Quarterly, Journal of Contemporary China, Pacific Affairs, Issues & Studies, Chinese Law and Government, and Zhongguo dalu yanjiu*, among others, and book chapters.

John F. Copper is the Stanley J. Buckman Distinguished Professor of International Studies at Rhodes College in Memphis, Tennessee. Dr. Copper is the author of more than twenty books on Asia and international affairs. In addition, he has written several monographs, edited one book, coedited one book, and cotranslated two books. He has also contributed to more than forty books and has published over seventy articles in academic journals and magazines. A number of his public addresses have been published. Professor Copper has testified several times before the Senate Foreign Relations Committee and the House Foreign Affairs Committee and its Sub-committee on Asia and Pacific Affairs. Dr. Copper was a member of the Board of Governors of the East West Center (an appointment made by the White House and the Secretary of State) from 1983 to 1989. He is currently on the Board of Directors of the American Association for Chinese Studies, and is a member of the editorial board of the journal *Asian Affairs.* Professor Copper is listed in *Who's Who in the World*, *Who's Who in America*, *Men of Achievement*, *Contemporary Authors*, *Annual Guide* *to Public Policy Experts*, and *Who's Who in Asian Studies*. In 1997, Dr. Copper was the recipient of the International Communications Award. Professor Copper has spent more than thirteen years in Asia teaching and doing research.

Lowell Dittmer received his PhD from the University of Chicago in 1971. His scholarly expertise is the study of contemporary China. He teaches courses on contemporary China, Northeast Asia, and the Pacific Rim. His current research interests include a study of the impact of reform on Chinese Communist authority, a survey of patterns of informal politics in East Asia, and a project on the China–Taiwan–U.S. triangle in the context of East Asian regional politics. Professor Dittmer's recently published books and monographs include *Sino-Soviet Normalization and Its International Implications* (University of Washington Press, 1992); *China's Quest for National Identity* (with Samuel Kim, Cornell University Press, 1993); *China Under Modernization* (Westview Press, 1994); and *South Asia's Nuclear Crisis* (M. E. Sharpe, 2005).

Bonnie S. Glaser has served as a consultant on Asian affairs since 1982 for the Department of Defense, the Department of State, Sandia National Laboratories, as well as other agencies of the U.S. government. She is also a senior associate at the Center for Strategic and International Studies (CSIS) in Washington, DC, and a senior associate with Pacific Forum CSIS in Honolulu, Hawaii. Ms. Glaser has written extensively on Chinese threat perceptions and views of the strategic environment, China's foreign and security policy, Sino–American relations, U.S.–Chinese military ties, cross-strait relations, Chinese assessments of the Korean peninsula, Sino–Russian relations, and Chinese perspectives on missile defense and multilateral security in Asia. Her writings have been published in *China Quarterly, Asian Survey, International Security, Problems of Communism, Contemporary Southeast Asia, American Foreign Policy Interests, Far Eastern Economic Review, the Korean Journal of Defense Analysis, the New York Times, the International Herald Tribune*, as well as various edited volumes on Asian security. Ms. Glaser is a regular contributor to the Pacific Forum quarterly Web journal *Comparative Connections*. She is currently a board member of the U.S. Committee of the Council for Security Cooperation in the Asia Pacific and a member of the Council on Foreign Relations, and she served as a member of the Defense Department's Defense Policy Board China Panel in 1997. Ms. Glaser received her BA in political science from Boston University and her MA with concentrations in international economics and Chinese studies from the Johns Hopkins School of Advanced International Studies.

Robert M. Hathaway has been director of the Asia Program at the Woodrow Wilson International Center for Scholars since 1999. Prior to that, he served for twelve years on the professional staff of the Foreign Affairs Committee of the U.S. House of Representatives, where he specialized in American foreign policy toward Asia. Dr. Hathaway has also been a member of the History Staff of the Central Intelligence Agency, and has taught at George Washington University and at Barnard, Middlebury, and Wilson colleges. He holds a PhD in American Diplomatic History from the University of North Carolina. He has authored three books and numerous articles on U.S. foreign policy since 1933. Recent coedited reports include *Hard Sell: Attaining Pakistani Competitiveness in Global Trade* (Wilson Center, 2008); *Fueling the Future: Meeting Pakistan's Energy Needs in the 21st Century* (Wilson Center, 2007); and *George W. Bush and East Asia: A First Term Assessment* (Wilson Center, 2005). He is a member of the Council on Foreign Relations and the National Committee on U.S.-China Relations.

Chih-Chia Hsu is Associate Professor at Ming Chuan University, Taiwan. His current researches focus on Chinese foreign policy, Chinese politics, international relations, and cross-strait relations. His recent publications include *Chinese Foreign Policy and Sino-American Relations* (in Chinese, 2004); *Chinese Foreign Policy Decision-Making Patterns in the Era of Deng* (in Chinese, 2000); "Foreign Policy Decision-Making Process in Deng's China: Three Patterns for Analysis" in *Asian Perspective* (1999), and several journal articles.

Steven Levine is Associate Director of the Maureen and Mike Mansfield Center at the University of Montana. He received his PhD from Harvard University and, over a thirty-five-year academic career, has also taught, inter alia, at American University, Columbia University, Duke University, and the University of North Carolina at Chapel Hill, where he was founding director of the Carolina Asia Center. He is widely published in the field of modern Chinese history, Chinese foreign policy, and East Asian international relations, and has translated several scholarly books from Chinese and Russian into English. He is now working with the Chinese scholar-essayist Zi Zhongyun on her English-language autobiography; with Michael H. Hunt on a book on America's Pacific Wars; and he is translating a new Russian-language biography of Mao Zedong by Alexander Pantsov, incorporating many new materials from Soviet and Comintern archives.

Christopher Marsh is Director of Asian Studies and Director of the Keston Center for Religion, Politics, and Society, as well as associate professor of political science and church–state studies, at Baylor

University. His research and teaching interests range from religion and politics to the role of identity in international relations. Professor Marsh's geographical focus is on China, Eastern Europe, and the former Soviet Union. Dr. Marsh is the author or editor of eight books, including *Unparalleled Reforms: China's Rise, Russia's Fall, and the Interdependence of Transition* and *U.S.-China Relations in the Twenty-first Century* (with June Teufel Dreyer). In addition, Dr. Marsh has authored over forty journal articles and book chapters, including those published in *The National Interest*, *Religion, State & Society*; *Nationalism and Ethnic Politics*; *Journal of Church and State*; and *Communist and Post-Communist Studies.* In his new book project, *One Nation Under God*, Dr. Marsh is exploring the intersection of ethnic, religious, and state identity in post–Communist societies. Dr. Marsh sits on the board of several journals, and serves as chairman of the editorial board of *Demokratizatsiya: The Journal of Post-Soviet Democratization*. He also works closely with the Institute on Culture, Religion, and World Affairs at Boston University, where he regularly directs research projects on religion and culture in Communist and post–Communist societies.

Robert Sutter specialized in Asian and Pacific Affairs and U.S. foreign policy in a U.S. government career of thirty-three years involving the Congressional Research Service of the Library of Congress, the Central Intelligence Agency, the Department of State, and the Senate Foreign Relations Committee. He was, for many years, the Senior Specialist and Director of the Foreign Affairs and National Defense Division of the Congressional Research Service. He also was the National Intelligence Officer for East Asia and the Pacific at the U.S. Government's National Intelligence Council, and the China Division Director at the Department of State's Bureau of Intelligence and Research. A PhD graduate in History and East Asian Languages from Harvard University, Robert Sutter taught part time for over thirty years at Georgetown, George Washington, and Johns Hopkins universities, and the University of Virginia. His current full-time position is Visiting Professor of Asian Studies at the School of Foreign Service, Georgetown University. He has published fifteen books, over one hundred articles, and several hundred government reports dealing with contemporary East Asian and Pacific countries and their relations with the United States. His most recent work is *China's Rise: Implications for U.S. Leadership in Asia* (East-West Center, 2006).

Liang Wang received his MA degree from the Elliott School of International Affairs, The George Washington University in 2007. A Young Leaders fellow with Pacific Forum, based in Hawaii, he has worked at Center for Strategic and International Studies in Washington, DC and the Chinese Academy of Social Sciences in Beijing. His academic interests include Chinese foreign policy, East Asian international relations, and environmental politics and civil society in China. His writings have appeared in *South China Morning Post* and *The Straits Times.* Mr. Wang received his MPhil degree from the University of Hong Kong, and BA degree from Foreign Affairs College in Beijing.

Introduction

Suisheng Zhao

At the Asia-Pacific Economic Cooperation (APEC) Summit held in Australia during September 2007, U.S. President George W. Bush addressed an audience of Pacific Rim business elite to discuss the war on terror, while Chinese President Hu Jintao talked about the business opportunities that China's growth was producing. One reporter captured this moment and suggested that the messages "underscore how Washington and Beijing are now being perceived in the Asia-Pacific region, where the U.S. role seems to be slipping, while China is seen as the power of the future." According him, "The terrorist attacks in 2001 and the war in Iraq drew Washington's attention from Asia, . . . just as China's historic reemergence gained critical mass."[1] This suggestion echoed the observation of an article two years earlier: "At gatherings such as APEC's annual summit, the US is suddenly no longer the only power to which lesser nations pay tribute. Strengthened by the relentless growth of its economy, China wields more influence among its Asian neighbors with every passing year."[2]

Is this observation accurate? This edited book attempts to address this controversial issue by exploring the implications of China's rise for U.S.–China relations, with a focus on their cooperation and competition in Northeast Asia. Located centrally in the Asia-Pacific region, Northeast Asia includes the main part of the Asian continent and wedges westward into the Eurasian heartland, borders northward on the Arctic Ocean, and, eastward, occupies the island chains of the western Pacific Ocean. Northeast Asia is the home of three great powers—China, Japan, and Russia—and two most dangerous hotspots left from the cold war era—the Korean Peninsula and the Taiwan Strait. While the United States is not geographically located in Northeast Asia, it has had a presence historically and strategically in this region in many ways, including current military stationing in Japan and South Korea.

China's steady rise to a global power status in the twenty-first century has fundamentally transformed the U.S.–China relationship in general, and the two great powers' relative positions in Northeast Asia in particular, and has raised many crucially important, but answered, questions. What are the challenges of China's rise for leaders in both Washington and Beijing in managing their bilateral relationship in the global, as well as the Asian, context? To what extent are the United States and China locked in a zero-sum competition or evolving into a stable and cooperative relationship? Has the rise of China produced the effect of power realignment among regional powers in Northeast Asia? How have the major Asian regional players responded to evolving U.S.–China competition and cooperation and made policy adjustments?

This book seeks answers to the controversial questions of competition and cooperation between China and the United States in Northeast Asia to help understand great power relations in the twenty-first century. It is not the intention of this book to find a consensus on these controversial questions, as it is not possible. The contributors to this book indeed try to address the different views and controversies concerning this critically important relationship at the global and regional levels. Chapter 1 provides a survey of the debates among Chinese and American scholars and policymakers about the implications of China's rise for U.S.–China relations at a global level, and the consequent policy responses by the leaders in Beijing and Washington to the transformation of U.S.–China relations. It finds that the key issue in the debate is whether to see China's rise as a zero-sum game or non-zero-sum game in international relations. A zero-sum game approach tends to result in a confrontational policy, while a non-zero-sum approach tends to produce a cooperative policy. Following China's rise, suspicions about each other's strategic intentions have made the zero-sum game approach appealing to many people in both countries, and has given rise to a perception of the "China threat" in the United States and a perception of the "U.S. threat" in China. This chapter argues that both perceptions are a threat to bilateral cooperation between the United States and China, as they have brought, and will continue to bring, fears that breed a sense of inevitability of conflict, which may, in turn, become one of the courses of conflict to divide the world into the dangerous new cold war.

Against the background of the general policy debate in the United States and China, Chapter 2 by Robert Sutter explores how China's rise has transformed U.S.–China relations in the Asia-Pacific context. Like at the global level, the transformation of U.S.–China relations in Asia is also a controversial issue. While some see that China's rise has resulted in a realignment of power against the United States in Asia, others argue that U.S. leadership is not shaken in the region. In response to a wide range of assessments and commentaries that depict an emerging Asian order led by a rising China, with the United States—the longstanding regional leader—playing an increasingly secondary role, Sutter shows that these assessments and commentaries tend to follow a pattern that emphasizes the strengths of China's rising power and the weaknesses of the United States. This pattern was followed in recent history and led to very wrong assessments of the challenge posed by the Soviet Union to U.S. leadership in Asia in the latter 1970s, and of the challenge posed by Japan's rise to U.S. leadership in Asia during the 1980s. According to Sutter, this pattern—emphasizing the rising power's strengths and U.S. weaknesses—is unbalanced. Trying to provide a more balanced and comprehensive assessment of China's rise and U.S. leadership in Asia that also considers China's weaknesses and the United States' strengths, his chapter sees China's rise as a less serious challenge to U.S. leadership in Asia. He points out that an important element to consider in assessing China's rise and its implications for U.S. leadership in Asia involves the role that the many independent-minded governments in Asia play in defining the Asian regional order. He argues that these governments are key decision-makers in determining the contemporary Asian order. Their reactions to China's rise have focused on maneuvers that sustain their independence. This has worked to support continued U.S. leadership in Asia.

Domestic politics and perceptions are important variables shaping U.S.–China relations. The next two chapters examine how domestic political dynamics in the United States and China have influenced their bilateral relations. It is interesting to see that the authors find that while the domestic politics in the United States has set many barriers for a policy emphasizing a stable and cooperative relationship with China, the domestic political environment and perceptions in China are largely in favor of a cooperative relationship with the United States. Chapter 3 by Robert Hathaway focuses on aspects of the U.S. domestic political context to explore the U.S.–China relationship, and indicates that U.S.–China relations have been on a roller-coaster since the end of the cold war. Periods of tension have alternated with moments of relative stability, which are inevitably followed by another cycle of acrimony, bitter words, and hard feelings. Looking beyond the specific irritants that loom so large at any given moment, he points out that the American political system is one variable that complicates management of the Sino–American relationship and makes this relationship volatile and difficult to inject long-term stability. The characteristics of the American political system, combined with Chinese behaviors that many Americans find offensive, have created nightmares for proponents of stable relations between the world's most populous country and its most powerful nation.

Chapter 4 by Chien-min Chao and Chih-chia Hsu analyzes the worldviews of China's fourth generation leadership and their implications for Sino–U.S. Relations. It indicates that China's fourth generation leaders are mostly technocrats and, therefore, are more pragmatic than their revolutionary predecessors. Nevertheless, most of the new leaders lack experience in handling external affairs. Domestic issues are their major concerns. As a result, the new leadership reacts passively rather than proactively to international challenges. While the Hu Jintao leadership has tried to create a peaceful and harmonious environment to resolve the daunting challenges from within, he has proposed the concept of a harmonious world and cooperation with the United States because working with the United States is a rational choice and in line with China's national interests. As a result, although differences of political systems between China and the United States have been an insurmountable obstacle, China's fourth generation of leaders has displayed tremendous enthusiasm in working with the United States to confront issues facing international society. To cope with the issue, China has advocated the idea of "democratization of international relations" to appeal to international society, especially the West, that the only answer to cultural differences is through mutual respect and toleration. A harmonious worldview would ease the apprehension that China might use its newly found powers to challenge U.S. hegemony and bully its neighbors.

No matter what kind of domestic environment that leaders in Washington and Beijing have found in their making of policies toward each other, they have to face the fact that China's rise has brought great opportunities for cooperation, as well as great challenges for strategic and geopolitical competition between the United States and China, not only on many difficult bilateral issues but also on increasingly complicated regional and global issues. Among the many issues that are central to Sino–U.S. cooperation and competition are the relations of the United States and China with other major powers in a regional context that may impact the course and tenor of the U.S.-China bilateral relationship. Perhaps no other powers in a region play a more important role in this regard than those in Northeast Asia, where the rise of China has inevitably produced an effect of power realignment among four major regional players: Japan, Russia, Korea, and Taiwan. While both Beijing and Washington have worked hard to redefine their relations with these regional players in Northeast Asia, these regional players, in turn, have struggled to find their proper places between the United States and China.

Chapter 5 by Steven Levine brings a major Northeast Asian regional player into the U.S.–China relationship by examining the Japan factor in U.S.–China relations during the period of a possible power transition as a rising China plays an increasingly active and assertive role in a world dominated since the end of World War II by the United States. Levine finds that, on the whole, except for dealing with the leaden burden of history, Japan has done a good job of responding to new realities by expanding its economic and cultural ties with China, adapting its alliance with the United States, and pursuing a more active regional diplomacy of its own. Looking at Japan's past and present relations with China and the United States in the context of regional and global politics, as well as at Japan's evolving sense of its place in the post–cold war world, Levine thus characterizes Japan's lack of political principles as one of the pillars of its politics. According to him, Japan is the first truly postmodern state—one whose policies are not fixed, but infinitely flexible and opportunistic, adaptable, and unconstrained by rigid principles or transcendent truths other than the bedrock of national interest defined as state power. In this case, he predicts that in the event of a United States to China power transition, Japan would accept and accommodate the new reality with little difficulty, while the United States would be left "sleeping single in a double bed, tossing, turning, trying to forget."

Like Japan, Russia is another important player in Northeast Asia that both the United States and China have to take into consideration in their bilateral relations. Chapter 6 by Christopher Marsh and Lowell Dittmer focuses on Sino–Russian relations and their implications for U.S. foreign policy in the twenty-first century. They argue that while Sino–U.S. relations remain complicated by China's military expansion,

U.S. military operations across the globe, and the future status of Taiwan, a Sino–Russian partnership is emerging. Meanwhile, the U.S.-Russian post–cold war marriage is over, and relations between the two have become so soured that Washington and Moscow are beginning to talk of a new cold war. In such a climate, China and Russia are warming up to each other in ways seldom seen in their histories. China has concluded that its own interests are best served by a stronger Russia that is capable of maintaining some degree of distance from the United States. Russia has pursued a policy of strategic partnership with China. While it is premature to conclude that either Beijing or Moscow wishes to create some sort of alliance against Washington, the United States must be careful with its dealings with both Russia and China, as its actions will continue to affect the course of the Sino–Russian relationship in the years to come.

Chapter 7 by Bonnie S. Glaser and Liang Wang uses the North Korea nuclear crisis as a case study of Sino–American cooperation from the beginning of the crisis in 2002 to the signing of the February 13, 2007 agreement. They find that the threat posed by North Korea's nuclear programs presented a rare strategic opportunity for close U.S.–Chinese cooperation that would prove to be the first successful collaboration on an international security issue since the collapse of the Soviet Union. Determined that the North Korean nuclear issue should be addressed multilaterally rather than bilaterally, the Bush administration sought to involve China from the inception of the crisis in July 2002. China's role evolved from a passive onlooker, to a reticent host, and, finally, to a mediator. The authors examine the reasons why the United States and China have, so far, been able to effectively cooperate despite differing perspectives on North Korea and divergences in their preferred approaches to persuading Pyongyang to abandon its pursuit of a nuclear deterrent. Among the many reasons is good communication at both the presidential and lower levels in the United States and China. The episode provides potential lessons for U.S.–China cooperation on other issues.

The Taiwan issue is arguably the most difficult and strategic issue in the U.S.–China relationship. Chapter 8 by John F. Copper studies how the U.S. Bush administration has turned from a policy in favor of Taiwan to one against Taiwan in the two terms of his administration. During the 2000 election campaign, George W. Bush and his foreign policy team promised better relations with Taiwan. Coming into office, they delivered and, consequently, U.S.–Taiwan relations improved markedly. But this situation changed rather quickly in a year or so, as Washington expressed displeasure, even anger, toward the

Chen administration. Copper suggests five reasons for this major shift in U.S.–Taiwan policy: (1) early close relations with Taiwan reflected more anti-Clintonism than an anti-China policy, pro-Taiwan stance; (2) U.S., China, and Taiwan policy changed perforce due to 9/11; (3) the Bush administration became alarmed that President Chen might provoke a conflict with China that would involve the United States; (4) there was serious U.S. disappointment with the Chen administration's governance; and (5) the view grew that the opposition was not likely to try to reunify Taiwan with China, or otherwise oppose U.S. interests.

This book is a selection of papers presented at the international conference, "The Challenge of China's Rise for US-China Cooperation/Competition in Asia-Pacific," which was held at the University of Denver from June 1–2, 2007, co-sponsored by the Institute of International Relations (IIR) at the National Cheng-chi University of Taiwan and the Center for China-US Cooperation (CCUSC) at Graduate School of International Studies, University of Denver. As the Executive Director of the CCUSC, I would like to take this opportunity to thank my co-sponsoring institution for the pleasant collaboration experience. I would also like to thank my executive assistant, Ms. Yvette Peterson, for her most able assistance that assured the great success of the conference.

NOTES

1. Charles Hutzler, "Hu's Up, Bush Down at Pacific Rim Summit," *Associated Press*, September 8, 2007.
2. John Burton, Victor Mallet, and Richard McGregor, "A New Sphere of Influence: How Trade Clout is Winning China Allies yet Stoking Distrust," *The Financial Times*, December 9, 2005.

Chapter 1

The Transformation of U.S.–China Relations

Suisheng Zhao

In a 1999 *Foreign Affairs* article, one Western scholar asked a highly controversial question at that time, "Does China matter?" and his answer was that, "at best, China is a second-rank middle power that has mastered the art of diplomatic theater."[1] This question has become less controversial since then, as China, today, is widely recognized as rising to the first-rank great power status in the twenty-first century. In a 2006 article on China's dramatic rise, one Western observer asserted that "Czarist Russia's emergence in the 18th-century European system and the respective rises of Germany and Japan at the end of the 19th century were comparatively of far less magnitude."[2] The controversial question today in the capitals of many Western countries and the Asia-Pacific is no longer "Does China matter?" but if, and how, China will use its rising global influence to challenge the current international system.

While appreciating "the fact that China's rise would have serious implications for other countries, especially the US" and that "China is likely to confront with growing suspicion and even resistance on the part of some countries especially the US,"[3] Chinese leaders have continued to emphasize that China is still a developing country facing considerable domestic and international challenges in its long march toward modernization. Indeed, if one focuses exclusively on China's domestic problems, or what has yet to be done to catch up with the developed world, particularly at per capital income level with a population of more than 1.3 billion, China's capacity to influence the international system on a massive scale can appear illusory. However, if one considers the speed of its economic growth, social transformation, and increasing global activism in the recent decades, while keeping in mind the Chinese empire's past cultural, economic, and political centrality in Asia, the question of China's global influence becomes obvious.

One of the most powerful nations in the world before the spread of the Industrial Revolution, China accounted for about one-third of the world's output as recently as the early nineteenth century. Its share of the global output began a steady decline in the twentieth century, as it plunged into chaos involving war, famine, isolation, and revolution. This trend is just opposite to that of the United States, which accounted for only about 1–2 percent of world output in the early nineteenth century, but shot up to about 20 percent and maintained this level in the twentieth century. U.S. Congressman Henry Hyde acknowledged this contrast in trends at a 2006 Congressional hearing: "While our founding fathers were waging their struggle for independence in 1776, China was already not only the most populous, but the wealthiest, nation in the world. From this apex of cultural, political, and economic influence, China plunged rapidly into two centuries of chaos involving war, famine, and revolution. Now, as this new century dawns, China has reemerged into its traditional position of influence in Asia and the world. . . . The Summer Olympics of 2008 is their symbol of this national reemergence from a dark cocoon of decline and isolation into the light of international recognition."[4] Indeed, with an average 10 percent economic growth rate, and increasingly proactive global engagement in recent decades, China is quickly reemerging to the status of a great power in the twenty-first century. If China is able to sustain the growth momentum during recent decades, it will ultimately match the United States, and regain the glorious position it enjoyed over two hundred years ago.

China's rise has transformed the most important bilateral relations in the twenty-first century. For more than a decade after the end of the cold war, the United States was the sole superpower in terms of economic, diplomatic, and military might. Now China has steadily stepped up to demonstrate rapidly rising economic, political, and military power as a counterweight to U.S. influence, both globally. and regionally in the Asia-Pacific. How have the leaders in Washington and Beijing responded to the challenges of China's rise to make policy adjustments in their bilateral relations? And will China's rise trigger an inevitable conflict between these two great nations? These are the crucially important questions that this chapter is going to seek answers to.

DEBATING THE IMPLICATIONS OF CHINA'S RISE FOR U.S.–CHINA RELATIONS

In spite of theoretical equality and anarchy in the modern nation-state system, a hierarchical power structure exists, and is acknowledged by national leaders. "This global hierarchy is constantly in flux, reflecting variations in relative power driven by differential nation-state growth rates and movements of capital and resources across frontiers."[5] A hegemonic state commends the dominant position over other states, resting on a robust economic base and military capabilities, supplemented and solidified by soft normative power. The hegemonic state, therefore, has vested interests in maintaining the status quo of the established international system, as their values and interests are universalized to the point where they largely conform to the rules, values, and institutions of the system. But there has never been a hegemonic power lasting for forever in world history. Rising powers often inevitably demand a change in the power hierarchy when their capacities approach that of the dominant power. In this process, they often become anti-status quo powers to challenge the established system because rising powers, unsatisfactory to a system created by dominant states, want to reshape the rules and institutions of the system according to their own interests and values. Defending its authoritative position, the hegemonic power most often has to confront the challengers in order to resist a power transition. The rivalry between a hegemon and a rising power, therefore, is fraught with dangerous conflicts, which are most probable as the two states reaches power parity.[6]

Indeed, the rise of great powers was, historically, often associated with transformation of the relationship between the rising powers and their more established counterparts, including restructuring the hierarchy, i.e., the power transition from dominant states to challengers in the international system. Whether or not a systemic power transition took place, the inevitable power competition between the rising powers and their established counterparts often caused disruptive conflicts and even large-scale wars. During the twentieth century, except the competition between the United States and the United Kingdom that resulted in a more or less peaceful power transition from a hegemonic Pax Britannica to a Pax Americana, all other great power competitions were violent and disruptive. The rivalry between Germany and the United Kingdom was one important cause leading to World War I; the challenge of rising Germany and Japan to the international system was followed by World War II; and the competition between the Soviet Union and the United States caused a prolonged cold war.

In today's world of hierarchy, the United States remains at the top as the dominant power. However, "US pre-eminence is declining *in relative terms*."[7] In the meantime, China has experienced remarkable economic growth in recent decades. Some predictions expect China's economy will be equal to, or surpass the size of, the U.S. economy in the foreseeable future. A 2006 survey by the Chicago Council on Global Affairs and the Asia Society revealed that "60% of Americans believe that China's economy will grow to be as large as the U.S. economy within two decades or so."[8] One 2007 *Financial Times* commentary even boldly suggested that "the era of American global dominance is coming to a close," and may be overtaken by China in about twenty years.[9]

Taking advantage of its rising economic power, China has significantly asserted its influence throughout Asia and expanded to other regions of the world. As a rising economic, political, and military power, China's diplomatic activism has been increasingly observed well beyond its neighboring Asian countries into Latin America, Africa, the Middle East, and Europe.[10] Although China has not reached the position of parity with the American power status, its rapid rise has profoundly transformed the Sino–U.S. relationship, and made the bilateral relationship increasingly strategic and globally significant. Consequently, a profound theoretic debate about the implications of China's great power aspiration for U.S.–China relations has taken place among scholars and policy makers in both the United States and China.

Liberal optimists see contemporary international politics as a non-zero-sum game. According to this view, the currently prevailing international system, built under the leadership of the United States after World War II, is different from the imperial systems of the past because it "is built around rules and norms of nondiscrimination and market openness, creating conditions for rising states to advance their expanding economic and political goals within it."[11] From this perspective, China's emergence as a global power may provide opportunities for expanding U.S.–China cooperation on a wide range of global and regional issues in a period of rapid globalization and growing strategic interdependence because "globalization has increased the common stakes for China and the United States. The two countries have a common interest on almost all important international issues, such as fighting terrorism, the proliferation of weapons of mass destruction, trade liberalization, environmental protection, energy, transnational crime, and pandemic diseases."[12] Strategic and economic interdependence, therefore, has become a positive force in integrating China into the established international economic and political system, in which economic self-interests and growing networks of international involvement will impose their own constraints on China and help ensure its emergence as a responsible stakeholder. As a result, "the rise of China does not have to trigger a wrenching hegemonic transition. The US-China power transition can be very different from those of the past because China faces an international order that is fundamentally different from that past rising states confronted. China not just faces the United States; it faces a Western-centered system that is open, integrated, and rule-based, with wide and deep political foundations."[13]

In this view, although China is not a fully satisfied power in the international system because of its historical grievances against the Western powers, and unresolved issues such as Taiwan, China is basically a status quo power, eager to be part of the international community, as it has benefited enormously from the international political and economic system since the late 1970s. "China's development is shaped by the international system and, most significantly, as an important participant, China is also helping to shape the changing international system at the beginning of the twenty-first century."[14] China's search for a greater role in world affairs, in this case, will not necessarily threaten U.S. interests, as the competition between China and the United States will not be a zero-sum game. This view is expressed by an American scholar, "Fortified by both globalization and its economic policies, China has thus become an ardent supporter of the existing international economic order. . . . In international relations, dominant states typically want to preserve the status quo and rising states want to change it. But today, it is China that wants to preserve key features of the current world order, whereas the United States, the lone superpower, seems bent on shaking it up by creating 'coalitions of the willing' assembled outside established international organizations."[15]

Realist alarmists, however, look at world politics as a zero-sum game and assert that "there will be no win-win situation in conflicts among international political entities accompanying the rise of China" because "the rise of a state's power status indicates an expansion of its political power. This in turn causes the fall of other states' power status and political power."[16] By this logic, China's rapid economic growth could transform not just into modern and effective economic power, but also into a resurgent foreign policy that would seek to alter the status quo in the international system, as a rising China will want to define its interests more expansively and seek a greater degree of influence in a somehow zero-sum game. If successful in fulfilling its expected potential, China will join a select group of modern great powers, including Great Britain in the nineteenth century, Germany and Japan during World War II, and the Soviet Union and the United States in the cold war. Each of these great powers used its rising power position to expand its influence, and pursued some form of hegemony to protect its interests, or even launched aggressive warfare against rival states. A rising China is likely to engage in an intense security competition with the United States to maximize its share of world power and lock into an epic battle over the leadership of the international system. This power competition will upset the balance of power and spark realignments in East Asia, as well as the world, because most of China's neighbors and other powers will have to make a decision about whether to join the United States or China in the new round of power competition.

Alarmists can easily find evidence of an unsatisfied China and suggest that China's rise will be fraught with tensions with the United States. China's links with the anti-American government in Venezuela, and Sudan's genocidal government that the United States has been trying to isolate, are often cited as evidence to support the assertion that China's rise will inevitably challenge U.S. interests, raising the specter of great power rivalry in the world, and forcing the realignment of international system. One study pointed out that China had adopted an increasingly aggressive policy to challenge the United States in various ways, including setting the goal in preventing intervention by the United States if China has to use force in its efforts of unification with Taiwan.[17] Another article suggested that China's new generation of leadership had begun a systematical challenge to the U.S.-led international system. "Current President Hu Jintao has shifted China in a new direction. Like Mr. Jiang, he believes that the country should assert itself. But unlike his predecessor, he seems to think that China should actively work to restructure the international system to be more to Beijing's liking. In short, the current leader appears to see his country mostly working against the U.S."[18]

Along with the theoretical debate, the rise of China has forced leaders in both Washington and Beijing to make policy adjustments in their relationship. In retrospect, the U.S.–China relationship has never been easy since their mutual diplomatic recognition in 1979. Harry Harding called it a "fragile relationship" in the 1980s, and Mike Lampton used "same bed different dreams" to characterize it in the 1990s.[19] This relationship has become more complicated after China's rise to a global power status in the twenty-first century. In addition to often sharp differences over many bilateral issues, such as the trade and human rights disputes and the Taiwan issue, political elites in both countries have become increasingly suspicious of each other's long-term strategic intentions, along with China's rise to be more competitive in the relationship with the United States. While some Americans become anxious about China's rise, many Chinese become concerned that the United States might try to keep China down. The mutual suspicions have given rise to a perception of a "China threat" in the United States, and a perception of a "U.S. threat" in China. "Opinion polls indicate that one-third of Americans believe that China will 'soon dominate the world,' while nearly half view China's emergence as a 'threat to world peace.' In turn, many Chinese fear that the U.S. will not accept their 'peaceful rise.'"[20] Both perceptions of the China threat and the U.S. threat are a threat to the maintenance of the established international system that the United States has urged China to integrate into as they have brought, and will continue to bring, that is, fears that breed a sense of inevitability of conflict, which may, in turn, become one of courses of conflict to divide the world into the dangerous new cold war. Political leaders in both the United States and China, therefore, face serious challenges with China's rise, and are forced into making policy adjustments accordingly.

The Policy Challenge to the United States

For about a century before China's recent emergence, the United States either engaged or confronted China for various purposes, but it always regarded China as secondary, important simply in the context of rivalry with other powers, such as with imperial Japan during the Pacific War and with the Soviet Union during the cold war. China's rise has changed the strategic thinking of China in the United States from "a weak China" to "a strong China," and from "the theory of a crumbling China" into "the theory of a rising China" in the most recent decade.[21] Acknowledging China's coming global power status in recent years, for the first time, the United States has to deal with China for its own sake. This change has given rise to a sense of fear among some in the United States about whether a rising China will become the post—World War II Soviet Union or the nineteenth-century Germany to challenge the international system.

The anxiety about the China threat has been intensified by China's continuing military modernization. For example, the Pentagon's 2001 *Quadrennial Defense Report* (QDR), a geopolitical blueprint issued right after the September 11 attacks, took a capacity-based approach to define enemies, and believed that "military competitor with a formidable resource will emerge in the region" and become the long-term threat to the United States. Although everyone knew the identification, the report did not mention the name "China."[22] The 2006 QDR, however, explicitly states that "of the major and emerging powers, China has the greatest potential to compete militarily with the United States and field disruptive military technologies that could over time offset traditional U.S. military advantages absent U.S. counter strategies."[23] In this case, it has become a concern among some Americans how China, as a great power, will use its influences at both global and regional levels.

At the global level, although China once acted as a revolutionary state against the established international system in the 1960s and 1970s, it was weak and isolated and, therefore, unable to pose serious challenges to U.S interests at a global scale at that time. China's rise in the twenty-first century has raised the bar for strategic rivalry between the United States and China on some important global issues in recent years. For example, as China's rapid economic growth has brought it to an unprecedented shortage of energy, the United States has become alarmed to see China going around the globe in search of raw materials and trying to lock up energy supplies from many parts of the world, including pursuing deals with countries under U.S. sanctions or with U.S. security concerns, such as Venezuela, Sudan, and Iran. This new development has raised concerns among some Americans that China is not only challenging the United States' historic dominance in many parts of the world, but also undermining Western efforts to promote transparency and human rights, thereby damaging U.S. interests and values.

In the Asia-Pacific region, a Middle Kingdom in East Asia before the nineteenth century, the Chinese empire disintegrated and Chinese power declined after its defeat at the Opium War in 1840–42. Now that China is reemerging as a great power, concerns have arisen about China's aspirations in the Asia-Pacific region. It is an unanswered question whether or not China will seek to restore the position of its ancient dominance in the region and develop a sphere of influence over its periphery for greater security. Another question is, should greater Chinese capacities enable Beijing to pursue a regional dominance, whether or not it would challenge U.S. strategic relationships with East Asian allies and diminishes U.S. strategic presence? If China were aspired to become a dominant power in the Asia-Pacific, it would certainly heighten U.S.–China conflict and cause region-wide instability.

In addition, three variables inside China have exacerbated the sense of unease among some Americans about an increasingly powerful China. One is the lack of transparency of China's rapid military modernization program. China has strived to modernize its military forces along with economic modernization, but has not told the world about how far it has gone, and will go, in its military modernization program, and what its grand strategy is. One unanswered question here is whether or not China will seek to become the leading military power and challenge U.S. predominance regionally and globally. As the 1996 QDR pointed out: "Secrecy envelops most aspects of Chinese security affairs. The outside world has little knowledge of Chinese motivations and decision-making or of key capabilities supporting its military modernization."[24]

The second variable is the rise of popular nationalist sentiments in China. Many in the United States are troubled by China's aspirations for great power status, drawing upon strong nationalism linked with the victim conviction of a "century of shame and humiliation" in the hands of imperialist powers. A rising China driven by this type of nationalist sentiment would be anything but peaceful. China's international behavior would be irrational and inflexible. It is not difficult to find evidences of rising popular nationalist sentiments in China. For example, many foreign observers were shocked to see more than twenty million Chinese signatures gathered on the Internet in early 2005 to oppose Japan's bid for the permanent membership of the United Nations' Security Council, and thousands of Chinese protesters demonstrated in major Chinese cities against Japan's approval of history textbooks that protestors claimed whitewashed Japan's wartime atrocities, as well as Japan's recent pledge to help the United States defend Taiwan in the event of a Chinese attack. Many Americans still remembered freshly about the massive anti-American demonstrations in front of U.S. diplomatic missions after the accidental bombing of a Chinese embassy in Belgrade by a U.S.-led North Atlantic Treaty Organization (NATO) force in May 1999. Many observers were astonished, at the time, by the quick and automatic conviction by the Chinese people that the U.S. bombing was deliberate.[25]

The third variable is China's reluctance to open its domestic political competition and adopt a liberal democratic polity. Many in the West have raised the question about whether China's authoritarian government could sustain its robust economic growth. The lack of effective political institutions to represent diverse social interests and reconcile competing political demands could pose a serious challenge to the Communist Party's efforts to maintain political stability, a precondition for rapid economic growth. In this case, the communist leadership may attempt to blame political instability and economic slowdown on foreign influence and seek foreign conflicts to divert attention from domestic problems. This action would be a classic case—predicted by democracy peace theory—that authoritarian governments are more prone to plunge into wars than democracies. Even if China's authoritarian system can sustain its rapid economic growth, many American policymakers would have another worry that China's performance could challenge the "Washington consensus" concerning free markets and liberal politics with a "Beijing consensus" promoting authoritarian governments, guiding economic policy to produce rapid growth with social stability.[26]

These concerns have brought about a profound policy debate in the United States about how to respond to the prospect of China's emergence as a great power. Ever since coming into office, the Bush administration has struggled to define its stance on the critical long-term issue facing the United States: whether to view China as a strategic threat and plan accordingly, or to see it as a strategic partner and work with it to shape the future international system. The Bush administration's policy toward China has moved from treating China as a threat to as a partner in the recent years.

To distinguish his Republican administration from the previous Democratic administrations, George W. Bush called China a strategic competitor, rather than a strategic partner, in his presidential election campaign. The Bush administration reversed many of the Clinton administration's China policies and took a tougher position against China on some sensitive issues during his first year of presidency. On the most sensitive Taiwan issue, the Bush administration studiously avoided mentioning Clinton's "three no's" policy: not recognizing two Chinas or one China, one Taiwan; not supporting independence for Taiwan; and not backing Taiwan to join international organizations that require sovereignty for membership. Instead, he repeatedly talked about America's obligation to the defense of Taiwan according to the Taiwan Relations Act. On April 23, 2001, Bush approved the largest package of arms sales to Taiwan since Bush, Sr., sold 150

F-16 fighters to the island nearly a decade ago. Abandoning Clinton's strategic ambiguity involving Taiwan, Bush unequivocally stated in a television interview on April 27, 2001, that his administration would take whatever actions necessary if the People's Republic of China were to attack Taiwan.

A midair collision of a Chinese jetfighter with a U.S. Navy reconnaissance plane over the South China Sea on April 1, 2001, touched off a tense, eleven-day crisis. While the incident created negative feelings and stoked nationalist sentiment in both countries, it provided an opportunity for the Bush administration to seriously look at the importance of U.S.–China relations early in his term. After a face-saving resolution for both sides was finally reached, U.S.–China relations began to improve.

The September 11 terrorist attacks further softened Bush's position because, dealing with the urgent danger of terrorism in other parts of the world, he had to work with Beijing in order to build a global coalition against terrorism. Proposing a "constructive, cooperative, and candid" relationship with China, Bush made two visits to China within a half-year after September 11, 2001. While it was unprecedented that a U.S. president visited China twice within a half-year, a third summit meeting took place in Crawford, the Bush family ranch in Texas, on October 25, 2002, roughly a year after the first summit. This was the highest frequency of meetings between the top leaders of the United States and China in history. Since then, while the Bush administration has hedged against possible China challenges,[27] it has cooperated with China on many strategically important issues, including sustaining progress in the Six-Party Talks, combating weapons of mass destruction (WMD) proliferation, supplying inexpensive goods to U.S. consumers, and responding to the growing nontraditional threats to international security, such as poverty and disease, because it has come to the realization that the two countries have a complicated relationship with a mix of cooperative and competitive interests.

At a May 2005 press conference, President Bush characterized the U.S.–China relationship as a complex one, and said that "Americans ought to view it as such." His Deputy Secretary of State, Robert Zoellick, elaborated on the complexity of the relationship in an important policy statement on September 21, 2005. On the one hand, Zoellick raised the concern about how China will use its power, criticized China's "involvement with troublesome states" and its "mercantilist" attempts to "lock up" energy resources, and urged China to adopt democratic reforms. In particular, he challenged the realist view of Chinese leaders by suggesting that the true partnership would depend upon the development of common values, not merely common interests. On the other hand, he disagreed with those who viewed China solely through "the lens of fear," and called for a cooperative relationship with China in the years ahead on a wide range of global challenges. He therefore emphasized important common interests between the two countries that could be pursued through cooperation, and proposed a U.S. policy goal of urging China to become a "responsible stakeholder" in the existing international system. to pursue the "shared interest in sustaining political, economic, and security systems that provide common benefits."[28] His successor, John Negroponte, reconfirmed this position at a U.S. Senate hearing on his confirmation when he stated: "I think we need to engage China on all levels and I think that ought to be our approach to that country, not one of confrontation but engagement."[29]

Indeed, as a 2007 *New York Times* article indicated, "the Bush administration has found a diplomatic crutch in an unlikely place: China." George W. Bush, who spent most of his presidency with a swaggering, go-it-alone style, has increasingly turned to China on problem after problem: from North Korea to Darfur to the repression of pro-democracy demonstrators in Myanmar. The *Times* article quotes Christopher R. Hill, Assistant Secretary of State for East Asian Affairs, as saying that "China has become the first stop for any American diplomacy."[30] Working so extensively with China, the Bush administration has taken a radical swing in its China policy on many issues, including the sensitive Taiwan issue. While the previous U.S. administration had very deliberately taken no position on the matter of sovereignty over Taiwan, Dennis Wilder, a senior Bush aide, said during his trip with the president to the April 2007 Asia-Pacific Economic Cooperation (APEC) Summit in Sydney that "Membership in the United Nations requires statehood. Taiwan, or the Republic of China, is not at this point a state in the international community."[31] The statement was a response to China's warning about Taiwanese President Chen Shui-bian's persistence in wanting to hold a referendum on whether it should apply for UN membership under the name "Taiwan." To preempt China's concern over this issue, in August 2007, Deputy Secretary of State John Negroponte once again expressed that Washington opposed Chen's referendum, and in December, Secretary of State Condoleezza Rice repeated that "we think that Taiwan's referendum to apply to the United Nations under the name Taiwan is a provocative policy."[32] An American commentator explained the Bush administration policy shift toward China in terms of that "national interests make strange bedfellows."[33]

THE POLICY CHALLENGE TO CHINA

For some time since the end of the cold war, two often contradictory self-images of a great power and a developing country constantly tested China's foreign policy makers.[34] While they cherished China's rising power status and wanted to play a role accordingly, China kept a low profile in international affairs and played down its pretense to being a global power while emphasizing that "the existing gap between China and the developed countries, and the United States in particular, is enormous in terms of national wealth, standard of living, education, and science and technology."[35] In this case, although China's great power aspiration sparked anxieties and hot debate in almost all world capitals, the topic remained delicate in China until very recently. A twelve-part television series with an explicit title—"The Rise of Great Powers"—broadcast twice on China's Central Television during the last two months of 2006, caught a lot of attention as the series closely looked at the ascendance of nine great powers, including Britain, Germany, Japan, and the United States, and the lessons that China could draw from their rise. The message was that "China is on the verge of the same historic rise."[36] The broadcasting was interpreted by Western media as if Chinese people were encouraged "to discuss what it means to be a major world power" and the Chinese leadership "largely stopped denying that China intends to become one soon."[37] This observation was supported by the 2006 Chicago Council on Global Affairs and the Asia Society survey, which found that 87 percent of Chinese respondents thought that China should take a greater role in world affairs. Most Chinese believed that China's global influence would match that of the United States within a decade.[38] In this case, a Western reporter suggested that although the Chinese leaders still coyly insist that China is merely a developing country, "a growing number of Chinese scholars and commentators are discarding the old bashfulness and beginning to talk openly of China's rising power."[39]

Gradually accepting China's rising power status, Beijing's leaders have insisted that China will pursue a road of peaceful development, and China's rise, therefore, will not be a threat to the United States. The concept of "China's peaceful rise" was saliently put forward for the first time by Zheng Bijian, a senior aid to Chinese President Hu Jintao, at the April 2003 Boao Forum—an annual high-level gathering of political and business leaders from Asia-Pacific countries on China's Hainan Island. Premier Wen Jiabao endorsed this concept in his New York City speech in December 2003. Since then, however, many Chinese scholars and officials have expressed their concerns about whether using the word "rise" may intimidate some of China's Asian neighbors as "the word 'rise' implies attaining superpower status."[40] As an alternative, President Hu Jintao used the words "peaceful development" in his speech at the 2004 Boao Forum. In a way to reconcile "rise" and "development," Zheng Bijian, in his 2005 Boao forum speech, elaborated that "China has chosen a strategy to develop by taking advantage of the peaceful international environment, and at the same time to maintain world peace through its development. This is a strategy of peaceful rise, namely, a strategy of peaceful development."[41] Whether using the term "peaceful rise" or "peaceful development," Chinese officials have attempted to assure China's neighbors and other major powers that, as a peace-loving and responsible power, China's rise as a global power will bring opportunities and benefits, instead of threats to peace and stability. In other words, China's rise is not a zero-sum game. The ultimate message in this concept is that China is seeking an accommodative, rather than confrontational, approach toward the United States and other powers in the process of its rise.[42]

Indeed, Chinese leaders have hoped to maintain a friendly and cooperative relationship with the United States because China's continuing rise rests on the maintenance of a favorable international environment, the most important element of which is a cooperative relationship with the United States, the unwieldy superpower holding the key to China's future of economic modernization. In this case, China has accepted the Bush characterization of the U.S.–China relationship as "complex," and welcomed Zeollick's invitation for China to become a "responsible stakeholder" in the international system. As A *China Daily* commentary suggested, the invitation as a "responsible stakeholder" indicates that the Bush administration, just as the previous six U.S. administrations, has come to see China as a "strategic partner." Chinese leaders particularly liked Zoellick's remarks that the "China of today is simply not the Soviet Union of the late 1940s: it does not seek to spread radical, anti-American ideologies; it does not see itself in a twilight conflict against democracy around the globe. It does not see itself in a death struggle with capitalism; it does not seek to overturn the fundamental order of the international system."[43] In this context, Chinese leaders were pleased to see the Bush administration move from a confrontational to a cooperative posture toward China in its second term. In particular, China was delighted to work with the Bush administration in the effort to stop Taiwan's drift toward independence. As a Chinese scholar, Wang Jisi, said: "While Taiwan's President Chen Shui-bian and his political party have pursued the island's formal secession from China; President Bush made crystal clear his opposition to a declaration of Taiwanese independence. Chinese see Washington as playing a role in restraining Taipei's separatist movement, although U.S. military ties to the island and its praise for Taiwan's democracy remain discordant cadences in U.S.-China relations."[44]

Although Chinese leaders have seen the Sino–U.S. relationship as the most crucial and important one in all of China's foreign relations and made an effort to maintain it, they have also been suspicious about American geopolitical intentions, and found working with the United States the most frustrating foreign policy challenge in recent decades. During the cold war, the United States confronted the Soviet Union and treated China as friendly nonally in the bipolar system. Now that the cold war is over and China is rising, Chinese leaders are not sure if the United States sees China as an ally, a rival, or an enemy. In the post–September 11 world, China has enjoyed the best international and neighboring environment since the establishment of the People's Republic of China (PRC). But concerns and anxieties have remained because Beijing not only sees that the United States needs cooperation from the major powers in its war against terrorism, but also the fact that the U.S. strategic objective is world hegemony. The United States still treats China as a "potential threat," and has never given up on the policy of containing China. One Chinese policy analyst believes that "because the US has clearly redefined China from a big developing country (*fazhanzhong daguo*) to a rising great power (*jueqi de daguo*), it has increasingly guarded against and tried to constrain China."[45] In this case, while some Americans have talked about a China threat, Chinese leaders are concerned about a "U.S. threat" arising mostly from the following two aspects of potential conflict between the two countries.

The first is a potential ideological conflict between China as the largest "communist" state left in the post–cold war world and the Western democracies, particularly the United States. Chinese leaders have worried that ideologues in the United States may want to subvert China's political system and the Chinese Communist Party (CCP) regime in the name of spreading democracy. A Chinese scholar, Zi Zhongyun, suggested that one of the basic urges of Americans in dealing with China throughout the years was to influence, educate, and change China to its liking. In this case, the difficulty in the Sino–U.S. relationship came from the fact that the development of China often took its own course beyond the control of the United States.[46] Second is the potential structural conflict between China as a rising power and the United States as the incumbent superpower. Chinese are concerned that the United States would try to do everything it could to prevent China from rising as a peer power. As a Chinese policy analyst suggested, "China's rise has led the rapid development of the structure conflict between the U.S. and China. Many previously hidden issues have begun surfacing saliently, such as economic and trade issues, geopolitical frictions, foreign policy conflict, etc. Some new issues, such as energy and environment, have come up one after another."[47] Although many in the United States have claimed that the main point of friction with China is ideological, and thus press for human rights, freedom, and democracy in China, Chinese analysts have wondered whether or not conflict will remain and grow perhaps starker, even if China rises to become democratic because they are not sure if the United States wants to see that China, even a democratic China, becomes richer and stronger than America.

To cope with the U.S. threat, Chinese leaders have made a two-pronged strategy. On the one hand, they have adopted a *taoguang yang-hui* (hide brightness and nourish obscurity) policy designed by Deng Xiaoping in the early 1990s. This policy emphasizes that China must keep a low profile in international affairs, bide its time, never take a lead, and build up its capabilities. Chinese leaders have stressed that even though the world is moving toward multipolarization, as one of the weaker poles, China cannot afford to confront the United States and exhaust itself. Facing many new challenges at home and abroad as a rising power, China is particularly concerned about possible U.S. actions to contain its continuing rise. To cope with these new challenges, Beijing abandoned the old position against the superpower hegemony and, instead, proposed "constructive strategic partnerships" with the United States, as well as all other major powers, on a more or less equal footing. In the words of a Chinese scholar, China has tried "learning to live with the hegemon," that is, making adaptation and policy adjustment to the reality of U.S. dominance in the international system.[48]

Chinese leaders have emphasized the common interests and the opportunities for cooperation between these two countries. In a speech to an American audience in Washington, DC, Zheng Bijian listed four aspects of opportunities for U.S.–China cooperation. The first "comes from a high degree of convergence of their national interests and mutual needs in the age of globalization." The second "comes from the new security concepts of major country cooperation in response to increased nontraditional security threats." The third "comes from their interest in settling regional hot spots and their joint efforts to maintain international order." And the fourth comes from the coexistence of, and interaction between, the two civilizations.[49]

On the other hand, China has tried to develop its comprehensive national strength (*zhonghe guoli*), composed of international competitiveness, an efficient and flexible diplomacy, and a compatible military capability. Because comprehensive national strength grows out of economic power, Chinese leaders have set economic modernization as the overarching national objective and pursued it enthusiastically since China decided to open up to the outside world in the late 1970s. At the sixteenth CCP Congress in October 2002, the Hu Jintao leadership reconfirmed the objective by presenting the goal of quadrupling the 2000 GDP by 2020, and transforming China into a *xiaokang* society, where the Chinese people would enjoy a much more abundant and comfortable life. Pursung this objective, China has boasted the world's fastest-growing economy in recent decades. China's rapid economic growth has transformed its position in relations with both developing countries and major powers. As one reporter pointed out: "Along the way Beijing has picked up influence, preaching a business-first message that multinationals like and that avoids the security and democracy issues the Bush administration dwells on."[50]

In this context, Chinese strategists have been particularly sensitive to *liliang duibi* (balance of forces) in the world, a Chinese term similar to the concept of distribution of power in Western international relations literature. Since the end of the cold war, while admitting the U.S. dominant power position and making pragmatic accommodations to the U.S. dominated unipolar system, China has also envisioned and promoted a multipolarization, as they see that the United States has failed to effectively control the globe unilaterally, and other big powers have adopted more or less independent policies. To actively push for a multipolar world, China has designed a network of global partnerships practically covering all the major powers and regional blocs, including Russia, France, the United States, the United Kingdom, the Association of Southeast Asian Nations (ASEAN), the European Union (EU), and Japan. Within the framework of partnership, Chinese leaders have appealed to their counterparts to abandon the cold war mentality and actively identify common interests, with the hope that differences and contradictions in political systems and values would not affect the healthy development of state-to-state relations.[51] Holding that its relationship with Washington is the most important one among all of China's bilateral relationships, Beijing has envisioned the China–U.S. relationship within a framework of strategic partnerships, with a group of great powers to balance against one another, in a multipolar world that it has perceived and promoted.

Beijing's efforts to build strategic partnerships with many major powers are to prevent their participation in any potential U.S. actions to contain China. China believes that "in the long term, the decline of US primacy and the subsequent transition to a multipolar world are inevitable, but in the short term, Washington's power is unlikely to decline, and its position in the world affairs is unlikely to change." China, therefore, has sought to maintain a stable relationship with the United States. It is, in the meantime, aware of the fact that "the Chinese-U.S. relationship remains beset by more profound differences than any other bilateral relationships between major powers in the world today."[52] Admitting the existing gap between the two countries in national power and fundamental differences between their political systems, China has set a policy priority to prevent U.S. actions from harming China's vital national interests. Taking advantage of its increasing strategic and economic assets as a rising power, China has tried to work with the United States and defend its interests in both cooperative and coercive ways. As one Chinese scholar indicates, while China has utilized its strategic assets to cooperate with the United States on issues that are of mutual interest, thereby exchanging benefits and altering the United States' negative impression on China, it has also utilized its strategic assets to thwart U.S. objectives, including using or threatening to use force, forming alliances to curb U.S. power, and voting against proposals favorable to the United States in international organizations. In the meantime, China has used its economic resources, such as market access, not only to meet the economic needs of the United States, but also to undermine U.S. economic well-being through trade embargoes, trade barriers, and so on.[53]

Chinese leaders have proposed a concept of a "world of harmony" to help reduce U.S. anxieties about China's rise, and to facilitate the strategic partnerships with other powers. The concept was presented to the international community by President Hu Jintao in his September 15, 2005, speech at the United Nations General Assembly. Derived from traditional Chinese thinking that "harmony" was at the core of dealing with everything from state affairs to neighborly relations, the concept emphasizes the peaceful coexistence of countries with different political systems and ideologies. According to a discussion among Chinese foreign affairs specialists, the world of harmony signifies, first of all, the importance of the coexistence of diversified civilizations as a very powerful driving force for the progress of the human being. Tolerance, which is free of restrictions by any ideologies and social systems, plays a role of paramount importance in bringing about peaceful coexistence of different civilizations. Applying this concept to international politics means consultation among all countries involved, not unilateralism driven by hegemonic ambitions. Big powers can play a key role in building the world of harmony as they waged fully fledged wars and the cold war in the twentieth century. Chinese analysts see big powers may alternately encounter times of strained relations and enjoy relaxed exchanges in the twenty-first century. Although the possibility of a deterioration of relations should not be ruled out, the big-power relations are poised to develop in a benign direction. The international community should help make this happen because the nature of relations between the leading global powers will determine war and peace on the world stage, and the smooth running of world affairs and upheavals.[54]

CONCLUSION

In a 2007 *Washington Post* article, Richard Holbrooke, who was Assistant Secretary of State for East Asia at the time of normalization of relations between China and the United States, stated that although the United States and China have vast differences in many areas, and profoundly different views on some fundamental issues, "there are many areas in which common interests can create opportunities. This was the concept in 1971 when Richard Nixon and Henry Kissinger opened the modern-era relationship over a shared concern about the Soviet Union, and in 1978 when Jimmy Carter established full diplomatic relations with China. Today we have a different set of issues, but they are no less pressing."[55] Indeed, in spite of the persistence of the perceptions of the "China threat" in the United States, and the "U.S. threat" in China, the U.S.–China relationship has transformed more toward cooperation. This is because while the current international system has demonstrated its remarkable capacity to facilitate Chinese integration as a rising power, the Chinese government has gradually accepted post–Cold War international reality and decided that it was not in China's interests to challenge the international system that has enabled its success and integration. If China and the United States can continue to work together for China's peaceful integration into a truly liberal international system and for China to become a stakeholder, the rise of China needs not lead to a violent power transition.

Seen in this light, mutual threat perceptions are dangerous because they could lead to the inevitable conclusion of U.S.–China conflict. Throughout history, whenever a rising power creates fear among its neighbors and other great powers, that fear becomes a cause of conflict. Joseph S. Nye reminds us of Thucydides' warning more than two millennia ago that "belief in the inevitability of conflict can become one of its main causes. Each side, believing it will end up at war with the other, makes reasonable military preparations which then are ready by the other side as confirmation of its worst fears."[56]

Consequently, it is crucially important that leaders in both Beijing and Washington not let the "threat" suspicions dictate their policy and lead the two great nations coming to a dangerous confrontation that is in the interest of neither. As Aaron Friedberg, a former senior advisor to Vice President Dick Cheney, indicated in an article of *International Security*: "Whether for good or ill, the most significant bilateral international relationship over the course of next several decades is likely to be that between the US and the PRC."[57] Joseph S. Nye also indicated that "maintaining good US-China relations will be a key determinant of global stability in this century."[58] As far-reaching as it is, leaders in both Washington and Beijing have to demonstrate their wisdom to overcome the pervasive mutual suspicions and use their political skill to communicate with each other on sensitive issues in order to assure that China's growing power produces cooperation, rather than confrontation, in the years to come. A stable U.S.–China relationship would benefit not only the United States and China, but also the broad international community for sustaining world peace and prosperity.

NOTES

1. Gerald Segal, "Does China Matter?" *Foreign Affairs*, September–October 1999, 24.
2. David Gosset, "A New World with Chinese Characteristics," *Asian Times Online*, April 7, 2006.
3. Jia Qingguo, "Learning to Live with the Hegemon: Evolution of China's Policy toward the U.S. since the End of the Cold War," *Journal of Contemporary China* 14, no. 44 (August 2005): 407.
4. "Congressional Views of China's Resurgence" *PacNet* 21–21A, May 15, 2006.
5. Ronald I. Tammen, "The Impact of Asia on World Politics: China and India Options for the United States," *International Studies Review* 8, no. 4 (December 2006): 564.
6. There is rich literature on power transition in international relations. Among them, see R. J. L. Tammen and J. Kugler, eds., *Power Transition: Strategies for the 21st Century* (New York: Deven Bridge Press, 2000); J. Kugler and D. Lemke, *Parity and War: Evaluations and Extensions of*

the War Ledges (Ann Arbor, MI: University of Michigan Press, 1996); and B. Bueno de Mesquita and D. Lalman, *War and Reason: Domestic and International Imperatives* (New Haven, CT: Yale University Press, 1992).

7. Ronald I. Tammen, "The Impact of Asia on World Politics: China and India Options for the United States," *International Studies Review* 8, no. 4 (December 2006): 564.
8. The Chicago Council on Global Affairs and the Asia Society, *The United States and the Rise of China and India: Results of a 2006 Multination Survey of Public Opinion* (Chicago, IL: The Chicago Council on Global Affairs, 2006), 15.
9. "Will China Really Overtake America?" *Financial Times*, June 11, 2007.
10. Phillip C. Saunders, *China's Global Activism: Strategy, Drivers, and Tools* (Washington, DC: National University Press, 2006), 2.
11. G. John Ikenberry, "The Rise of China and the Future of the West, Can the Liberal System Survive?" *Foreign Affairs* 87, no. 1 (January–February 2008).
12. Jianwei Wang, "Can 'Stakeholder' Hold U.S.-China Relations?" *PacNet*, May 11, 2006, p. 17A.
13. Ikenberry, "The Rise of China and the Future of the West," 24.
14. Zhiqun Zhu, *U.S.-China Relations in the 21st Century: Power Transition and Peace* (London: Routledge, 2006), 173.
15. David M. Lampton, "The Faces of Chinese Power," *Foreign Affairs* 86, no. 1 (January–February 2007): 117.
16. Yan Xuetong, "The Rise of China and Its Power Status," *The Chinese Journal of International Politics* 1, no. 1 (2006): 13.
17. Eric A. Posner and John Yoo, "International Law and the Rise of China," *Chicago Public Law and Legal Theory Working Paper*, no. 127, The Law School, the University of Chicago, May 2006, 2, 5.
18. Gordon G. Chang, "China Flexes Its Muscles," *The Wall Street Journal*, January 2, 2008.
19. Harry Harding, *A Fragile Relationship: The United States and China since 1972* (Washington, DC, Brookings Institution, 1992); David M. Lampton, *Same Bed Different Dreams: Managing U.S.-China Relations, 1989–2000*, Berkeley, CA: University of California Press, 2001.
20. Joseph S. Nye, "Taiwan and Fear in U.S.-China Ties," *Taipei Times*, January 14, 2008, p. 8.
21. David M. Lampton, "Paradigm Lost: The Demise of 'Weak China,'" *National Interest*, Fall 2005, 67–74.
22. U.S. Department of Defense, *Quadrennial Defense Report*, September 30, 2001, http://www.defenselink.mil/pubs/qdr2001.pdf.
23. U.S. Department of Defense, *Quadrennial Defense Report*, February 6, 2006, 29, http://www.qr.hq.af.mil/pdf/2006%20QDR%20Report.pdf.

24. Ibid.
25. Suisheng Zhao, "China's Pragmatic Nationalism: Is It Manageable?" *Washington Quarterly* (Winter 2005/2006), 131–44.
26. James Mann, "China's Dangerous Model of Power," *Washington Post*, May 20, 2007.
27. Sherman Katz and Devin Stewart, "Hedging Against the China Challenge," *PacNet* 43, September 29, 2005.
28. Robert B. Zoellick, "Whither China: From Membership to Responsibility?" *NBR Analysis* 16, no. 4, December 2005.
29. "Incoming Rice Deputy Seeks U.S. "'Engagement' with China," Agence France Presse, January 31, 2007.
30. Steven Lee Myers, "Look Who's Mr. Fixit for a Fraught Age," *New York Times*, October 7, 2007.
31. P. Parameswaran, "Taiwan Referendum Plan Triggers Shift in U.S. Policy," Agence France Presse, September 8, 2007.
32. "U.S. Opposes Taiwan Referendum to UN as 'Provocative,'" Agence France Presse, December 21, 2007.
33. Barry Schweid, "U.S., China Chart Parallel Courses on New Int'l Crises," *Associated Press*, March 3, 2007.
34. Wu Xinbo, "Four Contradictions Constraining China's Foreign Policy Behavior," *Journal of Contemporary China* 10, no. 27 (May 2001): 293.
35. Wang Jisi, *China's Changing Role in Asia*, The Atlantic Council of The United States, January 2004, 2.
36. Geoffrey York, "Self-confident China Sees its Own Star Rising," *Global and Mail*, December 5, 2006.
37. Joseph Kahn, "China, Shy Giant, Shows Signs of Shedding Its False Modesty," *New York Times*, December 12, 2006.
38. The Chicago Council on Global Affairs and the Asia Society, *The United States and the Rise of China and India: Results of a 2006 Multination Survey of Public Opinion* (Chicago, IL: The Chicago Council on Global Affairs, 2006), 33.
39. Geoffrey York, "Self-confident China Sees its Own Star Rising," *Global and Mail*, December 5, 2006.
40. Yan Xuetong, "The Rise of China and Its Power Status," *The Chinese Journal of International Politics* 1, no. 1 (2006): 12.
41. Cheng Bijian, "China's Peaceful Rise and New Role of Asia," *China Forum* (Autumn 2005): 3.
42. Xiaoxiong Yi, "Chinese Foreign Policy in Transition: Understanding China's Peaceful Development," *The Journal of East Asian Studies* 19, no. 1 (Spring–Summer 2005): 85–86.
43. Xue Fukang, "Hedging Strategy Won't Do Relationship Good," *China Daily*, November 21, 2005, p. 4.
44. Wang Jisi, "Reflecting on China," *The American Interest* 1, no. 4 (Summer 2006): 75.

45. Yuan Peng, "Mei dui hua jueche huanjing de bianhua ji yingxiang" [The change and influence of the China policy making environment in the U.S.], *Zhongguo Zhanlie Guancha* [China strategic review], no.8 (2006): 7.
46. Zi Zhongyun, "The Clash of Ideas: Ideology and Sino-U.S. Relations," in *Chinese Foreign Policy: Pragmatism and Strategic Behavior*, ed. Suisheng Zhao (Armonk, NY: M. E. Sharpe, 2004): 224–42.
47. Yuan Peng, "Mei dui hua jueche huanjing de bianhua ji yingxiang" ("The Change and Influence of the China Policy Making Environment in the U.S."), *Zhongguo Zhanlie Guancha* (*China Strategic Review*), no.8 (2006): 7.
48. Jia Qingguo, "Learning to Live with the Hegemon: Evolution of China's Policy toward the U.S. since the End of the Cold War," *Journal of Contemporary China* 14, no. 44 (August 2005): 395–498.
49. Zheng Bijian, *China's Peaceful Rise: Speeches of Zheng Bijian, 1997–2005* (Washington, DC: Brookings Institution Press, 2005), 10–12.
50. Charles Hutzler, "Hu's Up, Bush Down at Pacific Rim Summit," *Associated Press*, September 8, 2007.
51. Joseph Y. S. Chen and Zhang Wankun, "Patterns and Dynamics of China's International Strategic Behavior," in *Chinese Foreign Policy: Pragmatism and Strategic Behavior*, ed. Suisheng Zhao (Armonk, NY: M. E. Sharpe, 2004), 179–206.
52. Wang Jisi, "China's Search for Stability with America," *Foreign Affairs* 84, no. 5 (September–October, 2005): 40, 46.
53. Sun Xuefeng, "The Efficiency of China's Policy towards the United States," *Chinese Journal of International Politics* 1, no. 1 (2006): 59.
54. Lun Tan, "China's Dream of Harmonious Existence," *China Daily*, November 11, 2005, p. 4.
55. Richard Holbrooke, "China Lends A Hand," *Washington Post*, June 28, 2007, p. A25
56. Joseph S. Nye, Jr. "The Future of U.S.-China Relations," *PacNet* 10, March 16, 2006.
57. Aaron L. Friedberg, "The Future of U.S.-China Relations: Is Conflict Inevitable?" *International Security* 30, no. 2 (Fall 2005): 8.
58. Joseph S. Nye, "Taiwan and Fear in U.S.-China Ties," *Taipei Times*, January 14, 2008, p. 8.

Chapter 2

China's Rise and the Durability of U.S. Leadership in Asia

Robert Sutter

How Does China's Rise Affect U.S. Leadership in Asia?

China's rising importance in world affairs, and especially in neighboring Asian countries, represents a major change in Asian affairs in the early twenty-first century. China's impressive economic growth and attentive diplomacy have generally fit in well with the interests of Asian countries and ongoing Asian efforts to develop multilateral mechanisms to deal with regional and other issues. China's buildup of military power also advances at an impressive rate. Its significance tends to be played down by Chinese leaders seeking to reassure Asian neighbors of China's peaceful intentions.

Perhaps of most importance, China is now a manufacturing base and central destination in the burgeoning intra-Asia and international trading networks producing goods, notably for export to developed countries. China is the world's third largest trader and about half of its trade, including trade with Asian neighbors, involves trading arrangements where components and materials come from overseas and the finished products are sold abroad.[1]

There is also large-scale development of Chinese infrastructure. The massive investment in fixed assets—plant, property, and infrastructure—continues at an impressive rate. Capital investment, as a share of gross domestic product (GDP), is so high that the level is widely seen in both China and abroad as unsustainable, but nonetheless, it is continuing for the time being.[2] In Asia, China is a top trader with such key neighbors as South Korea, Japan, and Taiwan, and a number of Southeast Asian countries. China has emerged among the top ranks in the production of steel and other metals, cement, ships, cars, electronic goods, and textiles; and in the consumption of international raw materials.[3]

Based on recent trade growth averaging double the impressive rate of the Chinese economy, Chinese officials have built closer political ties with neighboring countries through effective and often high-level diplomacy that is attentive to the interests of neighboring Asian governments. Putting aside or narrowing differences in the interest of broadening common ground, Chinese diplomacy has been welcomed by most neighbors, especially as it contrasts positively with the sometimes maladroit and disruptive Chinese policies of the past. Chinese leaders have notably put aside past suspicion of Asian multilateral organizations and have strongly embraced burgeoning Asian groupings—some excluding the United States and other non-Asian powers—to the satisfaction of other regional participants.

The Chinese approach to Asia has developed gradually in the post-cold war period and most Chinese motives appear clear to outside observers. Chinese leaders want to secure their periphery in Asia and maintain stable relations in order to focus on key Chinese domestic issues involving economic growth and political stability. Needing economic growth at home, Chinese leaders endeavor to maximize effective economic interchange with neighboring countries. Strong Chinese nationalism and Taiwan's moves toward independence prompt Chinese leaders to step-up efforts to isolate Taiwan in Asia. Chinese leaders are also anxious to reassure neighbors and offset fears and wariness stemming from the rapid rise of China's economic and related military power. While there is broad agreement on the above Chinese motives, there is debate among specialists over how much influence China actually exerts in Asia and what this means for U.S. interests.[4]

The majority of commentaries and assessments of China's rise and Asian regionalism tends to highlight China's strengths and U.S. weaknesses.[5] Commentators often contrast growing Chinese-Asian trade figures, diplomatic activities, and positive public opinion polls with the perceived decline in U.S. influence in Asia on account of U.S. preoccupations elsewhere, military assertiveness, and poor diplomacy. They see U.S. emphasis on geostrategic issues, notably combating international terrorists, much less attractive to Asian governments and people than China's accommodating geoeconomic emphasis.

There are some specialists who judge that these trends are not particularly adverse to U.S. interests.[6] A more prevalent view in the United States is one of serious concern. Chinese leaders have worked for over fifty years to rid their periphery of great power presence. The Chinese military continues to devote extraordinary efforts to purchase and develop weapons systems to attack Americans if they were to intervene in a Taiwan contingency. China also continues to offset and counter U.S. influence in a variety of ways through trade agreements, rhetoric, Asia-only groupings and other means that amount to a soft balancing against the U.S. superpower.[7]

China's rise amid growing Asian multilateralism adds to a common view in the United States, and elsewhere, that Asia—with China at the core—is emerging as a new center of geoeconomic and geopolitical activity where an "inside-out" model of regional governance is displacing the past half century's "outside-in" model led by the United States and supported by its regional allies.[8] In the 1980s, projections were common that forecast Japan's economic prowess displacing the United States as the region's anchor. The developments of the past decade, however, are said to be very different, and more seriously challenge U.S. leadership for several significant reasons. First, China is far larger than Japan, and its rise coincides with Japan's relative decline. Japan was, and remains, a staunch U.S. ally, whereas China's current rapid military buildup is considered threatening to important U.S. security interests in the region.

Moreover, all the significant states in the region—China, Japan, India, Russia, South Korea, Indonesia, Thailand, and others—are each playing a role in advancing Asian multilateralism as means to pursue regional solutions to regional problems. In this context, U.S. leadership is seen to have been eroded by the region's growing self-confidence along with the spread of anti-Americanism, due to concerns particularly over trends in U.S. foreign policy. Unlike in the past, genuine Asian diplomatic institutions, with China in the lead, are growing in number and strengthening, often to the exclusion of the United States. For example, the 2005 East Asian summit set conditions on participation in the East Asia summit that have the effect of excluding the United States.[9]

A key question for this chapter is: how seriously does China's rise in Asia challenge U.S. interests in maintaining a leadership role in Asia? The United States has been the leading power in the Asia-Pacific region since World War II. U.S. policy has seen this continued leading role as important in support of longstanding U.S. interests in maintaining a balance of power in Asia favorable to the United States, allowing free U.S. economic access to the region, and promoting American political, religious, and other values in Asia. In what ways, and to what degree, does China's greater role in Asia challenge these interests?

Lessons of History

The record of U.S. relations with Asia reveals several findings of relevance to answering the question, how seriously does China's rise challenge U.S. leadership in Asia?[10]

U.S. Interests: Economy, Values, and Strategy Focused on Northeast Asia

Historically, U.S. relations with Asia were grounded in advancing trade and economic interests, and promoting religious and other American values. The U.S. Navy sometimes preceded U.S. diplomats in opening U.S. relations with Asian governments in the nineteenth century, but the Navy's mission focused heavily on fostering and protecting American commercial, missionary, and related interests.

Northeast Asia, especially China and Japan, was the focus of U.S. interest and has remained the top priority of the United States in Asia. The acquisition of the Philippines in the late nineteenth century gave the United States a modest stake in Southeast Asia. The United States generally cooperated with British, French, and other European colonial powers in Southeast Asia and in South Asia. Central Asia was the preserve of Tsarist Russia, and later, the Soviet Union.

U.S. Reluctance to Lead; Major Costs and Risks of Leadership.

The United States came late to leadership in the Asia-Pacific. After World War I, despite its position as a major world power and one of two leading powers in East Asia (Japan was the other), the United States was reluctant to undertake the risks, costs, and obligations of leadership. The United States used diplomatic efforts in attempts to curb Japanese expansion in East Asia following World War I and the collapse of Russia, and the weakening of Britain, France, and other European powers. These failed by the early 1930s. Nonetheless, the United States remained very reluctant to confront Japanese expansion.

The Japanese attack on Pearl Harbor put the United States in the leading role in the war effort to destroy Japan's military power and to create a new order in Asia and the Pacific. The scope of U.S. interests spread widely to include Northeast and Southeast Asia, Australia and New Zealand. and many Pacific Island countries. South Asia was still ruled by U.S. ally Great Britain, and Stalin's Soviet Union controlled Central Asia.

U.S. ambitions for a post-World War II order in the Asia-Pacific region initially featured a strong and united China, friendly to the United States and newly independent countries in Southeast and South Asia. These ambitions ran aground on realities of Chinese division and weakness, refusal of European colonial powers to withdraw from Southeast Asia, and emerging cold war competition with the Soviet Union and its allies and associates. Reflecting a reluctance to bear the continued cost of strategic leadership in Asia, the U.S. government rapidly demobilized its military forces in the Asia after World War II. U.S. occupation forces did remain in Japan.

Repeated Challenges to U.S. Leadership in the Asia-Pacific.

U.S. calculations of military withdrawal and continued peace in Asia, and U.S. interests in Asia, were fundamentally challenged by the emerging cold war in Asia. The Soviet Union and China backed North Korean assault on South Korea in June 1950. This followed the failure of U.S. policy in China with the rise of a Communist administration hostile to the United States in 1949 that aligned with Stalin's Soviet Union in a pact directed at the United States in February 1950. The war in Korea saw three years of U.S. hard combat against mainly Chinese forces in Korea that resulted in thirty-five thousand U.S. dead. The experience reinforced, in blood, U.S. determination to take the lead over the next two decades, pay the costs, and run the risks in building and maintaining strategic, economic, and political bulwarks to "contain" the spread of Chinese and Soviet-backed Communist expansion in Asia.

American leadership in Asia was repeatedly and seriously challenged. U.S.-backed French forces failed in Indochina in 1954 in the face of Chinese-backed Vietnamese Communists. The United States moved in and became more directly involved as the main backer of the non-Communist regime in South Vietnam, leading, by the 1960s, to the commitment of hundreds of thousands of U.S. troops to the war there against Chinese and Soviet-backed Vietnamese Communist forces. China militarily confronted Chiang Kai-shek and U.S.

forces in the Taiwan Strait twice in the 1950s; it developed a nuclear bomb by 1964; and it widely promoted insurgencies and "wars of national liberation" against U.S.-backed governments in Southeast Asia and elsewhere.

The nadir of U.S. influence in Asia, and the most serious challenge to U.S. leadership in Asia since Pearl Harbor, came with the collapse of U.S.-backed governments in Cambodia and South Vietnam in 1975. These developments marked the defeat of U.S. efforts in Indochina—despite enormous U.S. costs, including over fifty thousand dead. They came amid a major U.S. economic crisis partly caused by the oil shocks and energy crisis of this time, and the weak and divided U.S. government following the resignation of President Nixon and his pardon by President Gerald Ford. Anxiety among U.S.-backed governments in Northeast and Southeast Asia saw them maneuver internationally, and take measures at home in order to compensate for the obvious decline in U.S. power. The United States and China also cooperated together to deal with the rise of Soviet-backed power in the Western Pacific, Southeast Asia, and South Asia. They anticipated continued decline in U.S. regional power and influence in the Asia-Pacific region as Soviet power and dominance grew.

Faulty Forecasts of U.S. Decline in the Asia.

Forecasts of U.S. decline in the Asia proved incorrect. U.S. economic and military power at home and abroad rose markedly during the early 1980s. American resolve, backed by strong allies in Europe and Japan, prompted a new Soviet leadership of Mikhail Gorbachev to seek to ease tensions and reduce military competition and confrontation with the United States.

Nonetheless, a new challenge to U.S. leadership emerged in this period. For over ten years, a wide range of respected specialists and commentators argued that the United States could not keep pace with Asia's rapidly rising great power—Japan. Japan was seen as so competitive in Asian and world markets that it was widely asserted that Japan was emerging as Asia's dominant power, and that the United States was gradually falling to second place in Asian affairs. Such predictions lasted into the first years of the post-cold war period. They did not cease until Japan experienced several years of economic stagnation and deflation, and U.S. economic and military power rose to new prominence in the 1990s.

Current Challenges in Light of the Past.

Current challenges to U.S. leadership in Asia, posed by China's rise, are reviewed in this article and they appear to be serious. However, they have not reached the level of the challenges faced by the United States in the Asia at the start of the cold war, during the Vietnam War, after the U.S. defeat in Indochina in 1975, and in the face of Japan's rise in the late 1980s. Most notably, unlike in those past instances, today, U.S. military predominance and the continued growth of a massive and globally influential U.S. economy undergirds an ability to exert continued strong U.S. leadership in Asian and world affairs.

Past assumptions of U.S. decline, in the face of rising powers and challenges, tended to exaggerate the U.S. weaknesses without adequately assessing U.S. strengths, and they tended to exaggerate the strengths of the rising powers and challenges to U.S. leadership without adequately assessing their weaknesses and limitations. Credible assessments dealing with contemporary U.S. difficulties in the Asia would appear to call for better balance in considering contemporary U.S. weaknesses and strengths, as well as similar balance in assessing the power and influence of rising China and the challenges it poses to U.S. leadership in Asia. That is a main purpose of this chapter.

China's Rise in Asia: Strengths and Weaknesses

Changing Priorities and Current Goals

An overview of the highpoints of Chinese interaction with Asia in the post-Mao (d. 1976) period shows twists, turns, and adjustments.[11] At first, for over a decade, Deng Xiaoping focused on dealing with Soviet power and influence seen to encircle and pressure China. This priority did not end until Soviet policy began to change under Mikhail Gorbachev, and the USSR began to take steps to meet Deng's demand that Moscow must meet China's "three conditions" before there could be significant improvement in Sino-Soviet relations. Those conditions involved withdrawal of Soviet forces from Afghanistan and Mongolia, and the withdrawal of Soviet-backed Vietnamese forces from Cambodia.

The prolonged Western isolation of China following the Tiananmen crackdown in 1989 surprised Chinese leaders, and Deng advised that China should adopt a low profile in world affairs as it sought to gradually build Chinese economic, military, and political power, and preserve the leadership of the Communist Party administration in China. Chinese leaders reached out to Asian neighbors and other non-Western countries for diplomatic and other exchanges in order to demonstrate to audiences at home and abroad that China was not isolated, as many in the West supposed.

Now freed from the Soviet threat, Chinese leaders were more forthright in asserting territorial claims against Asian neighbors like Japan and Southeast Asia, whose support China had previously sought in alignment against the USSR. Chinese leaders were surprised by the U.S. decision to allow Taiwan President Lee Teng-hui to visit the United States in 1995, and reacted with nine months of tension in the Taiwan Strait that was punctuated by repeated large-scale Chinese military exercises designed to intimidate Taiwan and its U.S. supporters. China's demonstration of military force and its strong assertion of territorial claims headed the list of reasons why neighboring Asian governments were concerned about China's intentions in the region.

Chinese party leader Jiang Zemin gradually consolidated power in foreign affairs as Deng's health declined and he died in 1997. Under Jiang's leadership, Chinese foreign policy in Asian and world affairs became more active and prominent, seeking a variety of "strategic partnerships" and other formal interactions. The Chinese administration proposed a New Security Concept to guide post-cold war foreign relations. This plan represented a reworking of the features of the Five Principles of Peaceful Coexistence that had been periodically used by China since the mid-1950s whenever the Beijing government sought to emphasize peaceful intentions and reassurance to China's neighbors and others. The result was a marked increase in China's positive engagement with Asian neighbors, endeavoring to reassure them of China's "good neighbor" intentions as China and the Asian countries built mutually beneficial economic, political, and military relationships.

In this context, Chinese officials gave less emphasis to asserting territorial claims that infringed on the claims of Asian neighbors. They worked hard to reassure Asian countries that what they said was a "China threat" theory, publicized by enemies of China, was incorrect, as China sought to live in mutually beneficial peace with its neighbors. While developing positive relations with most neighbors, China remained firm in opposing Taiwan independence and the Taiwan government's efforts to broaden official international contacts and relations. It also continued an impressive buildup of Chinese military forces that appeared to be focused most immediately on deterring Taiwan from taking further steps toward political separation from China.

Meanwhile, Chinese officials remained strongly vocal in criticizing what they saw as U.S. hegemonism in Asian and world affairs. They averred that Asian neighbors should be wary of U.S. military presence and alliances that Chinese officials said represented American "cold war thinking" at odds with the more positive and constructive proposals seen in China's New Security Concept. They were particularly critical of the U.S.-Japan alliance that was being strengthened by U.S. and Japanese leaders at that time.

Chinese officials found that many Asian governments did not want to choose between their more constructive and growing relations with China and their important relations with the United States. The Chinese officials also recognized that the incoming George W. Bush administration in the United States was prepared to take strong and concrete action in response to Chinese efforts to confront the United States rhetorically, politically, militarily, or otherwise. By mid-2001, well before the September 11, 2001, terrorist attacks on America, China shifted away from publicly emphasizing criticism of U.S. hegemonism in Asian and world affairs.

By late 2003, Chinese leaders articulated a new foreign policy emphasis on China's "peaceful rise" that was said to pose many opportunities, but no threats, to Asian neighbors and other concerned powers, including the United States. Some debate among Chinese officials ensued, particularly over whether China should highlight China's "rise" in world affairs. By late 2005, China officially emphasized, in an authoritative government statement, that Chinese foreign policy would follow a long-term strategy emphasizing "peace and development." By late 2007, Chinese officials were emphasizing China's strong interest in fostering a "harmonious" world order that mirrored Chinese administration efforts to develop a more harmonious order inside China.

By this time, the goals of China's approach to Asia seemed clear. They were:

- To promote stability and a "peaceful environment" conducive to domestic Chinese economic development and political stability.
- To seek advantageous economic contacts and relationships.
- To reassure China's neighbors about the implications of China's rise.
- To isolate Taiwan.
- To gain regional influence relative to other powers (e.g., Japan, India, and the United States).

These goals sometimes worked at cross-purposes, complicating China's emphasis on a moderate and accommodating posture toward Asian neighbors and concerned powers, notably the United States. The buildup of Chinese military forces, focused on Taiwan, and strong Chinese efforts to isolate Taiwan in Asia concerned some Asian neighbors. The military buildup was seen by U.S. and Japanese military planners as posing a direct threat. Meanwhile, Chinese nationalism continued to be strongly emphasized in Chinese media and education, making it difficult for Chinese leaders to manage historical, territorial, and other disputes in order to sustain a moderate stance to Japan. Japan remained very important in the Asian order as its economy, by conventional measure, had half the wealth of Asia; the Japanese government was America's key ally in Asia and possessed an impressive array of modern military power.[12]

China's Advances and Accomplishments

In much of the post-cold war period, the foreign trade of China's export-oriented economy grew at about twice the rate of China's impressive overall economic growth. The result in Asia was that China became the leading trading partner, or one of the leading trading partners, of its Asian neighbors. The advanced economies of South Korea, Taiwan, and Japan saw China emerge as their largest and increasingly important trading partner. China grew in importance in Southeast Asia and caught up with Japan and the United States to become the region's leading foreign import and export destination. China's trade grew with India and South Asian nations, and with Central Asian countries, though geographic distance and the low level of development of many of those economies limited the scope and importance of these economic connections. China became increasingly important to Russia and Australia, major exporters of energy and raw materials needed by China's manufacturers.

The trading patterns that emerged among China and its neighbors created webs of relationships and dependencies. Asian producers of energy and raw materials found China to be a ready market for their goods. Asian manufacturers of consumer products and industrial goods often found it difficult to compete in international and domestic markets with low cost and good quality Chinese manufacturers. They tended to integrate their enterprises with China by joining the wave of foreign investors that made China the largest, or one of the largest, recipients of foreign direct investment in the world. The developed economies of Asia accounted for the majority of the $60–70 billion annual influx of foreign direct investment to China in recent years.[13]

What resulted were webs of trading relationships characterized by so-called processing trade, which accounted for half of China's overall trade each year. In the case of China, this processing trade had the following characteristics involving Asia. Led by foreign invested enterprises in China, consumer and industrial goods would be produced in China with components imported from foreign enterprises in other parts of Asia. It was often the case that the developing product would cross the Chinese border, sometimes several times, before it was completed. Also, China would often be the final point of assembly, and the value added in China would be relatively small in relation to the total value of the product. And the final product would frequently be exported to advanced Asian economies, or even more frequently, to China's largest export markets—the United States and the European Union.

The result was that China's importance as a recipient of Asian investment, a leading trading partner, and an overall engine of economic growth rose dramatically in Asia. China's important economic position was underscored by its rising trade surpluses with the world, and unprecedented current account surpluses (that included foreign direct investment as well as large and growing trade surpluses) that showed China to be the largest holder of foreign exchange reserves in the world. The advanced economies of Asia and other Asian export-oriented economies relied increasingly on trade and investment in China to sustain their economic growth.[14]

Adroit diplomacy that followed the lines of China's evolving "good neighbor" policy toward Asian countries greatly improved Chinese relations with most Asian neighbors.[15] High-level Chinese leaders were very active and attentive in frequent bilateral and multilateral meetings with Asian counterparts. Senior Chinese leaders were backed by an array of well-qualified and effective diplomats, and other officials who followed a "win-win" approach to Asian neighbors. This approach held that China and Asian partners should seek mutual benefit by focusing on developing areas of common ground while putting aside differences. China made few demands on Asian countries. With few exceptions, it did not expect them to do anything that they would not ordinarily do, and by the same token, China was not expected to do anything that it would not ordinarily do. The exceptions involved China's strong opposition to foreign official interaction with Taiwan, and foreign contacts with the Dalai Lama and the Falun Gong spiritual movement that was outlawed by the Chinese government.

China's approach was greeted positively by Asian neighbors, many of whom remembered and sought to avoid repetition of the assertive and disruptive Chinese policies of the past. Southeast Asian governments used Chinese involvement with the Association of Southeast Asian Nations (ASEAN) regional organization and other means as part of a so-called "Gulliver strategy," designed to tie China with a web of commitments and relationships that would insure continuation of its recent moderate and accommodating approach. South Korea found that China's attentive diplomacy included an approach to the problems posed by North Korean development of nuclear weapons that seemed more respectful of, and consistent with, South Korean policy than that of South Korea's ally, the United States. Amid marked deterioration of U.S.-South Korean relations in the first years of the George W. Bush administration, China followed an effective diplomatic approach that expressed understanding and support for South Korean policies that was warmly appreciated by South Korea public opinion. The Chinese ambassador to Australia enjoyed celebrity status in Australian media, as she rode a wave of positive publicity associated with an export boom of Australian energy and other raw materials to China.

China's diplomacy emphasized willingness to trade with, and to provide some aid, investment, and military support to, countries with "no strings attached." This meant that, unlike Western governments, China imposed few conditions on Chinese economic or other support. This approach was well received by Asian governments in Burma, Cambodia, and elsewhere, which needed foreign economic and other help, but were loath to meet the conditions imposed by Western donors.[16]

Another feature of Chinese diplomacy has been an emphasis on Chinese language, culture, and personal exchanges. This has included Chinese support for Confucius institutes throughout the region and the world that promote the teaching of Chinese language and Chinese culture. It also involved facilitating ever-larger numbers of Chinese tourist groups traveling to neighboring countries and other foreign destinations.[17]

Regarding China's relations with major powers in Asia, significant differences in Chinese relations with India were managed in ways that allowed the two governments to emphasize the positive aspects of their growing relationship. After the marked decline in official Chinese rhetoric critical of U.S. "hegemonism" in Asian and world affairs in mid-2001, the two countries managed to build a business-like relationship that featured continued emphasis on the positive aspects of

U.S.–China relations. China's relations with the Russian administration of Vladimir Putin developed in important military and energy areas, though they did not appear as close as during the hey-day of the China-Russia strategic partnership during the latter years of the Yeltsin administration.[18]

A salient feature of Chinese diplomacy was more flexibility and activism in multilateral organizations and groups involving Asian affairs.[19] In the past, Chinese leaders were seen to be wary of interaction with such bodies, out of concern that they would hamper Chinese freedom of action and might be used by the United States and other powers to force change and commitments unwelcome by the Chinese administration. Prevailing assessment by international specialists showed that the new Chinese approach to such multilateral groups was designed to reassure China's neighbors that rising China was not a threat they needed to balance against, to expand overall Chinese influence and prominence in the region, and to establish webs of regional relationships that would make it more difficult for the United States to win regional support for renewed pressure or so-called "containment" of China.

Chinese leaders and officials worked assiduously to build relations with ASEAN and with Asian groupings based on ASEAN. China set the pace of international involvement with ASEAN by being the first to propose a free trade agreement with ASEAN and the first to sign ASEAN's Treaty of Amity and Cooperation. It reassured the ASEAN countries, many of whom have claims South China Sea islands also claimed by China, by reaching an accord on how to manage the disputes.

China supported the ASEAN + 3 regional grouping, which also involved Japan and South Korea, as its favored East Asian group. By definition, the group excluded the United States, an advantage for China in the view of foreign observers. China had favored a more exclusive membership for the East Asian Summit that emerged in 2005, but was compelled to acquiesce to efforts by Japan, Indonesia, Singapore, and others to broaden the scope of membership to include India, Australia, and New Zealand, and to leave an opening for possible U.S. membership. China was the driving force and main backer behind the Shanghai Cooperation Organization that included Russia and central Asian states, involved Mongolia, India, Pakistan, Afghanistan, and Iran as observers, but excluded the United States.

China also worked actively in important regional groupings that included, and were favored by, the United States, such Asia-Pacific Economic Cooperation (APEC) and the ASEAN Regional Forum.

China also worked very closely with the United States in the Six Party Talks that dealt with the problem of North Korea's nuclear weapons development.

Chinese efforts to reassure neighboring countries that rising China does not threaten them saw public statements of Chinese officials and those of most Asian states play down the significance of China's impressive military buildup. Chinese military officers engaged in active diplomacy with regional counterparts, endeavoring to build trust and reinforce China's moderate and accommodating posture despite the buildup of Chinese forces. China's military modernization placed an important emphasis on power projection involving substantial increases in China's air and naval capabilities. Prevailing assessment judged that China has emerged as Asia's leading military power. This military advance presumably enhanced China's power and influence in Asia, even though it was not frequently discussed in these terms by Chinese officials in interaction with Asian counterparts.[20]

The overall record of Chinese relations with neighboring countries in recent years has witnessed a major improvement in Chinese relations with much of Southeast Asia, South Korea, and Australia. Public opinion and leadership statements in these areas reflect positively on China. China's relations with Russia and central Asian countries also continue to advance in various ways, as do Chinese-Indian ties. China's reputation in Asian multilateral groups is one of an active participant that often sets the agenda for new initiatives.

Chinese Limitations and Weaknesses

Heading the list of limitations and shortcomings in China's rising influence in Asia was China's relations with both Japan and Taiwan.[21] The negative record in recent years showed that China was unsuccessful in winning greater support in either country, despite many positive economic and other connections linking China and each state. The negative record also had a negative effect on China's overall influence in Asia.

China's efforts to isolate Taiwan included strong pressures on Asian governments to avoid contacts with Taiwan that China opposed. This was resented by some Asian governments, although it caused few major controversies and imposed few major obstacles in China's improving relations with Asia.

China's efforts to isolate Japan from the rest of Asia over disputes involving history, territorial issues, Japan's growing military role in the enhanced U.S.-Japan alliance, and Japan's seeking a permanent seat in the UN Security Council had significant negative costs for China's influence in Asia. These costs continued despite efforts since 2006 to improve China-Japan relations. Asian governments maintained strong connections with Japan, and were reluctant to side with China against Japan. Chinese pressure on them to do so generally was not welcomed and appeared to undercut China's efforts to foster a benign and accommodating image in Asia. The Chinese efforts also energized Japanese efforts to work with the United States, Australia, India, and other powers, and to use multilateral groupings and Japan's substantial economic, trade, and aid interactions in order to foster an Asian order where rising China would not be in a position to dominate Japan.[22]

Strong Chinese nationalism and territorial claims complicated Chinese efforts to improve relations with Asian neighbors. South Korean opinion of China[23] declined sharply from a high point in 2004 because of nationalist disputes over whether an historic kingdom controlling much of Korea and northeast China was Chinese or Korean. South Korean officials dealing with China over the historical dispute privately voiced sharp criticism of China's stance. Their concern over China's hard stance on this issue influenced their view of China's intentions toward North Korea. Many South Korean officials came to view China's strategy toward North Korea as intended to foster a continuation of an independent North Korean state under the economic, political, and security influence of China. Such an approach was seen as directly at odds with South Korea's prevailing so-called sunshine policy that envisioned an eventual peaceful reunification of North Korea with a dominant South Korea. This South Korean concern with China's perceived approach to North Korea made the Seoul government more wary of China.

Chinese nationalism and territorial claims underlined a tough Chinese posture regarding differences with Japan. The anti-Japanese demonstrations in China in April 2005 involved several days of violence against, and destruction of, Japanese diplomatic and private property in China that the Chinese authorities failed to suppress. Disputed island and resource claims in the East China Sea, along with competing interests in Taiwan, were accompanied by naval and other military maneuvers and statements by Japan and China that were seen as provocative, threatening, and indicative of a protracted rivalry between the two powers.

Chinese diplomacy endeavored to play down Chinese territorial disputes in Southeast Asia and with India, but clear differences remained unresolved. On balance, the continued disputes served as a drag on Chinese effort to improve relations with these countries.

China's remarkable military modernization, and its sometimes secretive and authoritarian political system, raised suspicions and wariness on the part of a number of China's neighbors. They sought more transparency regarding Chinese military intentions. They were not reassured by China's refusal to join at a senior level with the United States and other Asian defense leaders at an annual conclave known as the Shangri-La Forum meeting in Singapore.[24]

China's past record of aggression and provocative assertiveness toward many Asian countries remained hard to live down. It also meant that China had few positive connections on which to build friendly ties with its neighbors. As a result, and also reflecting the state-led pattern of much of Chinese foreign relations, Chinese interchange with Asian neighbors depended heavily on the direction and leadership of the Chinese government. Non-government channels of communication and influence were very limited.

An exception was the so-called Overseas Chinese communities in Southeast Asian countries. These people tended to be comparatively well-to-do and entrepreneurial members of their respective countries. They provided important investment and technical assistance to China's development, and represented political forces supportive of their home country's good relations with China. At the same time, however, it was clear to observers in Southeast Asia that evidence of growing influence of this group, and evidence of close Chinese government association with them, ran the risk of a strong backlash. The dominant ethnic, cultural, and religious groups in Southeast Asia often had a long history of wariness of China and sometimes promoted violent actions and other discrimination against the economic and political power and influence of ethnic Chinese.[25]

The areas of greatest Chinese strength in Asia—economic relations and diplomacy—also showed limitations and weaknesses.[26] Chinese trade figures were exaggerated because of double counting associated with processing trade. Such double counting was estimated to account for 30 percent of China's trade with Southeast Asia.[27] That half of Chinese trade was conducted by foreign invested enterprises in China, that the resulting processing trade saw China often add only a small amount to the product, and that the finished products often depended on sales to the United States or the European Union also appeared to undercut China's image in Asia as a powerful trading country.

The large amount of Asian and international investment that went to China did not go to other Asian countries, hurting their economic development. China invested little in Asia, apart from Hong Kong. While Chinese investment abroad grew fairly rapidly, it did so from a low base, amounting to $16 billion for Chinese investment to the entire world in 2006. Chinese aid to Asia was very small, especially in comparison to other donors, with the exception of North Korea and Burma. China's large foreign exchange reserves served many purposes for the authoritarian Chinese administration that was trying to maintain stability amid massive internal needs. They did not translate to big Chinese grants of assistance abroad. China's attraction to Asian producers of raw materials was not shared by Asian manufacturers. These entrepreneurs tended to relocate and invest in China and they appeared to do well, but their workers could not relocate to China and appeared to suffer.[28]

By definition, China's "win-win" diplomacy meant that China would not do things that it ordinarily would not do. The sometimes-dizzying array of meetings, agreements, and pronouncements in the active Chinese diplomacy in Asia did not hide the fact that China remained reluctant to undertake significant costs, risks, or commitments in dealing with difficult regional issues.

U.S. Weaknesses and Strengths

The weaknesses of the American position in Asia have been well publicized.[29] Prevailing discourse on the United States in Asia focused on the widespread negative image of the United States in public and elite opinion, and among many government officials in the region. The main cause of the negative image was the foreign policy of the U.S. government. Heading the list was the U.S. war in Iraq, which was strongly opposed by popular and elite opinion throughout the region. Until recently, the hard-line U.S. stance toward North Korea was widely criticized. This has moderated along with evidence, since late 2006, of much greater U.S. flexibility toward North Korea in the Six Party Talks. The U.S. support of Israel and its stance in dealing with the Palestinian Authority and the Middle East peace process has been widely criticized. U.S. unilateralism in other international affairs in dealing with Iran, Burma, global warming, and other issues was widely resented.

The United States government has been seen as narrowly focused on the war on terrorism, prodding Asian governments to do more to curb international terrorists. Asian opinion often saw the causes of terrorism differently than the U.S. government. Asian governments focused more on needs for economic development and effective nation building, but saw the forceful U.S. stance against terrorism as myopic and counterproductive. Perceived U.S. arrogance and unilateralism also led to resentment over U.S. reluctance to join with Asian states in seeking a variety of Asian multilateral groupings to deal with Asian problems and issues.[30]

In this atmosphere of negativism surrounding U.S. government actions and policies in Asia in recent years, it was sometimes hard to discern evidence of U.S. strengths in Asia. Several of these strengths were publicly noted in media, and in specialist and scholarly assessments, and they are duly noted below. More important for this assessment were private interviews conducted with 175 Asian affairs experts in the governments of eight Asian Pacific governments during three trips to the region in 2004–6. An assumption behind the focus on interviewing Asian officials knowledgeable about the Asian order is that, in Asia, governments are seen as the key decision makers in foreign affairs. On the whole, the governments of Asia are strong, the people look to the governments to make key foreign policy decisions, and government officials do so on the basis of careful consideration of their national interests. The findings of these interviews were reinforced in public speeches with audiences (amounting in total to approximately two thousand to three thousand) of informed Asian-Pacific elites in these eight countries during the course of two seven-week speaking trips in 2004 and 2006.[31]

These interviews—reinforced by the above noted public speeches—underlined twin pillars of U.S. security and economic strength in the Asian region. The United States continues to undertake major costs, commitments, and risks that are viewed by Asian officials as essential to the stability and well-being of the region. No other power, including rising China, is even remotely able and willing to undertake these responsibilities, in the view of these officials. America thus remains the indispensable leading power of Asia.

Asian government officials interviewed during the 2004–6 research trips were almost uniform in emphasizing the positive importance of the United States' leading role as Asia's security guarantor and vital economic partner. The few exceptions included a Communist Party of India (Marxist) official, and to a degree, some Chinese officials who criticized the U.S. security role in Asia.

Regarding security concerns, Asian government officials hold the view that Asian governments generally do not trust each other. The kind of suspicion and wariness one sees today between China and

Japan characterizes most relationships between and among Asian governments. And yet, the Asian governments need stability in order to meet their nation-building priorities. Economic development associated with effective nation building is seen as critically important to the legitimacy of most Asian governments. In this context, the United States looms very large in their calculations. Unlike their Asian neighbors, the United States does not want their territory and does not want to dominate them. It, too, wants stability and, in contrast with China's and other power's inability or reluctance to undertake major risks and commitments, the United States is seen to continue the massive expenditure and major risk in a U.S. military presence in Asia. This U.S. role is viewed as essential in stabilizing the often-uncertain security relationships among Asian governments.

Not only does the United States continue to occupy the top security position as Asia's "least distrusted power," the United States also plays an essential economic role in the development priorities of Asian governments. Most of these governments are focused on export-oriented growth. The United States continues to allow massive inflows of Asian imports essential to Asian economic development despite an overall U.S. trade deficit over $700 billion annually. Against this background, when asked if overall U.S. power and influence in Asia were in decline, Asian officials were uniform in saying "no."

The interviews in Asia appeared in stark contrast to the widely held perception of decline of U.S. power and influence in world affairs evident since the string of setbacks and failures of the U.S. military occupation of Iraq. However, more detached assessments see the consequences of the Iraq failure for U.S. security commitments and power in Asia as limited.[32] They appear to support the judgment of the interviewed Asian officials' that the overall U.S. military power and the U.S. leading security role in Asia have not diminished.

Meanwhile, evidence of U.S. economic difficulties and decline is widely seen in the United States, notably in the massive U.S. trade and government spending deficits. The argument here is that these problems will cause the United States to move in a decidedly protectionist direction that will significantly curb imports from Asia. Additional evidence was provided with the election of the Democratic party-led 110th Congress in 2006. Democratic leaders Speaker Nancy Pelosi and Majority Leader Harry Reid seemed to favor tougher and more restrictive trade measures against Asian exporters, especially China, the source of the largest U.S. trade imbalance. Nonetheless, more detached assessments showed Democratic Party divisions and weaknesses that made the adoption of significant protectionist measures unlikely. This suggested that the leading U.S. role as Asia's economic partner of choice would continue.[33]

Other strengths in the U.S. position, in comparison with that of rising China and other powers in Asia, were noted in media, and in specialist and scholarly assessments.[34] They included the following:

- Unlike China, the United States has not depended so heavily on government connections and government-led initiatives to exert influence in Asia. The United States has developed an extensive network of nongovernment connections developed over many decades that undergird U.S. influence in Asia. They have involved extensive business, educational, religious, and foundation connections. They have also involved an extensive web of personal connections that followed the U.S. decision in 1965 to end discrimination against Asians in U.S. immigration policy. This step resulted in the influx of many millions of Asians who settled in the United States and entered the main stream of U.S. society while sustaining strong connections with their country of origin.
- The U.S. military, in recent years, was by far the most active U.S. government component in Asia. It followed quiet and methodical methods to develop ever-closer working relations with most Asian governments, while endeavoring to reinforce the U.S. alliance structure in Asia.
- After the U.S. shift toward a more flexible posture toward North Korea in late 2006, the U.S. government was seen in a generally positive light in Asia, as it ensured that the three major hot spots in the region do not lead to war. The hot spots are the crisis caused by North Korea's nuclear weapons program, the conflict between Taiwan and China, and the conflict between India and Pakistan over Kashmir.
- The U.S. government developed a more active and positive stance toward multilateral groups in Asia, especially with ASEAN. Despite notable lapses in high-level U.S. leaders attending scheduled ASEAN meetings, the United States strongly supported the ASEAN Regional Forum (ARF), the primary regional forum for security dialogue. The Bush administration also strongly supported APEC. In November 2005, President Bush began to use the annual APEC leaders' summit to engage in annual multilateral meetings with attending ASEAN leaders. At that meeting, the leaders launched the ASEAN-U.S. Enhanced Partnership, involving a broad range of economic, political, and security cooperation, and in July 2006, a five-year Plan of Action to implement the partnership was signed.

In other steps, the United States enhanced investment, trade, and diplomatic relations with ASEAN.

- The Bush administration's success in improving U.S. relations with the great powers in Asia has added to the strength of U.S. leadership in the region, and reinforced the U.S. government's ability to deal with crises on the Korean peninsula and other regional difficulties, as well as negative implications coming from the rise of China in Asia. The United States having good relations with Japan and China at the same time is very rare. The United States being the dominant power in South Asia and having good relations with both India and Pakistan is unprecedented, as is the current U.S. maintenance of good relations with both Beijing and Taipei.
- Effective U.S. policy toward China, emphasizing positive engagement, while continuing to balance and "hedge" against negative implications of China's rise, has helped to reinforce China's emphasis on peace and development and to constrain past Chinese objections and pressure against Asian governments interacting with the United States in sensitive areas. The prevailing circumstances in U.S.-Chinese relations have allowed the United States and Asian countries very sensitive to Chinese preferences and pressures (e.g., Vietnam, Mongolia) to develop closer relations involving such sensitive areas as military cooperation and related intelligence and information exchanges.

ASIAN "HEDGING"

There appears to be a contradiction between assessments of an emerging China-centered order in Asia and the prevailing post-cold war regional pattern characterized by many proud and nationalistic Asian governments seeking greater prominence and hedging warily against powers and trends, including a rising China, which might curb their independence and nationalistic goals. While it appears that the latter pattern has both positive and negative effects on China's rising influence in Asia, at bottom, such hedging curbs Chinese ability to dominate or lead Asia to the exclusion of other powers, particularly the United States.

The post-cold war Asian order has witnessed a tendency, on the part of most Asian governments, to emphasize nationalistic ambitions and independence. They eschew tight and binding alignments of the past in favor of diverse arrangements with various powers that support security and other state interests in the newly fluid regional environment.[35]

On the one hand, China's generally constructive and accommodating approach to Asian neighbors is welcomed by Asian governments seeking to diversify international options and to integrate rising regional forces in accordance with their national interests. On the other hand, Asian governments respond to China's rising influence by taking steps to work with one another and other non-Asian powers, notably the United States, to insure that their interests and independence will be preserved in the face of China's growing role in regional affairs. Both tendencies, to integrate and cooperate with China on the one hand, and to work with one another, the United States, and other powers to hedge against possible negative implications of China's rise on the other, have strengthened as China has become more prominent in regional affairs in recent years. One conclusion that comes from this is that few Asian leaders or Asian states appear ready to adhere to a Chinese-led order in Asia, and that China's rise adds to reasons for them to sustain and develop close relations with the United States and other powers useful in hedging against China's greater influence in Asian affairs.

Asian government officials consulted in private interviews during 2004–6 agreed that China's rise adds to incentives for most Asian governments to maneuver and hedge with other powers, including the United States, in order to preserve their independence and freedom of action. A Singapore official in May 2006 said that "hedging is the name of the game" in Southeast Asia, while an Indian official in June 2006, said that Asian governments "are not going to put all their eggs in one basket." Asian officials made clear that their governments hedge against the United States and other powers as well, but their recent focus has been on China's rise. The governments tend to increasingly cooperate with China in areas of common concern, but they increasingly work in other ways, often including efforts to strengthen relations with the United States, to preserve freedom of action and other interests in the face China's rise.[36]

In an Asian order featuring continued strong U.S. security and economic power and influence, such hedging by Asian governments adds to factors that are seen to preclude Chinese leadership or dominance in Asia and that reinforce U.S. leadership in Asia. The majority of Asian government officials that were interviewed privately assumed that China sought eventual "preeminence" in Asia; Chinese officials said "no," though Chinese foreign policy specialists said that secret Chinese Communist Party documents over the years have continued to refer to a general goal of Asian leadership. When asked in May 2006 whether China sought leadership or domination in Asia, a senior

Chinese official acknowledged the complications of U.S. power and influence and the role of many independent-minded Asian governments. He responded that "China can't dominate Asia; there are too many governments in Asia." He nonetheless went on to advise that China's influence in the region would grow as China's "weight" would become increasingly important to the governments in the region and China would have increasing success in reassuring Asian governments of Chinese intentions.[37]

In sum, the nationalistic ambitions of Asian governments generally make them wary of coming under the dominant influence of their neighbors, most of whom they do not trust. This fact undermines concrete advances for Chinese influence in Asia. An inventory of Chinese influence compared with that of the United States, detailed in recent assessments and scholarship, shows that major regional powers like Japan, India, and Russia continue to take measures to maintain their leadership ambitions and guard against coming under strong or dominant Chinese influence. South Korea and a number of Southeast Asian states also have national and regional ambitions that require maneuvering and hedging to avoid coming under China's sway. As the most important power in the region, and one with no territorial, or few other, ambitions at odds with Asian governments interested in nation building and preserving a stable regional status quo, the United States looms large in the hedging calculus of Asian states dealing with rising China.

CONCLUSION

The above assessment endeavors to be more comprehensive than many recent assessments of the emerging order in Asia that have emphasized the strengths of rising China and the weaknesses of the current leading power in Asia—the United States. It endeavors to carefully consider both the strengths and weaknesses of the Chinese and U.S. positions in Asia. It also considers the implications for the Asian order of the practices of Asia's many independent-minded governments that seek to maximize their influence and freedom of action amid the more fluid situation in Asia after the cold war. The findings of the assessment are:

- China is rising in influence in Asia, the part of the world where China has always exerted its greatest influence; but China also has major limitations and weaknesses, and has a long way to go to compete for regional leadership.

- The power and interests of the United States and most Asian governments work against China ever achieving dominance in Asia.
- The U.S. image in Asia has declined in recent years and U.S. foreign policy continues to be widely criticized. However, U.S. ability and willingness to serve as Asia's security guarantor and its vital economic partner remain strong and provide a solid foundation for continued U.S. leadership in the region. Overall, U.S. power and influence in the region has not declined, according to Asian officials interviewed from 2004 to 2006.
- Most Asian governments maneuver and hedge against China's rise, and they find a strong U.S. presence in Asia fundamentally important and reassuring.

NOTES

1. "China Becomes No 3 Trading Nation," *Asia Pulse*, January 12, 2005 (http://www.taiwansecurity.org); Thomas Lum and Dick Nanto, *China's Trade with the United States and the World.* (Washington, DC: The Library of Congress, Congressional Research Service Report RL 31403, March 14, 2006).
2. Wayne Morrison, *China's Economic Conditions (*Washington, DC: The Library of Congress, Congressional Research Service Report RL 33534, October 11, 2007); Morris Goldstein and Nicholas Lardy, *Don't Hail China's Soft Landing Too Soon* (Washington, DC: Institute for International Economics, October 5, 2004).
3. Morrison, *China's Economic Conditions;* Lum and Nanto, *China's Trade;* Paul Blustin, "China Passes U.S. in Trade with Japan," *Washington Post*, January 27, 2005, E1.
4. David Shambaugh, ed., *Power Shift (*Berkeley: University of California Press, 2005); Robert Sutter, *China's Rise in Asia: Promises and Perils* (Lanham, MD: Rowman and Littlefield, 2005); Phillip Saunders, *China's Global Activism: Strategy, Drivers, and Tools* (Washington, DC: Institute for National Strategic Studies, 2006); Fu Ying, "China and Asia in New Period," (Beijing) *Foreign Affairs Journal* 69 (September 2003): 1–7; Asia Pacific Center for Security Studies, *Asia's China Debate*, December 2003, http://www.apcss.org; Herbert Yee and Ian Storey, *The China Threat: Perceptions, Myths, and Realities* (London: Routledge, 2002); Bates Gill, *Rising Star: China's New Security Diplomacy (*Washington, DC: The Brookings Institution, 2007); Joshua Kurlantzick, "Pax Asia-Pacifica? East Asian Integration and Its Implications for the United States," *The Washington Quarterly* 30, no. 3 (Summer 2007): 67–77.
5. Gill, *Rising Star*; Kurlantzick, "Pax Asia-Pacifica?"; David Shambaugh, "China Engages Asia: Reshaping the Regional Order," *International*

Security 29, no. 3 (Winter 2004–5): 64–99; *China-Southeast Asia Relations: Trends, Issues, and Implications for the United States (*Washington, DC: Congressional Research Service of the Library of Congress Report RL 32688, April 4, 2006); Morton Abramowitz and Stephen Bosworth, *Chasing the Sun: Rethinking East Asian Policy* (New York: The Century Foundation Press, 2006); Michael Vatikiotis and Murray Hiebert, "How China is Building an Empire," *Far Eastern Economic Review*, November 20, 2003, 30–33; Jonathan Pollack, ed., *Asia Eyes America: Regional Perspectives on U.S. Asia-Pacific Strategy in the 21st Century* (Washington, DC: U.S. Government Printing Office, 2007); David C. Kang, *China Rising: Peace, Power, and Order in East Asia (*New York: Columbia University Press, 2007); Joshua Kurlantzick, "How China is Changing Global Diplomacy," *The New Republic*, vol. 232. June 27, 2005, 16–21. Exceptions that give greater emphasis to U.S. strengths in Asia include: Michael Yahuda, *The International Politics of the Asia-Pacific (*New York: RoutledgeCurzon, 2005) and G. John Ikenberry, "America in East Asia: Power, Markets, and Grand Strategy," in *Beyond Bilateralism: U.S.-Japan relations in the new Asia-Pacific, ed.* Ellis Krauss and T. J. Pempel (Stanford, CA: Stanford University Press, 2004), 37–54.
6. David Michael Lampton, "China's Rise in Asia Need Not Be at America's Expense," in Shambaugh, ed., *Power Shift*, 306–28.
7. Michael McDevitt, "The China Factor in U.S. Defense Planning," in *Strategic Surprise*? ed. Jonathan Pollack (Newport, RI: U.S. Naval War College, 2003), 149–58; Phillip Saunders, *China's Global Activism: Strategy, Drivers, and Tools* (Washington, DC: Institute for National Strategic Studies, 2006). U.S.-China Economic and Security Review Commission, *2005 Report to Congress (*Washington, DC: U.S. Government Printing Office, 2005), 143–90; Hugo Restall, "China's Bid for Asian Hegemony," *Far Eastern Economic Review*, May 2007, http://www.taiwansecurity.org.
8. Vatikiotis and Hiebert, "How China is Building an Empire"; Shambaugh, "China Engages Asia"; Restall, "China's Bid for Asian Hegemony."
9. Dick Nanto, *East Asian Regional Architecture: New Economic and Security Arrangements and U.S. Policy (*Washington, DC: The Library of Congress, Congressional Research Service, Report RL33653, September 18, 2006).
10. Akira Iriye, *Across the Pacific: An Inner History of American East Asian Relations* (New York: Harcourt, Brace and World, 1967); Ernest May and James Thompson, eds., *American-East Asian Relations, A Survey* (Cambridge, MA: Harvard University Press, 1972); Tyler Dennett, *Americans in East Asia, A Critical Study of United States Policy in the Far East in the 19th Century* (New York: Barnes and Noble, 1963); Warren Cohen, ed., *Pacific Passage: The Study of American-East Asian Relations on the Eve of the Twenty-First Century* (New York: Columbia University Press, 1996); Bruce Cummings, *Parallax Visions: Making Sense of*

American-East Asian Relations at the End of the Century (Raleigh-Durham, NC: Duke University Press, 1999); Warren Cohen, *East Asia at the Center: Four Thousand Years of Engagement with the World* (New York: Columbia University Press, 2000); Warren Cohen and Nancy Bernkopf Tucker, "AHR Forum: America in Asian Eyes," *The American Historical Review* 111, no. 4, October 2006, http://www.historycooperative.org/journals/ahr/111.4/cohen.html.

11. Shambaugh, ed., *Power Shift;* Sutter, *China's Rise in Asia: Promises and Perils*; Shambaugh, "China Engages Asia"; Wang, "China's Changing Role in Asia"; Fu "China and Asia in New Period"; Asia Pacific Center for Security Studies, *Asia's China Debate;* Yee and Storey, *The China Threat: Perceptions, Myths, and Realities;* Lowell Dittmer, "Assessing American Asia Policy," *Asian Survey* 47, no. 4 (July–August 2007): 521–35; Bronson Percival, *The Dragon Looks South: China and Southeast Asia in the New Century* (Westport, CT: Praeger Security International, 2007); Thomas Christensen, "Fostering Stability or Creating a Monster? The Rise of China and U.S. Policy Toward East Asia," *International Security* 31, no. 1 (Summer 2006): 81–126; Yahuda, *The International Politics of the Asia-Pacific*, 276–77; Ian Story, *The United States and ASEAN-China Relations: All Quiet on the Southeast Asian Front* (Carlisle Barracks, PA: U.S. Army War College Institute for Strategic Studies, 2007).
12. Robert Sutter, *Chinese Foreign Relations: Power and Policy Since the Cold War* (Lanham, MD: Rowman and Littlefield, 2007), 1–15.
13. Lum and Nanto, *China's Trade with the United States and the World.*
14. David Shambaugh "The Rise of China and Asia's New Dynamics," in Shambaugh, ed., *Power Shift*, 1–21; Hideo Ohashi, "China's Regional Trade and Investment Profile," in Shambaugh, ed., *Power Shift*, 71–95; Robert Ash, "China's Regional Economics and the Asian Region: Building Interdependent Linkages," in Shambaugh, ed., *Power Shift*, 96–134.
15. Robert Sutter, *China's Rise: Implications for U.S. Leadership in Asia* (Washington, DC: East-West Center, 2006), 35–39.
16. Kurlantzick, "How China is Changing Global Diplomacy."
17. Joshua Kurlantzick, *Charm Offensive: How China's Soft Power is Transforming the World* (New Haven, CT: Yale University Press, 2007).
18. Sutter, *China's Rise in Asia: Promises and Perils*, 107–24, 231–48.
19. Yahuda, *The International Politics of the Asia-Pacific*, 298–305; Gill, *Rising Star*, 21–73; Jianwei Wang, "China's Multilateral Diplomacy in the New Millennium," in *China Rising: Power and Motivation in Chinese Foreign Policy, ed.* Yong Deng and Fei-Ling Wang (Lanham, MD: Rowman and Littlefield, 2005), 159–200.
20. David Shambaugh, "China's Military Modernization: Making Steady and Surprising Progress," in *Strategic Asia 2005–2006*, ed. Ashley Tellis

and Michael Wills (Seattle, WA: National Bureau of Asian Research, 2005), 67–104

21. Yun-han Chu, "The Evolution of Beijing's Policy toward Taiwan during the Reform Period," in *China Rising*, ed. Deng and Wang, 245–78; Richard Bush, "Taiwan Faces China: Attraction and Repulsion," in Shambaugh, ed., *Power Shift*, 170–86; Mike Mochizuki, "China-Japan Relations: Downward Spiral or a New Equilibrium?" in Shambaugh, ed., *Power Shift*, 135–50.
22. Richard Samuels, *Securing Japan: Tokyo's Grand Strategy and the Future of East Asia* (Cornell University Press, 2007); Susan Shirk, *China: Fragile Superpower* (Oxford: Oxford University Press, 2007), 140–80; Michael Mochizuki, "Japan's Long Transition: The Politics of Recalibrating Grand Strategy," in *Strategic Asia 2007–2008: Domestic Political Change and Grand Strategy*, ed. Ashley Tellis and Michael Wills (Seattle, WA: The National Bureau of Asian Research, 2007), 69–112; Christopher Hughes, *Japan's Security Agenda: Military, Economic, and Environmental Dimensions* (Boulder, CO: Lynne Reinner, 2004).
23. Sutter, *China's Rise in Asia: Promises and Perils*, 49–51; Samuel Kim, *The Two Koreas and the Great Powers* (New York: Cambridge University Press, 2006), 63–97; David Shambaugh, "China and the Korean Peninsula," *Washington Quarterly* 26, no. 2 (Spring 2003), 43–56; Denny Roy, *China and the Korean Peninsula*, Asia Pacific Center for Security Studies 3, no. 1 (Honolulu: Asia Pacific Center for Security Studies, 2004); Jae Ho Chung, "From a Special Relationship to a Normal Partnership?" *Pacific Affairs* 76, no. 3: 549–68.
24. Evelyn Goh, *Meeting the China Challenge: The U.S. in Southeast Asian Regional Security Strategies*, East-West Center Washington Policy Studies, no. 16 (Washington, DC: East-West Center Washington Policy Studies, 2005).
25. Sheng Lijun, "China's Influence in Southeast Asia," *Trends in Southeast Asia Series* 4 (Singapore: Institute of Southeast Asian Studies, 2006).
26. Sutter, *China's Rise: Implications for U.S. Leadership in Asia*, 17–24.
27. "Chinese Diplomacy and Optimism about ASEAN," *Comparative Connections* 8, no. 3, October 2006, http://www.csis.org/pacfor.
28. "Cebu Meetings, UN Veto on Myanmar," *Comparative Connections* 9, no. 1 (April 2007) http://www.csis.org/pacfor.
29. Abramowitz and Bosworth *Chasing the Sun;* Kurlantzick, *Charm Offensive;* Gill, *Rising Star;* Vatikiotis and Hiebert, "How China is Building an Empire"; Shambaugh, "China Engages Asia"; Restall, "China's Bid for Asian Hegemony."
30. Bruce Vaughn and Wayne Morrison, *China-Southeast Asia Relations: Trends, Issues, and Implications for the United States.* Report RL32688, Washington, DC: Congressional Research Service of the Library of Congress, April 6, 2006. Evelyn Goh, "Southeast Asian Reactions to

America's New Strategic Imperatives," in Pollack, ed., *Asia Eyes America*, 201–6.

31. These interviews are highlighted in Sutter, *China's Rise in Asia: Promises and Perils*, and Robert Sutter *China's Rise and U.S. Influence in Asia: A Report from the Region* (Washington, DC: Atlantic Council of the United States Issue Brief, July 2006).
32. Phillip Saunders, "The United States and East Asia after Iraq," *Survival* 49, vol. 1 (Spring 2007): 141–52.
33. Robert Sutter, "The Democratic-Led 110th Congress: Implications for Asia," *Asia Policy* 3 (January 2007): 125–50.
34. Yahuda, *The International Politics of the Asia-Pacific;* Ikenberry, "America in East Asia: Power, Markets, and Grand Strategy"; Daniel Twining, "America's Grand Design in Asia," *Washington Quarterly* 30, no. 3 (Summer 2007): 79–94; "South Korea's Election: What to Expect from President Lee," *International Crisis Group Update Briefing: Asia Briefing 73*, December 21, 2007; Percival, *The Dragon Looks South;* Christensen, "Fostering Stability or Creating a Monster?"; Storey, *The United States and ASEAN-China Relations: All Quiet on the Southeast Asian Front*; Nick Bisley, "Asian Security Architectures," in *Strategic Asia 2007–2008: Domestic Political Change and Grand Strategy*, ed. Ashley Tellis and Michael Wills (Seattle, WA: The National Bureau of Asian Research, 2007), 341–70; Victor Cha, "Winning Asia: Washington's Untold Success Story," *Foreign Affairs* 86, no. 6 (November–December 2007), http://www.foreignaffairs.org/current/; Donald Weatherbee, "Strategic Dimensions of Economic Interdependence in Southeast Asia," in *Strategic Asia 2006–2007: Trade, Interdependence, and Security*, ed. Ashley Tellis and Michael Wills (Seattle, WA: The National Bureau of Asian Research, 2006), 271–302.
35. On post–cold war Asian regional dynamics, see Yahuda, *The International Politics of the Asia-Pacific*; and Robert Sutter, *The United States and East Asia: Dynamics and Implications* (Lanham, MD: Rowman and Littlefield, 2003). On some smaller Asian nations hedging against China, see Evelyn Goh, *Meeting the China Challenge.*
36. Robert Sutter *China's Rise and U.S. Influence in Asia: A Report from the Region*, 4.
37. Ibid.

Chapter 3

U.S. Domestic Politics and the China Policy Rollercoaster

Robert M. Hathaway

Relations between the United States and the People's Republic of China (PRC) have been on a roller-coaster ever since the end of the cold war nearly two decades ago. Periods of tension have alternated with moments when the two nations have managed to maintain some stability in their relations, prompting scholars to write of "the loves-me-loves-me-not swings" in ties between the two.[1] The sanctions that Washington imposed on China in 1989 after Tiananmen Square were followed by efforts by the George H. W. Bush administration to patch up the relationship. Bill Clinton then came into office, promising that it would not be "business as usual" with the "butchers of Beijing." Clinton made a highly publicized effort to link economic ties to improvements in China's human rights record, thereby placing new strains on the relationship without noticeably contributing to better Chinese behavior. Soon enough, he had to reverse course, and by the time Clinton left the White House, an uneasy stability had returned to U.S.–China ties.

George W. Bush, in turn, blasted Clinton for being soft on China and pledged that a Bush administration would recognize Beijing for the "strategic competitor" it actually was. Almost immediately, the midair collision between an American reconnaissance aircraft and a Chinese fighter, and the subsequent detention of the U.S. crew, added new tensions to the relationship. That same month, April 2001, the White House announced the most provocative arms sale to Taiwan since the establishment of diplomatic relations with Beijing in 1979. The inexperienced Bush used the occasion to assert that the United States would do "whatever it takes" to defend Taiwan from Chinese attack. The pronouncement appeared to move U.S. policy well beyond the ambiguity that previous presidents—both Republican and Democrat—had deliberately cultivated. In the early months of the Bush presidency, then, it seemed like the bottom was about to fall out of the U.S.–China relationship. But, of course, nothing of the sort happened. U.S.–China ties since mid-2001 have displayed a stability few would have dared predict when Bush entered the White House. As John Copper and others have pointed out in this volume, Bush dropped the "strategic competitor" term as soon as he became president. By the end of Bush's first term, then Secretary of State Colin Powell could claim that U.S.–China relations were the best they had been since the days of Richard Nixon three decades earlier.[2]

On the Downward Slope

During Bush's second term, however, American anxieties about China, and anger at Beijing, resurfaced, placing new strains on the relationship. Denunciations of China increasingly came to permeate daily discourse in Washington. Congress was awash in bills proposed to counter one threat or another posed by the PRC; according to *The Economist* of April 7, 2007, almost a dozen anti-China bills had already been introduced in the U.S. Congress since the beginning of that year.[3] Washington and Beijing engaged in tit-for-tat bans on imports of foodstuffs and other goods. Newspapers and policy journals were saturated with articles predicting a serious crisis in bilateral relations. China's rising influence in Asia, its rapid program of military modernization, its aggressive search for secure energy supplies, its periodic saber-rattling toward Taiwan, and its refusal, or inability, to clarify its ultimate intentions encouraged understandable fears about the security of American interests in Asia and beyond. The power equation in East Asia was shifting, in directions unknown, and the United States, as the preeminent power in the region, was naturally uneasy about a possible future less amenable to its interests than the present.

In February 2007, Vice President Dick Cheney took up a theme previously articulated by other senior American officials by publicly questioning the motives behind China's growing military reach.[4] Beijing's test of an antisatellite weapon in January 2007 rang alarm bells all over Washington. Conservative American think tanks produced a blizzard of analyses and policy memos highlighting the China threat. Over the past three years, according to a typically hyperbolic warning issued in 2005, Beijing had gained ten years on the United States in its quest to match American military capabilities.[5] Reflecting these security-related concerns, leading U.S. dailies trumpeted the existence of a vast Chinese spy apparatus in the United States. The *Wall Street Journal* quoted a senior FBI official to the effect that China represented the gravest espionage threat facing the United States today. There were, the paper warned, more than three thousand Chinese "front companies" in the United States established specifically to steal American military, industrial, and technological secrets.[6]

China's economic challenge also caused considerable anguish in both business and labor circles. Trade and currency-related frictions—including the perception of mounting U.S. job losses to Chinese laborers toiling for "slave wages," rampant copyright and intellectual property piracy, and a sense that Beijing was manipulating the value of its currency in a manner that gave Chinese goods an unfair advantage—were staples of the daily news. Elements in the U.S. business community—long a key proponent of stable U.S.–China ties—actively lobbied for legislative relief from Chinese competition. The 2006 trade deficit with Beijing reached a record $233 billion;[7] the 2007 deficit almost surely exceeded that figure.[8] While economists insisted that the failure of Americans to save was the real cause for the country's huge trade deficit, rather than unfair Chinese practices, this argument did not hold the political appeal that China-bashing carried. Reflecting this growing frustration with the PRC, the Bush administration imposed tariffs on Chinese paper imports and filed several complaints against China at the World Trade Organization in early 2007.[9]

In what remains the most authoritative Bush administration statement on China policy, Robert Zoellick, then the deputy secretary of state, noted in 2005 that "many Americans worry that the Chinese dragon will prove to be a fire-breather. There is a cauldron of anxiety about China."[10] A frustrated member of the U.S. House of Representatives complained that congressional sentiment on China was such that "if somebody's dog dies, it's China's fault."[11] Or, as Sen. Lisa Murkowski, the former chair of the Senate East Asia subcommittee, remarked, Washington was seized by a "fever pitch of concern" about China.[12]

How does one explain this up-and-down, roller-coaster character of U.S.–China relations? Why has a succession of American presidents—from both political parties—found it so difficult to create and maintain a stable relationship with Beijing?

One answer—many would claim this is the only answer necessary—is that Beijing does not make it easy. Quite simply, China, by its actions, its words, and its ideology, offends American sensibilities. Chinese policies and practices challenge American interests across a wide spectrum of areas. Chinese secretiveness encourages worst-case conclusions; Beijing might assuage American security anxieties were it to practice greater transparency in its defense spending, both as to the amount it budgets, and the limits, if any, on its modernization plans. Inflammatory rhetoric—on Taiwan, for instance, or as occurred several years ago when a senior Chinese general talked about nuking American cities—does not help. And always, there remains the undeniable fact that China is, in important though not all respects, an autocratic, one-party dictatorship with little regard for what most Americans think of as "American values." As the late California congressman Robert Matsui, who worked tirelessly to promote better relations with Beijing, once bemoaned, "China just gives you a lot of reasons if you want to vote no."[13]

THE AMERICAN POLITICAL CONTEXT

Less well understood, however, is that the U.S. domestic political context also complicates the management of this relationship. Looking beyond the specific irritants that loom so large at any given moment, it may make sense to step back from the problems du jour in order to understand why, over the years, it has been so difficult to maintain a stable U.S.–China relationship. Only by appreciating the role played by the American political system can we fully comprehend why this relationship has been so volatile, or hope to inject long-term stability into U.S. ties with China.[14]

What, then, are the characteristics of the American political system that combine with Chinese behavior to create nightmares for proponents of stable relations between the world's most populous country and its most powerful nation?

First, the nature of the American two-party system—the eternal rivalry between the party in power and the opposition party—provides institutional encouragement to China's critics. To a surprising degree, considering the highly polarized nature of U.S. politics today, China policy does not divide along either partisan or ideological lines. Republican–Democrat and conservative–liberal splits are largely meaningless in considering how American politicians deal with China. Indeed, for the better part of two decades, the China debate on Capitol Hill has seen the most conservative Republicans joining forces with liberal Democrats, in opposition to moderates of both parties. This, for instance, was the usual lineup during the annual congressional vote in the 1990s on whether to renew China's most-favored-nation (MFN) status. Clinton, otherwise so widely scorned by Republicans, was forced, year after year, to rely on GOP votes to secure MFN renewal. More recently, Senators Charles Schumer (D-NY) and Lindsey Graham (R-SC) have worked closely together on behalf of legislation to force China to revalue its currency.[15]

Every presidential administration since Nixon's, regardless of party affiliation or pre-White House pledges, has ended up working for stability in the relationship—promoting engagement with Beijing, emphasizing common interests, and looking for areas where the two could cooperate. And every political opposition promises to reverse the current administration's policy of engagement, to get tough with China, to "stand up for American values." So *China policy is more likely to be a contest between the "ins" and the "outs" than to reflect party or ideological labels.* And because one party in the American two-party system is always "out," that party can usually be counted upon to be pushing for a harder line on China.

Second, the *separation of powers* characteristic of the American system of government regularly interjects an element of contention into Sino–American ties. The China debate routinely pits the executive against the legislative branch. As veteran Washington Asia-watcher Chris Nelson, among others, has observed, every president since the 1970s has had a dual China problem: managing ties with Beijing while simultaneously countering congressional calls for a tougher policy toward the PRC.

This is not to suggest that the executive branch is always united in its approach to China. The Pentagon is consistently more alarmist than the State Department. Commerce is more apt to downplay disputes with Beijing than Treasury or the U.S. Trade Representative. Most of the major departments and agencies are themselves fractured; within the State Department, for instance, the human rights bureau is usually more confrontational than the regional bureau. Having conceded all this, however, it is still broadly true that the executive branch, stretching back to the Nixon era, has been more engagement-minded than the legislative branch.

Congress, unburdened with the day-to-day responsibilities of conducting policy, is far freer to criticize, to pick at the scabs in the relationship, to focus on single issues rather than considering the relationship in its totality. Many members of Congress, of both parties, complain that the executive is prepared to pay almost any price for China's friendship. Accusations that the White House elevates pragmatic concerns like trade over issues of principle, such as human rights or religious freedom, regularly emanate from the Hill. Entirely typical was the complaint lodged against the Clinton administration by Rep. Frank Wolf. "This country," the Virginia Republican observed, "has been blessed by God. We have to be faithful to our fundamental values. . . . We need to put back some morality in foreign policy."[16] Democrats who lambasted George H. W. Bush for conducting "business as usual" with Beijing after the Tiananmen Square massacre were essentially saying the same thing.[17]

The two branches of government also operate under differing time schedules. Diplomacy and negotiation, the business of the State Department, the U.S. Trade Representative's Office, and their sister executive branch agencies, encourage a long-term perspective and an incremental approach. "The best way to engage China is through dialogue and engagement, and not necessarily legislation," a senior official in the Bush Treasury Department has asserted.[18] Elected officials on Capitol Hill, on the other hand, pressured by constituents for immediate results, frequently look for the quick fix.

These two characteristics of the American political system—the never-ending struggle between "ins" and "outs," and the separation of powers that frequently finds the White House battling Capitol Hill—help explain why the Democratic victory in the 2006 congressional elections triggered predictions of a dramatic upsurge in U.S.–China tensions. The new Speaker of the House, Nancy Pelosi (D-CA), was a vocal critic of Chinese economic and human rights practices, and opposed MFN renewal even when a president of her own party, Bill Clinton, sought to build a constructive relationship with Beijing. Many of the new Democratic members of Congress reflected the increasingly protectionist leanings of their constituents—and China, of course, was an easy target for those worried about the loss of American jobs overseas. Publicly and privately, Bush officials used the Democratic capture of Congress as a lever in their dealings with Beijing: "Deal with us, or deal with Nancy Pelosi," was their unsubtle message.[19]

SPECIAL INTERESTS

The independent role accorded the U.S. Congress by the separation of powers is closely linked to a *third* factor making the management of this relationship difficult: the influence in American politics of single-issue interest groups. Few Americans view the U.S.–China relationship in a comprehensive or strategic sense. Geopolitical vision is not the strong suit of most people; few look at the connections among the many components of the U.S.–China relationship, or ask—to pick an example at random—how a decision to impose new trade sanctions on China might affect U.S. hopes to persuade North Korea to abandon its nuclear weapons aspirations. Americans, and their elected representatives in Congress, tend to focus on single issues, almost always contentious in their impact on U.S.–China relations. A very incomplete list of these hot button issues would include abortion, religious freedom, Tibet, labor rights, nonproliferation, trade competition, Taiwan, and human rights. Hollywood wants the Chinese to stop ripping off its movies. North Carolina textile workers want China to stop flooding the United States with cheap clothing. American religious groups oppose China's abortion policies and want Beijing to allow Chinese Christians to worship freely. Everyone has his own special concern and list of complaints against Beijing.

This is not to disparage the importance of these issues. Indeed, it is the insistence of the American people that these matters be given a prominent role in U.S. foreign policy that distinguishes American policy from that of other great powers throughout history.

Nonetheless, because most Americans, including their representatives in government, pay little detailed attention to foreign affairs, *special interest groups and single-issue lobbies wield a disproportionate influence in the conduct of U.S. foreign policy, and on U.S.-China relations.* The influence of single-interest groups is hardly a new phenomenon in American foreign policy, but the pervasiveness of that influence, and the multiplicity of interests seeking a voice in the foreign policy making process, is unprecedented. This adds an element of uncertainty to the management of U.S.–China relations today that was not nearly as prominent in previous eras. Moreover, single-issue activists are frequently uninterested in measured, nuanced responses. So American politicians and diplomats responsible for this key relationship face a challenge that their predecessors during the long cold war struggle with the Soviet Union did not have.

This American *tendency to consider China policy in piecemeal fashion*, to emphasize one or a small number of issues while giving short shrift to other important aspects of the relationship, helps explain why Sino–American ties have followed their roller-coaster trajectory. A classic example of this single-minded focus in America's China policy occurred in 1995, when Congress, by overwhelming votes, adopted legislation voicing its desire that the Taiwanese president, Lee Teng-hui, be permitted to attend his college reunion at Cornell University, notwithstanding long-established U.S. policy denying American visas to senior Taiwanese officials. The resultant Lee visit touched off a serious crisis in the U.S.–China relationship, eventually leading the Clinton administration to dispatch two aircraft carrier battle groups toward Taiwan waters.

In supporting Lee's desire to visit the United States, members of Congress were expressing quite appropriate indignation about PRC bullying of Taiwan, and reflecting views about fair play and support for democracies widely endorsed by the American public. The point is not that granting the visa to Lee Teng-hui was wrong. The point simply is that this failure to consider the China relationship in a comprehensive fashion, to ask how a visa for Lee would impact upon the broader tapestry of U.S.–China relations, underscores the manner in which a focus on single issues can complicate the conduct of America's China policy.

The important role played by single-issue groups links directly to a *fourth* factor influencing Washington's China policy: *the American political system offers few benefits for supporting good relations with Beijing, but many rewards for taking a tough approach toward China.* Each of the single-interest groups mentioned above, and many others, is mad at the Chinese. And for many activists, theirs is a litmus test issue—they will support or oppose candidates for office based solely upon the candidate's position on this single issue. If the issue enjoys enough backing, this gives candidates and elected officials a powerful incentive to support the get-tough-with-China position of these groups. Equally important, on many of these issues, there is no countervailing lobby or group pushing in the opposite direction. No one in America supports Beijing's coercive abortion policies; no one defends Chinese intellectual property piracy. In the 1990s, the U.S. business community often provided a countervailing influence, but in recent years, business itself has become much more ambivalent about China's growing economic muscle.

In a particularly revealing episode several years ago, well over one hundred members of the House of Representatives cast a vote in favor of a bill they thought was directed at China, only to take the unusual, if not embarrassing, step of reversing their vote upon being told by better informed colleagues that the bill would impose severe sanctions on European countries doing business with China. Originally advertised as a measure to keep American technology out of Chinese hands, the bill captured the anger with China felt by many legislators, who were all too happy to take a swipe at Beijing and saw no political or policy downside to doing so. But after learning that their anti-China gesture carried potentially sweeping consequences, they formally reversed the vote they had cast only minutes earlier.[20] Bemused observers found it an odd way for a superpower to make policy.

The congressional leadership understands the advantages of permitting rank-and-file legislators to take an anti-China stand, and uses this to advance other priorities. In July 2005, for instance, the House of Representatives was poised to vote on the Central American Free Trade Agreement (CAFTA). The House leadership feared it lacked the votes to pass this bill because of concerns held by some lawmakers that the pact would contribute to the loss of American jobs. In order to give its members political cover to vote for CAFTA, the leadership arranged to hold a vote one day before the CAFTA vote on legislation purportedly to curb unfair trade practices by China. In fact, no one seriously argued this legislation would protect American jobs or have any impact on Chinese practices; indeed, congressional insiders knew there was little chance the Senate would even take up the measure. Instead, everyone involved recognized this move as nothing more than an effort by the House leadership to give members a chance to cast a stand-up-for-American-workers vote prior to the CAFTA vote.

In other words, there is no downside to engaging in a bit of China-bashing if doing so serves other purposes. (Even in this case, however, a majority of House Democrats voted against the China legislation on the grounds that it was not tough enough.) Nor was the CAFTA incident unusual. The annual MFN votes in the 1990s frequently included a companion bill that castigated China for its shortcomings. Congressional leaders understood that their members should not be asked to support legislation that could be portrayed as pro-China (MFN renewal), without first being given an opportunity to shake a fist at Beijing.

Various congressional procedures and practices also tempt U.S. lawmakers to promote one-sided legislation. One chamber (often the House of Representatives) will feel free to adopt a bill that goes considerably beyond official U.S. policy in order to "send a message" to Beijing because its leadership knows that the other chamber is unlikely to pass the bill (i.e., that the second chamber will "provide adult supervision," some would say). Or, if both Houses do approve identical legislation, they can count on the president to veto it. Another favorite tactic is to adopt "sense of the Congress" language, indicating strong displeasure with China, but without requiring either the White House or Beijing to take any action. In legislative parlance, these are "cost-free" votes, which make a statement, articulate genuine concerns, prod a status quo-oriented White House, send a warning message to China, and please domestic constituencies—all without any costs, at least from the vantage point of Capitol Hill.

A *fifth* factor making the management of U.S.–China relations difficult relates to the fact that *the American political system is tilted in favor of the alarmists*, of those who see dangers to the American polity. Congressional human rights committees do not focus on those countries whose human rights record is exemplary. They focus on the problematic countries, a list where China figures prominently. Or consider the powerful congressional armed services committees. Generally speaking, conservatives and supporters of big military budgets dominate these panels. And the witnesses who are asked to testify at committee hearings are often those who reinforce the "China threat" message, who provide a justification for more U.S. defense spending. This tendency to alarmism even spills over into the area of pork barrel politics. A Connecticut legislator, a few years ago, pointed to the growth of China's submarine force to argue that the submarine base in his district not be closed. Here as well, there seemed good political reasons to raise the alarm about China, and little risk in doing so.

Nor is this built-in bias toward alarmism confined to the legislative branch. Congress, in recent years, has mandated numerous reports from the Pentagon on Chinese military capabilities, Beijing's threat to Taiwan, and related topics. In virtually every instance, the emphasis of these reports lies on those developments that cause the most concern for U.S. defense planners, not the areas that do not seem threatening. No Pentagon officer was ever denied a promotion for overestimating the threat from a potential adversary, and the system encourages worst-case scenarios. Such reports, or fragments taken out of context, are then used by congressional hawks to influence future spending decisions and probably exacerbate Chinese apprehensions as well.

The press is party to this predisposition to alarmism as well. The major news outlets these days are saturated with China-related stories. In a disproportionate number of cases, these reports highlight the problematic, the threatening, the unpleasant—those aspects of Chinese life and society that are most distasteful to American audiences. In the world of commercial journalism, there is little room for good news; good news is deemed no news. This condition is not the result of a deliberate press conspiracy, nor applicable only to China. Instead, it reflects a dollars-and-cents calculation as to what attracts readers and draws viewers. But here again, the system encourages news reports on China that are painted in the darkest hues, and accustoms Americans to think of the PRC in somber, if not threatening, terms.

UNINFORMED AND UNIMAGINATIVE

A lack of historical context in viewing the PRC, reflecting an ignorance about Chinese politics, history, and culture, is a *sixth* factor that has contributed to the volatility of U.S.–China relations. A few years ago, a delegation from the U.S. Congress met with a senior Chinese foreign ministry official at a time of considerable tension in the bilateral relationship. After briefing his visitors on the domestic and international challenges facing his country, the Chinese diplomat then invited questions. "I just want to know," one congressman asked, "if you've accepted Jesus Christ as your personal savior." Describing the incident later, another participant recalled that their Chinese host—an official representative of a militantly atheistic government—looked dumbfounded. The incident, unimportant in itself, suggests the wide gap in experiences and in perceptions, and the difficulties of communication between the two countries, that is aggravated by the lack of understanding each has of the other.

What is striking about American images of China is how one-sided and ahistorical they are. An astonishingly large number of American policy makers demonstrate little historical perspective when looking at China, little appreciation of the distinctly Chinese experience, and little recognition of how far—in some, though certainly not all, respects—China has traveled in recent decades. Nor is there an attempt to measure the PRC by anything other than American standards—or even a recognition that other standards exist. A failure to distinguish between the short-term and the long-term—the failure, for instance, to evaluate the arrest of a prominent political dissident against the backdrop of an increasingly open PRC—further handicaps Americans and American officials as they seek to comprehend this new Asian power.

Americans justly celebrate the collapse of Communism in the Soviet Union. China looks at Russia in the 1990s and sees a disorder that calls to mind earlier unhappy periods in China's own history. Whereas the United States applauds the introduction of democracy in the former Soviet Union, China sees it as a warning—a danger to be shunned. Similarly, the United States takes pride in the absence of an imperialist history in China. Beijing, on the other hand, views Washington's support for Taiwan today as the only factor preventing the PRC from removing the most emotional remaining relic of its nineteenth- and twentieth-century humiliation by outside powers. With such divergent perspectives, it is little wonder that the two find it difficult to communicate. Most Americans are unlikely to embrace the Chinese perspective, but until they at least understand that China's recent history leads Beijing to a fundamentally different view of the world, they will find it difficult to construct and maintain a stable U.S.–China relationship.

These divergent historical memories sometimes produce what many Chinese regard as an American double standard in its treatment of the PRC. Politicians and China analysts in Washington have focused on the robust increases in China's defense spending since the end of the cold war as an indicator of troubling, and possibly sinister, Chinese intentions. In a speech in Singapore in 2005, U.S. Defense Secretary Donald Rumsfeld, in tones reminiscent of the 2000 "China-as-strategic-competitor" Bush campaign, pointedly asked why Beijing was spending so much on its military, and other senior American officials have echoed his question. Such complaints appear hypocritical to the Chinese, conscious as they are that America's defense budget dwarfs China's.[21]

In another celebrated incident, Washington's China hawks have gotten considerable mileage out of the crude threat to nuke American cities issued by a senior Chinese general.[22] As offended as many Americans were by the heavy-handed comments of Gen. Zhu Chenghu, Chinese analysts saw little difference between Zhu's words and those of Gen. Michael Moseley, the senior U.S. Air Force commander, who, a few weeks earlier, had told a Senate committee that preparing for war with China was at the top of his list of priorities.[23] Similarly, the Chinese question the sincerity of American complaints about the jailing of Chinese political dissidents at a time when the newspapers are full of unsavory reports regarding the ill treatment of U.S. prisoners at Guantanamo and in Afghanistan and Iraq.[24] Beijing views American complaints about Chinese espionage in the United States against the backdrop of the discovery, a few years ago, that a Boeing aircraft built for the use of the Chinese president was riddled with eavesdropping and other spying devices. And, surely, no one in the Bush administration would grant China the right of preemptive or preventive war—against Taiwan, for instance—that the Bush White House has claimed for itself.

Of course, a compelling case can be made that American actions in each of the above cases are not really comparable to Chinese practices. The United States, for instance, is presently engaged in two wars and, moreover, has global interests and responsibilities that Beijing does not. Little wonder that its military budget is far larger than China's. Be that as it may, the Chinese perception that the United States is hypocritical, that it holds China to a higher standard than Washington demands of itself, is a further manifestation of the difficulty the two countries have in communicating. Even if they reject this Chinese perception of a U.S. double standard, Americans need to recognize that Beijing does not necessarily credit the United States with the sincerity and good intentions Americans routinely ascribe to their country and its government.

Seventh, the *failure of successive American presidents to give clear signals on China policy* has also hampered the conduct of U.S.–China diplomacy. For all the reasons mentioned already, U.S. presidents have been reluctant to speak out clearly and forcefully on the importance of Chinese–American relations and the cost to American interests in the absence of an at least modestly decent working relationship with Beijing. It is one thing for a secretary of state to speak about the necessity of getting this relationship right—people expect that. But it is an altogether different matter when the president of the United States lends the immense weight of his prestige to such a message. Given the passions surrounding this relationship, given frequent Chinese actions that heighten the anger or anxieties China already engenders in many Americans, and given the unique position in the American political system occupied by the president, there is no one else but the president who can credibly make the case for stable U.S.–China relations. Without direction from the White House, the individuals, the lobbies, the bureaucracies, and the activists who bear a (frequently legitimate) grudge against Beijing will highjack U.S. policy to promote their own objectives.

Clinton's policy toward China for much of his first term was thoroughly muddled. Even after the White House decided that a policy of engaging Beijing was the only realistic option, it failed to convey this decision in a manner that convinced many of the president's political allies, let alone the opposition Republicans. It took several years of pushing by pro-engagement forces within the administration and Congress before Clinton finally agreed to devote an entire speech to U.S.–China relations. The current occupant of the White House, seven years into his presidency, has yet to do so.[25]

Yet, even a firm presidential explanation of the stakes involved in the U.S.–China relationship carries dangers. Clinton ultimately oversold the purported benefits of engagement. He failed to adequately convey that engagement represented a long-term approach to relations with China, and that there would be many bumps and, indeed, some substantial setbacks along the way. By not preparing the Congress and the country for the inevitable difficulties and frictions in the relationship, Clinton, in the very act of trying to highlight the importance of the relationship, contributed to the cycle of excessive expectations, dashed hopes, and consequent feelings of betrayal and anger that continue to plague U.S.–China ties. Decisive presidential leadership, in other words, requires far more than a single speech. The White House must, on a regular basis, risk angering key constituencies—domestic groups, congressional allies, the Chinese—by providing continual high-visibility leadership on this issue.[26]

Finally, this emphasis on the American domestic political context that shapes the debate on U.S.–China relations should not be allowed to obscure one further important factor that makes managing this relationship so tricky—*the existence of genuine disagreement about what China's rise means, and what Beijing's ultimate intentions are.* The course of international politics over the next several decades will revolve around the answer to the question of what kind of China a strong China will be. Will a rising China be a disruptive force on the global scene, as Germany and Japan were in the previous century? Or will an increasingly powerful China become a force for stability within Asia and around the globe?

These are not easy questions. The stakes at issue are high. And the consequences for getting this relationship wrong could be considerable. China is not Albania of the 1960s, or Burma today. What happens in China, and how China evolves, will influence the lives of twenty-first-century Americans in ways profound as well as mundane. China counts, and Americans understand this, even if they are frequently hazy on the details. So it is not surprising that the passions surrounding Chinese–American relations are heated. This, too, makes maintenance of stability in this relationship more difficult.

Countervailing Forces

Nonetheless, the situation is not all discouraging. As Professor Steven Levine has aptly noted, roller-coasters have their ups and downs, but they seldom go off track. Counteracting these forces creating instability in the relationship are a number of factors that push in the opposite direction.

First, in the years since Tiananmen Square, institutional mechanisms and habits of dialogue, and even cooperation, have become an integral part of the Chinese–American relationship: the more or less regular summits between the U.S. and Chinese presidents; frequent dialogue on global issues such as Iran and Iraq; regularized ministerial-level exchanges; collaboration on regional problems such as North Korea; at least modest cooperation in the sensitive areas of security and intelligence, especially since 9/11; and bilateral dialogue on contentious issues such as human rights and trade irritants. The institutionalization and regularization of these contacts offer safety values and mechanisms for tension abatement at moments when relations between the two countries become particularly difficult.

Second, influential segments of the U.S. business community will almost surely continue to work for stability in U.S.–China relations, providing a countervailing force to the many groups whose agendas bring them into conflict with Beijing. While the business community is anything but monolithic, key components have provided ballast in the relationship over the years. U.S. businesses, for instance, played a key role in the annual congressional battles in the 1990s over MFN renewal. Business, especially large corporations with international operations, enjoys considerable clout in the American political system, and those firms with a multinational tint can be counted upon to continue making the case for engagement with China.

Third, Beijing will almost certainly remain focused on economic growth and internal development in the years ahead. For all the extraordinary progress China has achieved over the past quarter century, its leaders today are still acutely aware of the PRC's many weaknesses and vulnerabilities. To take just one example, China has almost no ability to protect the sea-lanes through which an increasingly larger portion of its oil supplies transit—a hostile America could deliver a crippling blow to the Chinese economy by cutting off these oil shipments. For the foreseeable future, the Chinese leadership will seek to avoid crises in its relations with the United States, although it will remain hypersensitive on issues relating to Taiwan, especially anything that hints of Taiwanese independence. Given even modest encouragement from Washington, Beijing is unlikely to challenge core U.S. interests. That, of course, does not preclude a Chinese misreading of what constitutes such interests. One must hope, therefore, that, over time, Beijing comes to develop a more sophisticated understanding of the Washington decision-making process, so as to make truly stupid actions less likely. (Again, Taiwan remains a special case, with its own dangers.[27])

Fourth, and perhaps most importantly, the absence of attractive options will push any U.S. administration in the direction of fostering stability in this relationship. This will be true especially so long as the United States finds itself tied down in the Middle East and southwest Asia, but it will continue to be the case beyond that time as well. Said differently, the costs for the United States, should this relationship fall apart, are too high for any American official to contemplate with equanimity. It is so obviously in the nation's interest to make this relationship work, at least tolerably well, that it is almost impossible to envision any U.S. leadership acting on any other assumption. American politicians are not stupid. They are, moreover, results-oriented. Traditional American pragmatism will push the nation's leaders to take pains to make this relationship work.

This, however, is simply another way of saying that the U.S.–China relationship is too important to allow a "politics as usual" approach. While the politics cannot be avoided, neither can they be permitted to determine policy. The challenge—it is an American challenge, but one with crucial consequences for the world—is how to manage the politics of the relationship so as to get the policy right.

NOTES

1. Thomas Donnelly and Melissa Wisner, "A Global Partnership Between the U.S. and India," August-September 2005, American Enterprise Institute, http://www.aei.org/include/pub_print.asp?pubID=23139.
2. http://en-1.ce.cn/National/Politics/200411/14/t20041114_2276574.shtml. For an earlier expression of the same sentiment, see Colin L. Powell, "A Strategy of Partnerships," *Foreign Affairs* 83, no. 1 (January–February 2004): 32. In their contribution in this volume (Chapter 7), Bonnie S. Glaser and Liang Wang show that Powell was using this formulation as early as September 2003.
3. "The Trade Two-step," *The Economist*, April 7, 2007, 27. This number rose substantially as the year progressed.
4. See Cheney's remarks at the Australian-American Leadership Dialogue, February 23, 2007, at http://www.whitehouse.gov/news/releases/2007/02/20070223.html. These comments echoed widely reported remarks by then Secretary of Defense Donald Rumsfeld in Singapore in 2005. For the Rumsfeld speech, see http://singapore.usembassy.gov/060405.html.
5. This claim, by the Heritage Foundation's John Tkacik, appeared in William Matthews, "U.S. Leaders Underscore Rising China Threat," *DefenseNews* (June 27, 2005): 10.

6. Jay Solomon, "FBI Sees Big Threat From Chinese Spies; Businesses Wonder," *Wall Street Journal*, August 10, 2005, p. A1. For similar articles, see Mark Magnier, "Defection Spotlights Chinese Way of Spying," *Los Angeles Times*, July 15, 2005, p. A3; "Espionage Targets Technology," *Roanoke Times*, January 16, 2007, at http://www.roanoke.com/business/wb/wb/xp-100267; Bill Gertz, "China a 'Central' Spying Threat," *Washington Times*, September 29, 2005, p. A4; and Bill Gertz, "China Taps into U.S. Spy Operations," *Washington Times*, December 21, 2007, p. A1. The *Los Angeles Times* article noted that the claim about 3,000 Chinese front companies was unsubstantiated.
7. By U.S. estimates; the Chinese, using different statistical measures, claim that the actual figure is significantly lower.
8. Preliminary U.S. government figures through November 2007 put the bilateral deficit at $237 billion. See http://www.census.gov/foreign-trade/balance/c5700.html#2007.
9. Note, as well, the frosty tone of the exchanges at the Strategic Economic Dialogue (SED), held in Washington in May 2007, and attended by the largest delegation of senior Chinese officials ever to visit the American capital. At the December 2007 SED talks, China warned that protectionist measures in Congress could trigger Chinese retaliation.
10. Zoellick's September 21, 2005, speech to the National Committee on U.S.–China Relations can be found at http://www.ncuscr.org/articlesandspeeches/Zoellick.htm.
11. The author was privy to the "dog dies" remark in an off-the-record conversation in June 2006. In the aftermath of the scare over contaminated pet food imports from China, the quip has assumed a poignancy the speaker did not intend.
12. Joel Brinkley, "Rice Warns China to Make Major Economic Changes," *New York Times*, August 19, 2005, p. A10.
13. Matthew Vita, "On Hill, Clinton Turns To Calif. Free-Trader," *Washington Post*, April 5, 2000, p. A17.
14. Helpful starting points on how U.S. policy toward China is fashioned include Jean A. Garrison, *Making China Policy: From Nixon to G. W. Bush* (Boulder, CO: Lynne Rienner, 2005), an historical overview that does not emphasize the structural and institutional factors highlighted in this essay; and Robert L. Suettinger, *Beyond Tiananmen: The Politics of U.S.-China Relations, 1989–2000* (Washington, DC: Brookings, 2003), by a former U.S. government official directly involved in shaping Washington's China policy during the presidencies of George H. W. Bush and Bill Clinton.
15. The weekly *National Journal* awarded Schumer a 74.5 liberal rating (out of 100) in 2006, and Graham a 70.8 conservative rating; see "Senate Ratings," *National Journal* 39, no. 9 (March 3, 2007): 48–51. Schumer and Graham were joined by conservative Republican Charles Grassley

(IA) and moderately liberal Democrat Max Baucus (MT) in the 2007 version of the Graham-Schumer bill.

16. Miles A. Pomper, "The Religious Right's Foreign Policy Revival," *CQ Weekly*, May 9, 1998, 1210.
17. China, perhaps because its own National People's Congress is almost toothless, has been slow to recognize the important role in policy making toward China played by the U.S. Congress. As a consequence, over the years, Beijing has not been very effective in defending its positions on the Hill.
18. Peter S. Goodman, "Battle Rises Over China," *Washington Post*, June 14, 2007, p. D1
19. See, for instance, Edward Cody, "U.S. Warns China on Piracy, Market Access," *Washington Post*, November 15, 2006, p. D8. For an informed and less alarmist analysis of what Democratic control of Congress might mean for Washington's China policy, see Robert Sutter, "The Democratic-Led 110th Congress: Implications for Asia," *Asia Policy*, no. 3 (January 2007): 125–50. Sutter quite correctly argued that the Democratic Congress would be unable to force a major shift in U.S. policy toward China. This, however, did not preclude new strains in U.S.–China relations as a result of the Democrats' electoral victories in November 2006.
20. For details, see Martin Kady II, "Vote Switching Stalls Military Sales Bill," *CQ Weekly*, July 18, 2005, 1979.
21. The Chinese claim that their 2007 defense budget totaled $45 billion, a figure that almost certainly understates actual military spending. The U.S. Department of Defense asserts that total Chinese defense expenditures were two to three times this amount. Other estimates tend to fall somewhere between these two extremes. By way of contrast, the U.S. military budget will be in the range of $623 billion for fiscal year 2008. RAND analysts project that twenty years from now, China's defense spending will still be less than half of today's U.S. defense budget. For recent discussion of this issue, see Office of the Secretary of Defense, "Military Power of the People's Republic of China, 2007," Annual Report to Congress, May 23, 2007, available at http://www.defenselink.mil/pubs/pdfs/070523-China-Military-Power-final.pdf; Edward Cody, "China Boosts Military Spending," *Washington Post*, March 5, 2007, p. A12; C. Fred Bergsten, Bates Gill, Nicholas R. Lardy, and Derek Mitchell, *China: The Balance Sheet: What the World Needs to Know About the Emerging Superpower* (New York: Public Affairs, 2006), 149–54; Keith Crane, Roger Cliff, Evan S. Medeiros, James C. Mulvenon, and William H. Overholt, *Modernizing China's Military: Opportunities and Constraints*, RAND, May 19, 2005; Council on Foreign Relations, "U.S.-China Relations: An Affirmative Agenda, a Responsible Course," Independent Task Force Report No. 59 (April 2007), 47–54; and Donald G. Gross, "Transforming the U.S. Relationship with China," *Global Asia* 2, no. 1 (Spring 2007): 78–89.

22. For discussion of this remark (which almost certainly did not represent official Chinese policy), and more generally, for a look at the Taiwan issue as a potential trigger for U.S.–China conflict, see Richard C. Bush and Michael E. O'Hanlon, *A War Like No Other: The Truth about China's Challenge to America* (Hoboken, NJ: John Wiley & Sons, 2007), esp. 156.
23. For American reaction to Zhu's comments, see Joel Brinkley, "U.S. Rebukes Chinese General for His Threat of Nuclear Arms Use," *New York Times*, July 16, 2005, p. A8. For Moseley's testimony, see the Reuters report, "US Struggles on China-War Planning, Top Officer States," June 29, 2005, at http://english.epochtimes.com/news/5-6-29/29933.html.
24. See, for instance, the pointed comment by a 2007 Council on Foreign Relations task force: "The United States' ability to champion a human rights agenda with China has been severely impaired by the U.S. failure to live up to its own ideals of the rule of law and respect for human rights" (Council on Foreign Relations, "U.S.-China Relations," 91).
25. While they angered many Taiwanese, Bush's public warning to Taipei in December 2003 not to challenge the status quo between Taiwan and the mainland, and the administration's related statements in the run-up to the 2004 Taiwanese presidential election, were looked upon by many as precisely the sort of White House clarity that heretofore had been lacking. But these messages have been followed by others—Rumfeld's Singapore speech in 2005, for instance—whose cumulative impact has been to raise new doubts as to just how committed the Bush administration is to a policy that, even if current officials do not emphasize the term, looks much like Clinton's policy of engagement.
26. It is important to emphasize that this does not mean the president should refrain from criticizing China when its actions merit criticism. To the contrary, unless the White House demonstrates it is prepared to stand up to Beijing and to condemn China in a highly public fashion when necessary, it will be impossible to retain support from either Congress or the American people for a policy that seeks to build a tolerably decent working relationship with the PRC.
27. See, for instance, Ted Galen Carpenter, *America's Coming War with China: A Collision Course over Taiwan* (New York: Palgrave Macmillan, 2006).

Chapter 4

The Worldviews of Chinese Leadership and Sino–U.S. Relations

Chien-min Chao and Chih-Chia Hsu

China's fourth generation leadership is mostly made up of technocrats, who are therefore more pragmatic than their revolutionary predecessors. The new leadership includes firm supporters and practitioners of reform and open policies, and has reaped the benefits of these policies in witnessing their once isolated and backward country emerge as a dominant power on the world stage. Under this backdrop, the fourth generation leadership has developed unique views of the world.

There is no doubt that important policies were made only after consultation with the third generation leadership, at least at the beginning.[1] The new leaders in Beijing have already shaken off the shadow cast by Jiang Zemin and his cohorts, and they are the ones who are making China's policies now.

Most of the new leaders lack experience in external affairs, as domestic issues, especially economic development and social stability, are their major concerns. While putting up a "stay close to the people" (*qinmin*) policy, the new leadership reacts passively rather than proactively when facing challenges.[2] Under Hu Jintao's stewardship, China's foreign policy reflects the pragmatic inclination of technocrats.[3] "Rising peacefully" (*heping jueqi*) and "harmonious world" (*hexie shijie*) are embodiments of the new policy.

What is the cognitive map of the fourth generation leadership over world affairs? Do they offer new perspectives? What is the rationale and basis for this new thinking? Will Sino–American relations be affected by this new thinking? These are the issues that this chapter intends to explore. The chapter analyzes the worldviews of China's top leadership in an attempt to find clues into their making of important foreign policies.[4]

Contradictions, Realism, and Constructivism

China's foreign policy has been based on three sub-theories—the theories of contradiction, realism, and constructivism—and the theory of "harmonious world" is no exception.

For Mao Zedong, the world revolved around contradictions. According to their relevancy and importance, contradictions could be further broken down into primary and secondary contradictions, confrontational and nonconfrontational contradictions, and domestic and adversarial contradictions.[5] To him, incessant struggles were necessary, because of these contradictions.

Although China's foreign policies were made according to the contradictions it assessed in the world at the time, what decided the contradictions was not Marxist ideology, but rather, realist and constructivist's views.

Continuing the policy blazed by the paramount leader Deng Xiaoping, the fourth generation of leadership views peace and development as the primary contradictions in the nation's strive for modernization. A valid solution to this predicament is cooperation. The "harmonious world" theory has been designed specifically for that purpose.

Scholars differ on how realism is defined. As a paradigm, realism has different variations: classical realism, structural realism or neorealism, defensive realism, offensive realism, and neoclassical realism. Regardless of their differences, these variations do share some common assumptions: states are the main roles of international politics; the world is in a state of anarchy; states are rational actors with survival as the core value; international structure determines outcome and behaviors of nations.[6] For realists, states will be strengthened or weakened in the international system of powers.[7]

For realists, the international community is often anarchical. States are the main actors of international relations and their existence is for the pursuit of power and interests. States interact with each other through a delicate balancing of powers.

As pragmatic technocrats, national interests are an important consideration for the fourth generation of leadership in the making of foreign policies. The purpose for raising the idea of "respecting plural cultures" (*duoyuan wenhua*), a main component in the "harmonious world" theory, is to shield China's one-party dictatorship from undue outside influences. The trumpeting of a multilateral trading system and coprosperity is also in line with China's goal as a developmental state.

Constructivism was introduced to the study of international relations in the late 1980s. Although Chinese scholars did not get to know the theory until shortly before the end of the twentieth century, it soon became the most dominant school in the country's fledgling study of international relations. Chinese scholars are particularly interested in the works of Alexander Wendt. Like realists, Wendt treats nations as the main actor of analysis in world politics. Unlike the realists, super-national structures are decided by interactions between nations rather than by some other material measurements. Furthermore, national identity and interests are defined by social structure, instead of some other external factors within the system.[8] For the constructivists, international relations are constituted by social facts.[9] In other words, it is the agreements and norms reached and shared by the actors that are playing the major roles. Since international structure is determined by nations, security dilemma emerges due to a lack of trust among nations. If nations can share knowledge and thinking and construct trust, then wars are no longer needed as a means to resolve differences.[10]

Mao's ideology is long gone, but the legacy of the theory of contradiction lives on—it has been made part of the Hu Jingtao thinking. The main contraction now, as was suggested by Deng Xiaoping two decades ago, remains the one between development and nondevelopment. For Hu, to work with, rather than fight against, the major powers in the world system in a harmonious way is realistic and suits China's best interests.

To China, the current international system has been created by the major powers in the West. It is urgent that China and countries in the Third World take initiative to construct international norms catering to their own interests.[11] China is obliged to take a more active role in the shaping of the world order in the post-cold war era. Common security, coprosperity, and democratization of international relations are all meant for the construction of a new international political order.

WHY "HARMONIOUS WORLD"?

Deng Xiaoping broached the concepts of "peace and development" as the most critical issues facing the world in 1985.[12] For the first time in China's history, the main contradiction in the world was interpreted not from the ideological point of view, but from the developmental point of view. This new version of contraction has been the official policy for the new reform-minded Chinese leaders since the mid-1980s. Built upon the basis of the inherited policy, the "harmonious world" thesis was designed to cultivate a fitting environment to facilitate its domestic agenda and alleviate mounting pressure from the outside world as a result of China's rising economic strength.

A Rising but Threatening China

In a speech during a trip to the United States in December 2003, Premier Wen Jiabao broached the idea that China was "a big power in reform rising peacefully."[13] This was the first time that the term "peaceful rise" was made public. Later on, while commemorating the one hundred and tenth anniversary of Mao's birthday, Chinese Communist Party (CCP) Secretary General Hu Jingtao talked about "insisting on the path of development via rising peacefully."[14] However, the term was officially abandoned, because of concerns of China's intentions overseas, and a less intimidating "peaceful development" was resurrected.[15] However, the term "peaceful rise" continues to be in use in private.

Nourishing a peaceful environment—so that China can concentrate on the tall task of pulling its humongous 1.3 billion population out of poverty—remains the most sacred goal for the fourth generation leadership of China. China's economy has seen leaps and bounds since Deng Xiaoping started to reform its highly inefficient centrally commanded economic system. China's gross domestic product (GDP) doubled in the first four years under Hu Jintao's leadership, increasing from 10.23 trillion RMB in 2002 to 20.94 trillion in 2006, while foreign trade tripled in the same period from US$620.8 billion to US$1,760 billion (see Table 4.1). It is on this increase of economic power that a new foreign policy has been founded.

In the United States, how to treat an economically rising and yet politically repressive China was a touchy issue for the Bill Clinton administration in the late 1990s. Many participated in the great debate between policies of engagement and containment. Although the engagement school seemed to have the upper hand, and Clinton

Table 4.1 China's GDP and Foreign Trade, 2002–6

Year	GDP (RMB trillion)	Foreign Trade (US$ billion)
2002	10.23	620.8
2003	11.67	851
2004	13.65	1,154.7
2005	18.23	1,422.1
2006	20.94	1,760

Sources: GDP data are cited from *Government Work Report, 2003–2007*, http://www.gov.cn/test/2006-02/16/content_200719.htm; http://news.xinhuanet.com/misc/2007-03/17/content_5859480.htm. China's foreign trade information can be found in http://big5.china.com.cn/aboutchina/data/txt/2006-11/09/content _7335919.htm.

even went so far as to enter a "constructive partnership" with Jiang Zemin, the view that China remained a threat and a conflict in the future was inevitable with rife.[16] The theory of a "China threat" emerged in the early 1990s. It resulted from an array of reasons: a rising economic power armed with a one-party dictatorship and increasing military capabilities, fear of a collapse of China, and the visible strength of Chinese nationalism.[17] Implications of the rise and fall of China were issues often discussed in the academic world.

The 9/11 terrorist attacks changed U.S. security policy and priorities in the formulation of its foreign policy. Fighting against international terrorism became the most urgent task for the Bush administration. As such, the United States needs China, in its global strategy, to build a more secure external environment. Consequently, certain degrees of trust were reached between the two countries.[18] Under these circumstances the "threat of China" was bereft of its ideological basis and Sino–U.S. relations improved as a result.

To the Chinese leadership, the retreat of the "China threat" might only be transient, resulting from tactical cooperation between the two countries to fight a common enemy. It is not unlikely that once the threat of terrorism is removed, the "China threat" might be resuscitated due to the consistent rapid growth of China's economy. China replaced the United Kingdom as the fourth largest economy in 2005. The theory of "harmonious world" was created to partly preempt another wave of adversarial discourse in the international community, so that a favorable environment can be retained to continue the course of developing its economy.

Popular Expectation and Consolidation of Power

Economic strength has heightened nationalistic expectations from the Chinese people. A century of humiliation from Western imperialist powers (including Japan) has left an indelible imprint in the minds of Chinese leadership, as well as ordinary people. According to one survey, international standing outweighs economic growth, and is ranked one of the three major issues concerning the younger generation in China.[19] How to improve China's international profile is surely something Beijing's leadership needs to worry about, and economic might has provided China necessary wherewithal to improve its image abroad. Chinese elites are well aware of the need to increase their country's international recognition and for the improvement of relations with major Western powers like the United States.[20] Popular expectations have put pressure on the Chinese leadership to further improve its international standing.

Another important reason for the promotion of the theory of "harmonious world" is to consolidate powers. It is essential for the Chinese leadership to retain the right to ideological interpretation. Leaders have been using this weapon to legitimatize their policy lines and keep them from being accused of deviating from the right line. It is an important instrument on the way toward power consolidation. Mao Zedong, Deng Xiaoping, and Jiang Zemin have all had their idiosyncratic ideologies written into the party constitution. These guidelines were critical in building their respective regimes and strengthening their own power base. For Hu Jingtao, it is imperative that he comes up with his own version of ideology for the rationalization of his rule and for providing guidance in the writing of important policies.

For the fourth generation leadership, it is necessary to follow their reform-minded predecessors and formulate innovative thinking as part of the "practical ideology," so that the legacy of reforms can be continued. "Deng Xiaoping theory" (*Deng Xiaoping lilun*) put down the general principles on how a market economy can, and should, be a part of socialism. Jiang's "three represents" theory added a dimension of practicality by expanding the scope of socialism to include capitalists—the most pivotal part of the capitalist mode of production—into the ranks of its party. An easy way out for Hu in the fight to claim a niche in the Holy Grail is to address the social injustices stemming from a rapid reformation of the old system. This is the rationale for the advocating of the "harmonious society." The "harmonious world" is a variant of the theory on external affairs.

COLLECTIVE SECURITY, CO-PROSPERITY, AND DEMOCRACY

"Harmonious world" has been part of the new ideological underpinning to help the fourth generation of leadership consolidate its rule. The term appeared for the first time in a speech delivered by Hu Jingtao on April 22, 2005, at the Asia-African Summit Meeting. Hu stressed the need to "push for a harmonious world where different civilizations can coexist in good terms, dialogue in equality, and develop in prosperity."[21] A few months later, while attending the ceremony marking the sixtieth anniversary of the United Nations on September 15, Hu again included in his speech the intension to "strive to build a harmonious world with eternal peace and common prosperity." Chinese media has used expressions such as "new diplomatic policy" and "new development of diplomatic thinking" to describe the "harmonious world."[22] During the Central Working Meeting on Diplomacy held in August 2006, "harmonious world" was hailed as a guiding principle as well as an important task for external work.[23] Peace, development, and cooperation seem to be the three pillars of this new thinking on China's foreign policy.

Hu's "harmonious world" entails at least three contents:[24]

1. To achieve collective security through multilateralism: countries should abandon cold war mentality and promote new thinking on security based on mutual trust and benefits, equality, and cooperation. Disputes should be resolved through peace and negotiation.
2. To realize coprosperity through mutual benefits and cooperation: an open and fair multilateral trading system should be formed in which developed countries should open up their markets to the developing countries and transfer their technology, provide assistance, and reduce the burden of debts on the latter.
3. To build a harmonious world through democracy and inclusiveness: history, cultures, and different models of development should not be obstacles for international exchanges and reasons for animosity. More exchanges should be promoted between civilizations. International relations should be democratized.

Common security (*gongtong anquan*), mutual prosperity (*gongtong fanrong*), and harmonious relations (*hexie guanxi*) seem to be the three main ingredients to the concept of the "harmonious world."

According to Chinese logic, the purpose of common security is peace and it can be accomplished through multilateralism, such as the United Nations. It has to be done through peaceful means. Mutual prosperity resolves the problem of development through cooperation. Developed countries have to open up their markets, and harmonious relations resolve the issue of differences between cultures. This is possible only when mutual respect is honored by members of the global community. Therefore, international relations have to be democratized. It seems that the construction of a harmonious world is a goal. This goal will not be possible unless it is based on respect of cultures. International rules have to be drawn up on principles of democracy and multilateralism. Peaceful negotiation and cooperation are necessary as a means to reap mutual benefits.

A Realistic Way to Reconcile Systemic Differences with the West

As part of the effort to construct a "harmonious society under socialism," the "harmonious world" has successfully helped with the formation of an ideology on which Hu Jiantao has been able to base its ruling. However, major components of the theory—such as "new security" and "democratization of international relations"—are borrowed from the "new diplomacy" initiated by Hu's predecessor, Jiang Zemin.[25]

The goals entailed in the "harmonious world" are semantically no different from the five principles of the "peaceful coexistence" policy tailored by Mao at the height of the cold war period. In reality, there is a subtle difference. Mao was firmly convinced that a world war between the socialist camp and the capitalist camp was inevitable. For Deng, the inevitability of a war caused by ideological incompatibility was ridiculed as the two former rival camps started to converge amid economic reforms in the socialist countries. For the fourth generation of leadership, a draconian world war is not only unimaginable, but the dependence on the West for technology and capital for development is growing each day.

The seemingly idealistic theory—the "harmonious world"—projects the image that China is a peace-loving country. However, beneath this glorious proclamation lies a realistic consideration. It is designed to counter the apprehension that China's one-party dictatorship might be on a collision course with major democracies such as the United States.

Two decades of economic reforms have made China an integral part of the global economic order, but politically, China remains a country deeply immersed in a long tradition of autocracy. Differences over political systems and values have emerged as the biggest hindrance for furthering relations with countries in the West, particularly the United States. Nearly two decades after the tragic Tiananmen Square crackdown in 1989, the European Union still retains its arms embargo against China. China has to defend its record on human rights each year against accusations and excoriations coming from rights-conscious groups and nations. To some, differences over political systems can be irreconcilable.

The dictum of a "harmonious world" was coined to combat the ramifications of the "clashes of civilizations" theory first broached by Samuel P. Huntington. China is convinced that it is being treated unfairly because of the socialist system that it is holding onto. On the surface, concepts embodied in the "harmonious world" theory, such as peace and respect for different cultures and political practices, seem to run counter to those suggested by Huntington, but in fact, like Huntington's arguments, the theory also implies conflicts of cultures. Beijing stresses that although dialogue, exchanges, respect, equality, and peaceful coexistence have become norms in relations between countries, power politics is still the game in town and the democratization of international relations has yet to be realized.[26] This discourse mixes ideas of both realism and constructivism. China is well aware that the majority of countries in the Third World have adopted polities other than democracy, and it is possible to form an "alliance of willing," freeing themselves from pressure demanding change. For these countries, the respect for one's way of life is a fundamental belief that should be shared by all people.

A Participatory Worldview

Apart from the influence of realism, the "harmonious world" theory also bears resemblance of constructivism. At least two important ingredients—democratization of international relations and theory of new security—are direct proof of the linkage. In a speech at the UN Summit Meeting in September 2000, Jiang Zemin stated that "the principle of democracy has to be carried out whether it is to maintain world peace or to develop altogether."[27] Democracy was erected as a core value in China's handling of international affairs. A month later, Jiang raised the concept of "democratization of international relations" in the first meeting of the Sino–African Cooperation Forum, emphasizing that "the main force of world development is people; that management has to have the participation of the people; and that problems and challenges should be resolved collectively through mediation."[28] However, it is the fourth generation of leadership that has provided substance to these new diplomatic discourses.

In a speech delivered to Russians in a state visit in 2003, Hu Jingtao stressed "democratic spirit"—such as equal dialogue and friendly cooperation—as a means to world peace, stability, and prosperity.[29] Premier Wen Jiabao reiterated the proposition of multilateralism as a way to democratize international relations at the second Sino-African Ministerial Meeting in December 2005.[30] China seems to be interested in building a new international order by promoting common beliefs and collective interests.

"Mutual respect" seems to continue to be part of China's foreign policy thinking. What is different this time is that the concept has been broadened to include countries deemed as hostile in the past. In an Association of Southeast Asian Nations (ASEAN) Regional Forum meeting in March 1997, Beijing raised the term "new security" for the first time.[31] The idea is to connect interests through security so that a cooperative, rather than confrontational, common security system can be established.[32]

As a one-party dictatorship, it seems weird to advertise democracy. This contradiction can only be understood in dialectic logic. Since it is suggested that no war has been fought between democracies, and advocates of the democratic peace theory have often based on this theory to demand change for nondemocratic polities,[33] the purpose of the "democratization of international relations" is to reduce the adverse effects of "peaceful evolution."

Proactive Multilateralism and Good-neighborly Policy

From "peaceful rise" to "harmonious world," Hu and Wen have constructed meaningful foreign policy thinking. Although continuity is kept in China's foreign policy, as peace and development were phrases not uncommon in Mao and Deng's times, this new thinking does have something new in its own right. Basically, the "harmonious world" theory derived from a new foreign policy strategy starting from the mid-1990s. It has synthesized practices and experiences accumulated since.

Two important concepts of the "harmonious world,"—the "new security" and "democratization of international relations"—are borrowed from Jiang Zemin's foreign policy discourse. However, when presented individually, these concepts are not as effective in explaining China's current foreign policy thinking as the "harmonious world" theory. The latter seems to better illustrate what China faces in the global arena today and, furthermore, provides an answer to deal with them.

The "new security"—with key concepts such as mutual trust (*huxin*) and benefits (*huli*), equality (*pingdeng*), and coordination (*xiezuo*)—was initiated by Jiang in 1996 as a policy to cope with the complex situations in the post-cold war era.[34] "New security" was strategized at a time when China was cautiously expanding its foreign engagement. It was defensive realism in nature. The policy also reflected newly gained confidence after years of economic reforms and enlargement. "Harmonious world" points out a direction in which the "new security" should strive to achieve.

The concept of "democratization of international relations" reflects the mindset of constructivism. However, pushing democracy as a core value is not in line with the political reality back home. This contradiction could be bridged through the theory of "harmonious world." In addition to peace and development, the new theory has an additional element—cooperation—making it the third pillar in China's new international initiative.

Participatory Multilateralism

China's attitude toward major international organizations changed from that of a radical reformist in the 1950s, to that of maintaining status quo in the 1980s, and then on to more active participation since the end of the cold war system.

Although China's participation multiplied tremendously in quantitative terms under Jiang's stewardship, the drive was less than enthusiastic. The "harmonious world" theory sends a message that China, already an integral part of the world order in every respect, will shoulder its responsibilities willingly, and even lead when necessary.

The new activism is most fittingly reflected in China's policy toward the United Nations. For the first time, Beijing dispatched five military observers as part of the UN Truce Supervision Organization (UNTSO) peace initiative in 1990. A year later, China formed a UN Peace-Maintenance Office to handle the affairs.[35] According to

China's Defense White Paper, released in 2002, the country has taken part in ten such missions since 1990, sending 1,450 military personnel overseas for various peace causes. Data released in a conference held by the People's Liberation Army (PLA) in June 2007 put the number at 7,293 in seventeen UN peace missions.[36] The fourth generation of leadership has sent five times more personnel overseas to monitor the progress of peace in five years than their predecessors did in twelve years. With Beijing's endorsement, Margaret Chan Fung Fu-chun, Hong Kong's representative to the World Health Organization, was elected Secretary General of the world's highest health body, making her the first Chinese to head a UN-affiliated organization.[37]

For Hu and his cohorts, multilateralism is a tool to project China's image and expand influence abroad. Jiang Zemin was lukewarm to solving regional conflicts. Beijing opted an apathetic and noninterference policy during the nuclear crisis between India and Pakistan in 1999. However, Hu Jintao has been actively involved in the "Six-Party Talks" in an attempt to resolve a similar crisis on the Korean peninsula. The event has been earmarked as a watershed in changing China's foreign policy into a proactive offensive one. Responding to the urge by the Americans, China is showing signs of being a responsible stakeholder.

Diplomatic activism is abundantly clear. Hu Jingtao reversed Jiang Zemin's decision and attended the G8 summit meeting in 2003.[38] This was the first attendance by any Chinese leader. China was the first signatory country outside Southeast Asia to sign the Treaty of Amity and Cooperation in October 2003.[39]

The Shanghai Cooperation Organization (SCO) is another example of this new activism. The organization was proposed and formed by China in 2001 to promote economic welfare with its neighbors in the northwest, including Russia and five other Central Asian nations—Tajikistan, Uzbekistan, Kazakhstan, Kyrgyzstan, and Turkmenistan. Under Hu's stewardship, the SCO has been transformed into a formidable force to coordinate security interests in the region. In what is known as the "Shanghai spirit"—a term coined in the Declaration of the Fifth Anniversary of the organization—words such as mutual trust, mutual benefit, equality, and respecting cultures, and so on, are the embodiment of the theory of democratization of international relations.[40]

The Beijing Summit of the Forum on China-Africa Cooperation in November 2006 pushed China's new diplomatic initiative into high gear. The forum held its first ministerial meeting in 2000. The 2006 summit boosted attendance of heads from forty-eight African countries and a strategic partnership was announced. Eight aid programs were promised by Beijing, including writing off debts owed by the Africans and setting up a US$5 billion Sino-African Development Fund.[41] Most important of all, all assistance was made on the premise of "no interference of domestic politics."

Three-neighborly Policy

At the CCP's Sixteenth Party Congress, a "good neighbor" policy was proposed. "Befriending neighbors" (*yulin wei shan*) and "accompanying neighbors" (*yilin wei ban*) were the goals. More substance has been added to this good-neighbor policy. Now, it is called the three-neighborly policy—befriending the neighbors (*mulin*), enriching (*fulin*) the neighbors, and providing the neighbors with a secure environment (*anlin*)—corroborating to the activism in foreign policy.[42]

Under Hu Jingtao's leadership, China's relations with her neighbors have improved by leaps and bounds (see Table 4.2). Among the declarations and treaties reached of late are the signing of an all-round cooperative partnership with South Korea; the forming of a strategic partnership of peace and prosperity with India; the upgrading of relations with Mongolia to that of a partnership of neighborliness and mutual trust; the establishment of strategic partnership with Pakistan, Kazakhstan, Indonesia, and ASEAN; the redefining of Sino-Philippine relations to that of strategic cooperative relations for peace and development; and the declaring of strategic relations of mutual benefit with Japan.

In 2003, China signed a treaty with ASEAN to form the biggest free market in the world in 2011. A second treaty, the Declaration on Principles for Relations and Comprehensive Cooperation, was reached with India about the same time. Beijing removed Sikkim, annexed by India in 1975, from the list of nations recognized by China. Likewise, New Delhi acknowledged Tibet as part of China for the very first time. Bilateral relations between the two nations have made great progress.[43] In April 2005, the two former adversaries signed the Agreement on Guiding Principles for the Resolution of Territorial Disputes. Although border issues have not been eliminated in entirety, the two nations have evidently come out of the nadir of past relations of adversity. When Junichiro Koizumi was the prime minister, Sino–Japanese relations ebbed for a number of reasons, including the prime minister's insistence on visiting the controversial Yasukoni Shrine. Upon taking office in October 2006, Shinzo Abe started to revamp

Table 4.2 Forms of Cooperation between China and Its Neighbors

Country	Forms of Cooperation	Time
United States	Constructive and strategic partnership	1997
	Constructive and cooperative relations	2001
Mongolia	Long-term stability, healthy and mutual trust, neighborliness, and friendship into the 21st century partnership of neighborliness and mutual trust	1998 2003
Russia .	Coordinative strategic partnership	1994
North Korea	The Treaty on Friendship, Cooperation, and Mutual Assistance between China and N. Korea	1961
Vietnam	Long-standing stability, facing the future, neighborliness, and friendship, all-round cooperation	1999
Laos	Relationship of long-term stability, neighborliness, friendship, and mutual trust	2000
Burma	Mechanism for diplomatic consultations	1992
Nepal	Friendly and neighborly partnership of generations into the 21st century	1996
Sikkim	Removed Sikkim from the list of nations recognized by China	2003
India	Declaration on Principles for Relations and Comprehensive Cooperation	2003
	Strategic partnership of peace and prosperity	2005
Pakistan	An all-round cooperative partnership into the 21st century	1996
	Strategic and cooperative partnership	2005
Afghanistan	Declaration on Good-neighborly and Friendly Relations	2002
Tajikistan	Relations of neighborliness, friendship, and cooperation into the 21st century	2000
Kyrgyzstan	Treaty of neighborliness, friendship, and cooperation	2002
Kazakhstan	Strategic partnership	2005
South Korea	Cooperative partnership into the 21st century	1998
	An all-round cooperative partnership	2003
Japan	Partnership of friendship and cooperation for peace and development Strategic relations of mutual benefit	1998 2006
Philippines	Relationship of neighborliness, mutual trust, and cooperation into the 21st century	1996
	Strategic cooperative relations for peace and development	2005

Table 4.2 (*continued*)

Country	Forms of Cooperation	Time
Malaysia	An all-round relationship of neighborliness, friendship, and cooperation	1999
Brunei	Relations of neighborliness, friendship, and cooperation	2005
Indonesia	Relationship of neighborliness, mutual trust, and all-round cooperation Strategic partnership	1999 2005
ASEAN	Partnership of neighborliness and mutual trust Strategic partnership of peace and prosperity	1997 2003

Source: PRC Ministry of Foreign Affairs Web site, http://www.mfa.gov.cn/chn/gjhdq/default.htm.

the ruptured relations. China was the choice for his first overseas trip, and the two sides declared to form a "mutually beneficial relationship based on common strategic interests."[44] A few months later, Premier Wen Jiabao made concrete the contents of the new relationship in a return visit.[45] The two countries seem to have gradually weathered the storms that brewed in the past.

China signed a treaty with Russia in October 2004, resolving the territorial issues that had troubled the two countries for decades. On October 22, 2003, Chinese and Pakistani navies practiced joint rescue exercises in the East China Sea, the first such exercise that China has ever held with a foreign country. A similar drill was underway a few weeks later with India. Active engagement seems to distinguish the foreign policies under Hu from those in the past.

Culture as a New Diplomatic Instrument

Contrary to what used to be blamed as the main culprit in China's lagging industrialization behind its Western counterparts, Chinese culture has become an important instrument in the nation's advancing relations overseas. In a speech given in France in December 2005, Wen Jiabao reminded his audience that peace and harmony are essential parts of traditional Chinese culture.[46] In a government work report he delivered to the National People's Congress in March 2007, Wen declared cultural exchange, along with political equality and democracy and economic mutual benefit and cooperation, as critical ingredients in the building of a harmonious world.[47] The use of culture as a way for the advancement of a harmonious international order transcends the barriers created by ideological rigidity and national borders. The export of "Chinese culture with peaceful characteristics" has become an official policy. On November 21, 2004, the first Confucius school was established in Seoul, South Korea. As of May 2007, 155 such schools have been set up in fifty-three countries.[48]

In addition to stressing the role of China's culture in the forming of contemporary international relations, the Beijing leadership has also shown a positive spin on cultures with Western origin or influences. While touring the Lincoln Memorial in Washington, DC, in December 2003, Premier Wen Jiabao praised the building as symbol of unity, a value with unsurpassable importance for the federal system.[49] An analogy was meant for China's stand on Taiwan. In another trip to Japan in April 2007, Wen cited a Japanese saying to suggest stability in the often-troubled relations between the two nations.[50]

ALL IS NOT HARMONIOUS IN SINO–U.S. RELATIONS

"Harmonious world" provides an ideological pivot to facilitate cooperation with the sole hegemon—the United States. However, it should not be interpreted as a sign of weakness, for it also serves the interests of fighting against the superpower.

In the wake of the 1989 Tiananmen Square incident, Deng Xiaoping laid down the fundamental policy guidelines to regulate Sino–U.S. relations: to increase trust, reduce trouble, develop cooperation, and avoid confrontation.[51] Hu seems to loyally follow the policy set by Deng not to challenge the international orders prescribed largely by the United States at this stage. There is a subtle difference between Hu and Jiang, though. China became more actively involved in multilateral international organizations beginning in the early 1990s, but it was not until a few more years later, at the turn of the century, that China started to charge ahead with full steam.

China has been a willing partner of the United States in the fight against international terrorism. China has also been mostly cooperative in other forums of multilateralism. Wang Jisi suggests that, given the complexities of international relations, the traditional Chinese foreign policy thinking of distinguishing foes from friends is outdated. The United States is not China's eternal rival, nor does the latter wish to make an enemy out of the former.[52] Yang Jiemian contends that in the post-cold war era, cooperation in the Asia-Pacific region to reduce threats has not been as successful as those in the economic area. While the United States continues its bilateral security arrangements serving its own agenda, China wishes to construct a new multilateral framework under new security thinking. Yet, Yang sees complementarity in these two thinkings, proposing that cooperation in the areas of nonconventional security can be augmented.[53] Liu Huihua argues that both China and the United States are beneficiaries of the current international system, and therefore should work together to bear more fruition.[54]

For advocates of reconciliation and cooperation, China is a beneficiary of the international order and there is no reason to sabotage and destabilize the status quo. To work with the United States is a rational choice, and in line with China's national interests.

While meeting with U.S. Vice President Dick Cheney in Beijing in April 2004, Hu Jingtao stressed that the development of constructive and cooperative relations were to the best interests of the two countries. Hu went on to say that China was willing to strengthen strategic dialogue, increase trust, and deepen mutually beneficial cooperation.[55] When meeting with President George W. Bush in April 2006 on his first trip to the United States, Hu told his American host that the two countries should be more than stakeholders—they should be constructive cooperators.[56] China's fourth generation of leaders has displayed tremendous enthusiasm in working with the United States to confront issues facing the international society. Beijing's decision to work with the United States, rather than fight against its former nemesis, on the North Korean nuclear issue is a telling example. Even on the sensitive subject of the Taiwan Strait, Hu has been conciliatory. While meeting President Bush in Washington, DC in September 2005, Hu pledged to "work with the U.S. to maintain peace and stability in the Taiwan Strait and fight against so-called 'Taiwan independence.'"[57] Beijing's policy has changed from demanding no intervention from the United States to that of comanagement and collective responsibility.

The expansion and institutionalization of dialogue has been a marked achievement in China's rocky relations with the United States. Sino–U.S. Senior Dialogue was first proposed by the presidents of the two nations at an Asia-Pacific Economic Cooperation (APEC) summit meeting held in Santiago, Chili in 2004, and reaffirmed by U.S. Secretary of State Condoleezza Rice on a visit to China in March 2005. The dialogue is to be held annually between vice foreign ministers. In the first meeting, hosted by the Chinese in Beijing on August 1, 2005, it was decided to stall the motion sponsored by Japan, Germany, India, and Brazil for the expansion of the UN Security Council.

Sino–U.S. Strategic Economic Dialogue was initiated by U.S. Secretary of Finance Henry M. Paulsen. In September 2006, the two nations issued a declaration for activation of the mechanism. It is held twice a year and led by the U.S. Treasury Secretary and China's Vice Premier Wu Yi to discuss economic issues with bilateral or global concerns. The first meeting was held in December 2006.

As a country striving to improve its economy at all costs, China needs the United States to get this grand strategy on the ground. Sino–U.S. relations have come a long way from the cold war rivalry. Former U.S. Secretary of State Colin Powell once said the state of relations is the best since 1972.[58] However, the rise of China and uncertainties surrounding its future have alarmed some policy makers in Washington. China was considered a "potential rival" in the Pentagon's Quadrennial Defense Review Report of 2006.[59] The same assessment was retained in its Military Power of the People's Republic of China 2007.[60]

For the Chinese, "harmonious world" is more than a theory of peace. Beijing is content with being a status quo power for now, but that does not mean China is willing to subject itself to the mercy of the rules written by the Americans. The majority rule prescribed by the doctrine of "democratization of international relations" is an ingenious way to hold the American hegemonic status in check. The rules of engagement established by this new set of norms will also likely do away with systemic pressure imposed upon China by major powers.

Chinese academics will also occasionally drum out opinions with nationalistic rhetoric. This group of people continues the mantra that the United States has never stopped containing China and supporting Chinese dissidents. To them, even though China is not strong enough to prevent the United States from bullying the smaller powers, China should make its displeasure known, without reservation. Necessary measures should also be adopted so that the Americans understand that China is no pussycat.[61] China should stand firm against its big potential rival.

Reconciliation or not, both sides have based their reasoning on national interests. All agree that there are problems with Sino–U.S. relations. They differ, however, on how to deal with these problems. Since a framework of peace and stability in relations with the United States is the official policy, Chinese scholars have been rationalizing to its support.

It is nevertheless presumptuous to assume that the same constructive thinking is resonated by the general public. A public opinion poll shows that while half of the respondents consider the United States as China's competitor, only 10.4 percent of the Chinese deem the country as friendly. Only 11.7 percent of Chinese treat the United States as a model, and 25.6 percent consider the country worthy to work with.[62]

CONCLUSION

Lacking the halo enjoyed by leaders of the first two generations, the fourth generation of Chinese leadership needs to demonstrate their powers through ideological reinforcement. There is no major disagreement in foreign policy within China now, and it is easier to come up with coherent policy thinking. As structural reforms deepen, newly surfaced problems are starting to upset the existing social order. The leadership needs new thinking to unite the disintegrating old order.

To the fourth generation of Chinese leadership, "peace and development" are two goals in one, and the "harmonious world" theory paves the way for building wholesome connections with the outside world. To cultivate an environment favorable to economic development, China needs undivided attention both at home and abroad. Reconciliation has emerged as a main principle in enacting foreign policies. The new policy is composed of a stabilized international setting, friendly neighborly relations, mutually beneficial cooperation, a secure environment, and favorable media. China's international standing will be greatly heightened should these goals be realized.

"Harmonious world" has its foundation in both realism and constructivism. It is tinged with idealistic expectations. It will help with China's propaganda overseas by proclaiming peace, development, and cooperation as essential ingredients of China's new foreign policy. The aim is to convey the message that China is a status quo power and has no intention of destabilizing the international regimes and values established under Pax Americana. Democracy should be brought into the international community so that different cultures will be able to peacefully coexist, and a true multilateralism will be the norm where important decisions are made. A harmonious world will also champion mediation rather than conflict as a means of resolving differences.

The purpose of the "harmonious world" is to convey the message that a rising China is also a peace-loving country. It is certainly true that China is very much integrated into the international community, and the degree of cooperation with major powers is unprecedented. However, as Iain Johnston suggests, it remains to be seen whether China will become a revisionist power challenging the hegemon in due time.[63] "Harmonious world" theory provides China with an ideological fulcrum on which a more wholesome relationship with the outside world could be built. However, the theory itself also contains elements of discontentment. If history is any guidance, China will not be satisfied as a status quo power, dancing to the music orchestrated by other bigger powers.

NOTES

1. Susan Shirk, "The Succession Game," *Asia Program Special Report*, no. 105 (September 2002): 9. http://wwics.si.edu/topics/pubs/asiarpt105.pdf.
2. Hu Jintao raised his "stay close to the people" policy in February 2003, see "Hu Jintao: lingdao ganbu quan weimin suoyong qing weimin suoxi li weimin suomou" [Hu Jintao: Leading cadres should use powers for the people, feel for the people, and seek benefits for the people], *Nanfangwang*, February 18, 2003, http://big5.southcn.com/gate/big5/www.southcn.com/news/china/zgkx/200302180983.htm.
3. Cheng Li, *China's Leaders: The New Generation* (Lanham, MA: Rowman & Littlefield, 2001), 197–203.
4. Chih-Chia Hsu, "Zhonggong waijiao zhengce de yanjiu tujing" [Research approaches to the studies of China's foreign policy], *Wenti yu yanjiu* [Issues and studies] 36, no. 4 (April 1997): 55–56.
5. Mao Zedong, "Maodun lun" [On contradiction], *Maozedong xuanji 1* [Mao Zedong selected works], Vol 1 (Guangdong: Renmin chubanshe, 1991), 320–34; "Guanyu zhengque chuli renmin neibu maodun de wenti" ("On the Issue of Correctly Dealing with People's Inner Contradictions"), *Maozedong xuanji* [Mao Zedong selected works], *Vol. 5* (Shanghai: Renmin chubanshe, 1977), 363–65.
6. Yuan-Kang Wang, "Offensive Realism and the Rise of China," *Issues & Studies* 40, no.1 (March 2004): 175.
7. James E. Dougherty and Robert L. Pfaltzgraff, *Contending Theories of International Relations: A Comprehensive Survey, 3rd ed.* (New York: Harper Collins, 1990), 81.
8. Alexander Wendt, "Collective Identity Formation and the International State," *American Political Science Review* 88, no. 2 (June 1994): 385.
9. Emanuel Adler, "Seizing the Middle Ground: Constructivism in World Politics," *European Journal of International Relations* 3, no.3 (September 1997): 323.
10. John MacMillian and Andrew Linklater, eds., *Boundaries in Question: New Directions in International Relations* (New York: St. Martin's, 1995), 5.
11. Fang Zhangping, "Jiango zhuyi: Chuangxin, yiyi ji wenti" [Constructivism: Innovation, meaning and questions], *Shijei jingji yu zhengzhi*

[World economics and politics], no. 7, July 2004, http://www.irchina.org/news/view.asp?id=534.

12. Deng Xiaoping, "Heping he fazhan shi dangdai shijie de liangda wenti" [Peace and development are two major issues in the world], in *Dengxiaoping wenxuan* [Deng Xiaoping selected works], *Vol. 3* (Tienjin: Renmin chubanshe, 1993), 104.
13. "Wenjiabao hafo yanjiang tichu guangfan wenming duihua he wenhua jiaoliu" [Wen Jiabao addresses extensive civilization dialogue and cultural exchange], *Renminwang*, December 10, 2003, http://www.people.com.cn/GB/shizheng/1024/2239366.html.
14. "Hu Jintao zai jinian maozedong danchen 110 zhounian zuotanhui de jianghua" [Hu Jintao's speech at the symposium in memory of Mao Zedong's 110 Birthday], *Renminwang*, December 26, 2003, http://www.people.com.cn/GB/shizheng/1024/2267174.html.
15. Yuan Tiecheng, "Qian mei guofangbu fubuzhang cheng meiguo wuda shili zuoyou duihua zhengce" [Former U.S. Deputy Secretary of Defense said five powers determine the United States' China policy], *Zhongguo qingnien bao* [China youth daily], November 4, 2005, http://news.xinhuanet.com/world/2005-11/04/content_3728121.htm.
16. Bill Gertz, *The China Threat: How the People's Republic Targets America* (Washington, DC: Regnery, 2000), 199; Richard Bernstein and Ross H. Munro, *The Coming Conflict with China* (New York: Alfred A. Knopf, 1997).
17. Herbert Yee and Ian Storey, "Introduction," in *The China Threat: Perceptions, Myths, and Reality*, eds. Herbert Yee and Ian Storey (New York: Routledge Curzon, 2002), 2–5.
18. Nina Hachigian and James Mulvenon, "A Chance to Get Closer to China," *Los Angeles Times*, September 27, 2001.
19. See Yong Deng, "Better Than Power: 'International Status' in Chinese Foreign Policy," in *China Rising: Power and Motivation in Chinese Foreign Policy*, eds. Yong Deng and Fei-Ling Wang (Lanham, MD: Rowman & Littlefield, 2005), 51–72.
20. Yan Xuetong, ed., *Zhongguo jueqi: Guoji huanjing pinggu [*China rises: Evaluation of international environment] *(*Tianjin: Renmin chubanshe, 1998), 170–74.
21. "Jianshe hexie shijie: Zhongguo waijiao sixiang de xinfazhan" [Constructing harmonious world: The new development of China's diplomatic thought], *Banyue tan* [Bimonthly Talk], August 23, 2006, http://news.xinhuanet.com/world/2006-08/23/content_4993067.htm.
22. "Guoji zhoukan: Hexie shijie—zhongguo waijiao xinzhuzhang" [International weekly: Harmonious world—China's new diplomatic view], *Renmin ribao*, September 23, 2005, http://world.people.com.cn/GB/1030/3720226.html.
23. Guowuyuan bangongshi (Office of the State Council), "Ruhe lijie tuidong jianshe hexie shijie" [How to realize and push for the construction

of a harmonious world], *Zhongyang zhengfu menfu wangzhan* [Central government gate Web site], March 20, 2007, http://www.gov.cn/ztzl/2007zfgzbgjd/content_555815.htm.

24. "Hu Jintao zai lianheguo chengli 60 zhounian shounao huiyi shang de jianghua" [Hu Jintao's speech at the summit meeting of the 60th anniversary of the UN], *Xinhuawang* [Xinhua net], September 16, 2005, http://news.xinhuanet.com/world/2005-09/16/content_3496858.htm.
25. Evan S. Medeiros and M. Taylor Fravel, "China's New Diplomacy," *Foreign Affairs* 82, no. 6 (November–December 2003), 22–35.
26. "Hu Jintao zai lianheguo chengli 60 zhounian shounao huiyi shang de jianghua" [Hu Jintao's speech at the summit meeting of the 60th Anniversary of the UN].
27. Jiang Zemin, "Zai lianheguo qiannian shounao huiyi shang de jianghua" [Speech at the millennial head meeting of the UN], *Xinhuawang*, September 7, 2000, http://www.people.com.cn/GB/channel1/10/20000907/220934.html.
28. Jiang Zemin, "Zhongfei xishou hezuo gongying xinde shiji" [Sino-Africa cooperate to welcome the new century], *Xinhuawang*, October 10, 2000, http://big5.xinhuanet.com/gate/big5/news.xinhuanet.com/ziliao/2003-11/24/content_1195633.htm.
29. Hu Jintao, "Shidai mulin youhao gongtong fazhan fanrong—zai mosike guoji guanxi xueyuan de yanjiang" [Befriending neighbors, friendship, mutual development and prosperity for generations—speech delivered at the Moscow's State Institute of International Relations of MFA of Russia], *Zhongguo xinwen wang* [China news net], May 29, 2003, http://big5.chinataiwan.org/web/webportal/W5079024/Uadmin/A5080703.html.
30. "Wenjiabao zai zhongfei hezuo luntan fabiao chongyao jianghua" [Wen Jiabao delivered important address at the Sino-African Cooperation Forum], *Xinhuawang*, December 15, 2005, http://big5.xinhuanet.com/gate/big5/news.xinhuanet.com/world/2003-12/15/content_1232556.htm.
31. Chu Shulong, "Lengzhanhou zhongguo anquan zhanlue sixiang de fazhan" [The development of China's strategic thought on security in the post cold-war era], *Shijei jingji yu zhengzhi* 9 (September 1999): 12.
32. Huang Renwei, "Xin anquan guan yu dongya diqu hezuo jizhi" [New security and regional cooperation mechanism in East Asia], *Shijie jingji yanjiu* [World economics research], 2000, 25.
33. See Spencer R. Weart, *Never at War: Why Democracies Will Not Fight One Another* (New Haven, CT.: Yale University Press, 1998).
34. Zhonghua renmin gongheguo waijiaobu (Foreign Ministry of the PRC), "Zhongguo guanyu xinanquan de lichang wenjian" [China's position document about new security concept], Ministry of Foreign Affairs

of PRC, July 31, 2002, http://211.99.196.166/chn/wjb/zzjg/gjs/gjzzyhy/1136/1138/t4549.htm.

35. Wang Jing, "Zhongguo yong weihe xingdong chuilian shuaida budui weihe huiyi zhaokai" [To strive for the convening of a meeting for the peace mission by actions], *Dongfang ribao*, June 19, 2007, http://www.news365.com.cn/xwzx/gj/200706/t20070619_1457671.htm.
36. Dong Guozheng and Lu Desheng, "Wojun shouci weihe gongzuo huiyi kaimu" [The first meeting on maintaining peace by our military convenes], *Jiefang junbao*, June 19, 2007, 1.
37. "Chenfeng Fuzhen dangxuan shiwei zuzhi xinren zongganshi" [Chen Feng Fuzhen elected as the new secretary general of the World Health Organization], *Xinhuawang*, November 10, 2006, http://big5.xinhuanet.com/gate/big5/news.xinhuanet.com/world/2006-11/10/content_5311366.htm.
38. *New York Times*, March 28, 2003.
39. "Zhongguo zhengsi jiaru dongnanya youhao hezuo tiaoyue yu dongmeng huxin jiashen" [China formerly joins the Southeast Asia friendship and cooperation treaty and mutual trust with ASEAN deepens], *Renmin ribao*, October 8, 2003, http://www.people.com.cn/GB/shizheng/1024/2123245.html.
40. "Shanghai hezuo zuzhi wuzhounian xuanyan" [SCO declaration for the fifth anniversary], http://www.sectsco.org/html/01442.html.
41. "Zhongfei fenghui kaimu duifei jingyuan jiang fanfan" [Economic assistance to African states will double as the Sino-African summit meeting takes place], BBC, November 4, 2006. http://news.bbc.co.uk/chinese/trad/hi/newsid_6110000/newsid_6115800/6115886.htm.
42. "Wenjiabao zongli chuxi dongmeng shangye yu touzi fenghui bing fabiao yanjiang" [Premier Wen Jiabao attends ASEAN commerce and investment summit meeting and delivers a speech], *China Daily* (Beijing), October 8, 2003, http://www.chinadaily.net/gb/doc/2003-10/08/content_269949.htm.
43. Ruan Zongze, "2003 zhongguo waijiao zhi heping jueqi" [2003: Peaceful rise of China's diplomacy], *Liaowang zhoukan* (Utlook weekly, Beijing), http://worldol.com/huanqiu/html/2003/12/20031216201943-1.htm.
44. Xinhuashe (Xinhua News Agency), "Zhongri fabiao lianhe xinwen gongbao" [China and Japan issue joint communique], *Renminwang*, October 8, 2006, http://politics.people.com.cn/BIG5/1026/4891940.html.
45. "Wenjiabao tong anbei jinsan huitan queren zhongri zhanlue huhui guanxi neihan" [Wen Jiabao and Shinzo Abe reaffirmed contents of Sino-Japan mutually beneficial relationship based on common strategic interests], *Zhongguowang*, April 12, 2007, http://big5.china.com.cn/international/zhuanti/wjbfhr/2007-04/12/content_8103401.htm.
46. Wen Jiabao, "Zunzong butong wenming, gongjian hexie shijie—Wenjiabao zongli zai faguo bali zonghe ligong daxue de yanjiang" [Respect cultures and build a harmonious world—premier Wen Jiabao spoke in Ecole

Polytechnique De Paris], *Xinhuawang*, December 6, 2005, http://news.xinhuanet.com/world/2005-12/06/content_3885342.htm.

47. Wen, Jiabao, "Zhengfu gongzuo baogao: zai dishijie quanguo renmin daibiao dahui diwuci huiyi shang" [Government work report to the fifth meeting of the tenth national people's congress], *Xinhuawang*, March 17, 2007, http://news.xinhuanet.com/misc/2007-03/17/content_5859480_5.htm.
48. "Gedi kongzi xueyuan" [Locations of Confucius School] *The Office of Chinese Language Council International Web site*, June 15, 2007, http://www.hanban.edu.cn/cn_hanban/kzxy_list.php?state1=Asia.
49. He Hongze, "Wenjiabao zongli tan taiwan wenti: guo zhi dashang xiang zhi shenchou" [Premier Wen Jiabao talks about Taiwan issue: A huge sadness for the country and deep sorrow for the society], *Huanqiu shibao* [Global times], December 10, 2003, 2.
50. Wen Jiabao, "Weile youyi yu hezuo: Zai ribenguo guohui de yanjiang" [For friendship and cooperation: Speech at the Japanese parliament], *Xinhuawang*, April 12, 2007, http://big5.xinhuanet.com/gate/big5/news.xinhuanet.com/world/2007-04/12/content_5968135.htm.
51. Zhou Cipu, "Jiangzemin huijian meiguo zhongyiyuan tan zhongmei guanxi" [Jian Zemin meets the U.S. Congressmen talking about Sino-American relations], *Renmin ribao*, December 1, 2004, 1.
52. Wang Jisi, "Lengjing, lengjing, cai lengjing: Dui dangqian meiguo yu zhongmei guanxi de jidian guancha" [Calm, calm, and calm again: A few observations on the U.S. and Sino-American relations], *Guoji jingji pinglun* [International economic review], No. 9–10 (2004), http://www.irchina.org/news/view.asp?id=619.
53. Yang Jiemian, "Heping gongchu wuxiang yuanze he zhongmei guanxi" [Five principles of co-existence and Sino-American relations], *Guoji wenti yanjiu* [International studies], No. 4 (2004), http://www.irchina.org/news/view.asp?id=606.
54. Liu Huihua, "Zhuanxing shijie zhong de zhongmei hezuo" [Sino-American cooperation in the changing world], *Guoji wenti luntan* (*International Review*) (Winter 2005), http://www.irchina.org/news/view.asp?id=1156.
55. "Guojia zhuxi hujintao huijian meiguo fuzongtong qianni" [National chairman Hu Jintao meets the U.S. vice president Cheney], *Renmin ribao*, April 14, 2004, http://www.people.com.cn/GB/shizheng/1024/2447699.html.
56. "Hujintao tong bushi huitan: women juebu rongren taidu" [Hu Jintao meets Bush: We would not tolerate Taiwan independence], *Renmin ribao*, April 21, 2006, 1.
57. Zhang Zongzhi, "Hujintao hui bushi: gonghu taihai heping" [Hu Jintao meets Bush: Protecting the peace in the Taiwan Strait together], *Lienhe bao* (United daily, Taipei), September 15, 2005, http://gb.udn.com/gb/mag.udn.com/mag/news/storypage.jsp?f_MAIN_ID=136&f_SUB_ID=491&f_ART_ID=18906.

58. Glenn Kessler, "Powell Strongly Defends Bush's Foreign Policy," *Washington Post*, September 6, 2003, p. A15.
59. The original wording is "of the major and emerging powers, China has the greatest potential to compete militarily with the United States and field disruptive military technologies that could over time off set traditional U.S. military advantages absent U.S. counter strategies"; see U.S. Department of Defense, *Quadrennial Defense Review Report*, February 6, 2006, 29. http://www.defenselink.mil/pubs/pdfs/QDR20060203.pdf.
60. Office of the Secretary of Defense, *Annual Report to Congress: Military Power of the People's Republic of China 2007* (Washington, DC: Department of Defense, 2007), I. http://www.defenselink.mil/pubs/pdfs/070523-China-Military-Power-final.pdf.
61. Zhang Ruezuang, "Women weishenmo buleng jieshou zhongmei guanxi lishi zuehao de shuofa?" [Why couldn't we accept the statement that Sino-U.S. relations are at their best?], *Wenhui bao*, September 7, 2005, http://www.irchina.org/news/view.asp?id=984.
62. "Zhongguoren kan zhongmei guanxi" [Chinese view Sino-American relations], *Huanqiu shibao* (*Global Times*, Beijing), March 2, 2005, 1.
63. Iain Johnston, "Is China a Status Quo Power?" *International Security* 7, no. 4 (Spring 2003), 49.

Chapter 5

The Japan Factor in U.S.–China Relations

*Steven I. Levine**

For more than a century and a half, the U.S.–China–Japan triangle has been a constant, if frequently changing, feature of international politics in the Asia-Pacific region. Presently, the rise of China and the reinvigoration of Japan at a time when the United States is bogged down in another neocolonial war make this an appropriate time to look, once again, at the interactions of these three powers.[1] This chapter attempts two tasks. The first is to briefly review and assess the role that Japan plays in the U.S.–China relationship against the background of the past. The second, and necessarily much more speculative, undertaking, is to consider how Japan might respond in the event of a future global power transition from an international system marked by U.S. dominance to one marked by China's dominance.

Historical Background

During the three-quarters of a century from the Meiji Restoration in 1868 to the defeat of Japan in 1945, the United States stepped forward as the would-be protector of a weak and disintegrating China against a rapidly modernizing Japan with ambitions to dominate and eventually

*Dr. Dimon Liu generously provided me a number of helpful references in the course of my work that I would not otherwise have come across.

integrate its much larger neighbor into a Japanese imperium. Unfortunately, the protection was usually ineffective and always self-serving. Not until after the Japanese attack on Pearl Harbor on December 7, 1941, did American sympathies for China, an earlier victim of Japanese aggression, translate into effective military action to stop Japan. Then, as now, the key objective of U.S. policy was to prevent the emergence of a dominant power in East Asia bent on restricting or excluding American interests. Washington was even more concerned when, as in the case of Japan from 1936 to 1945, the Asian power was allied to an extraregional state as Japan was to Germany.

Postwar American hopes of stabilizing East Asia in concert with China, awarded an honorary Great Power degree by President Roosevelt, were quickly frustrated by the communist conquest of China in the context of a global cold war. By 1951, Japan was already well on its way to assuming the position it still occupies as the key American ally in the Asia-Pacific region under a succession of conservative governments. The shared purpose, of course, was to contain the perceived threat of the People's Republic of China (PRC), initially allied with the Soviet Union, and later, as an independent revolutionary state. It is no accident that Japan's major crisis of confidence in the security alliance with the United States coincided with the Nixon shocks of 1971 when the United States, without consulting its Japanese ally, moved to normalize relations with Mao's China and force the revaluation of the Japanese yen. Despite its not undeserved reputation for glacial decision-making, Japan quickly adjusted to this unanticipated new reality by normalizing its own relations with China in 1972. When, in the 1980s, the underlying American assumption that Japan would know and accept its subordinate place in an American-ordered universe was briefly challenged by Japan's economic success, the American reaction, typically excessive, verged on paranoia in certain quarters.[2] The bursting of Japan's economic bubble, and the political flux and economic stagnation of the 1990s, coupled with America's post-cold war triumphalism, put to rest American fears of an emerging Japanese superpower.[3] In the past few years, those same fears have now resurfaced with respect to China.

Mapping the Present

For the first time in its modern history, Japan faces a China, animated by an assertive nationalism, that has been growing much more rapidly than itself and whose active regional and, increasingly, global diplomacy has transformed it, in a generation, into a real global power. To be sure the authoritarian and repressive Leninist-capitalist hybrid that is contemporary China suffers from severe domestic political, environmental, and governance problems, but it is not alone in that respect. In the eyes of the world, the neon glitter of Shanghai obscures the many dark corners of a country where, for the time being anyway, the leaders have come up with a workable, if harsh, formula for holding on to power. On the whole, except for dealing with the leaden burden of history, Japan has done a good job of responding to this new reality by expanding its economic and cultural ties with China, adapting its alliance with the United States, and pursuing a more active regional diplomacy of its own, symbolized perhaps by the recent Japan-Australian security agreement.[4]

The short-lived premiership of Shinzo Abe (September 2006–September 2007), otherwise mostly notable for its failures, achieved an improvement in the atmosphere, if not the underlying reality, of Sino-Japanese relations. In his first trip abroad as prime minister—to China in October 2006—Abe expressed his interest in repairing a relationship that had frayed badly during the premiership of Junichiro Koizumu, whose insistence on visiting the Yasukuni Shrine made him a convenient whipping boy for Beijing. (The Yasukuni Shrine is home to the spirits of Japan's war dead, including officials responsible for Japanese aggression during World War II.)[5] In his reciprocal visit to Japan in April 2007, PRC Premier Wen Jiabao reinforced Abe's desire. Abe's successor as prime minister—the veteran politician Fukuda Yasuo—enjoys good relations with Chinese leaders, and is unlikely to provoke the Chinese by word or deed.[6] Yet, there are structural and other realities that prime ministers and summit diplomacy cannot alter, and that bear upon Japan's role in the U.S.–China relationship.

Prime among these is that, after more than a century of false starts and dashed aspirations, China is now on track toward winning the game of catching up with the West and Japan that it has been playing since the late Qing. (In this context, the Reform and Opening of the post–Mao era were the Chinese equivalent of the Meiji Restoration 110 years earlier in terms of development, cultural and technological borrowing, and integration into the international system. The Showa era denouement of Meiji modernization, namely, expansion and military aggression, is not, however, an encouraging parallel, which may be one reason why Chinese leaders repeat ad nauseam that theirs is a peaceful rise.) China's leaders are determined to wrest maximum international advantage from their economic success, and do not want to be upstaged by Japan. This is expressed, inter alia, in their opposition to Japan's candidacy for permanent membership on the UN Security Council.

One of the enduring problems in Sino-Japanese relations is that the Chinese and Japanese simply dislike and mistrust each other. A recent Pew Global Attitudes Project poll revealed that 70 percent of Japanese respondents disliked China; around the same percentage of Chinese respondents disliked Japan.[7] A somewhat earlier joint *Asahi Shimbun*-CASS poll indicated that under 10 percent of Japanese had a positive view of China, and a mere 7.8 percent of Chinese, a positive view of Japan, while 64.1 percent had negative views.[8] Polls conducted between April and October 2006 of the general public in China and educated elites in ten Chinese cities showed that approximately three-quarters of those surveyed viewed Japan as the country that most threatens China's interests. (The United States is second at around 60 percent.)[9] Yet only 5.32 percent of the general public surveyed considered Japanese militarism the greatest threat to world peace over the next five years. (Incidentally, American hegemonism scored at 24.77 percent.) Over 60 percent of the general public considered relations between China and Japan poor or very poor, and most cited historical issues—the Nanjing massacre in particular—as their reasons for disliking Japan.[10] Chinese memories of Japan's half-century of aggression against China (1895–1945) and the horrific atrocities against Chinese civilians committed by the Imperial Japanese Army during the Sino-Japanese War of 1937–45 constitute the history issue in Sino-Japanese relations. These memories, which Chinese media and the educational system regularly refresh, are like pieces of shrapnel embedded in the body politic of China that cannot be extracted and that periodically send shooting pains to every nerve and joint.

Anti-Japanese sentiment in China has been fostered by leading Chinese politicians and has periodically boiled over in the form of boycotts of Japanese goods and massive popular demonstrations that can take violent form, such as the protests in Beijing, Shanghai, Chengdu, and Shenzhen in April 2005 when demonstrators attacked the Japanese embassy and consulate as well as Japanese cars and restaurants.[11] That Japan has provided China with tens of billions of dollars in low-interest loans, official development assistance, and technical cooperation, as well as being a leading source of foreign direct investment, has not allayed the anger of the Chinese, but merely increased feelings of resentment at Japan's greater wealth. There is a kind of Gresham's Law that operates in Sino-Japanese relations. Negative symbolic interaction focused on the history issue—the political equivalent of debased currency—drives out the substantive positive interactions in the realm of trade, technology, and investment.

This negativity is not the result of isolation as, for example, was the case in mutual attitudes among Americans and Russians during the cold war. In 2006, there were 4.7 million visitors traveling between China and Japan, and in 2005, 110 thousand Chinese students studying in Japan and twenty thousand Japanese students in China.[12] This may be a case where familiarity breeds contempt. The fact of the matter is that the modern Chinese sense of national identity has been forged in opposition to Japan over a period of many decades. Meanwhile, mass circulation Japanese *manga* pander to and feed popular enmity toward, and resentment of, Chinese and Koreans by crudely racist depictions. Tsuneo Watanabe notes the popularity of the anti-China cartoons of Yoshinori Kobayashi that express rising nationalist sentiment.[13] Such attitudes are deeply rooted in the modern historical experience of both countries, going back to the late nineteenth century when Meiji modernizer Fukuzawa Yukichi stated that Japan must "escape from the bad company of Asia."[14] Japan's current "return to Asia" is both partial and ambivalent. It is colored by an attitude of condescension that derives, at least in part, from an insular *amour propre* that nearly a century and a half of contact with the world has only served to confirm.

This is one reason why I am skeptical of Brad Glosserman and Bonnie Glaser's recent suggestion that with bilateral relations—U.S.–China, China–Japan, U.S.–Japan—in reasonably good shape all around "Washington, Tokyo, and Beijing have a unique opportunity to build genuinely trilateral relations and, in particular, transform Chinese perceptions of the U.S.-Japan alliance." They list such "non-traditional security issues" as energy, weapons of mass destruction (WMD), disaster relief, problems of aging, and maritime security as conversation starters.[15] The problem, as I see it, is that even were such a trialogue to take place on these issues at, say, the deputy ministerial level, it is doubtful it would do much to assuage the core security and status anxieties that each party entertains toward the others, since these are grounded not in misperception, but in prudent suspicion. Although it may not be too late to attempt to head off a regional arms race centered on missiles and missile defense systems, such a regional arms race is more likely than are arms control agreements in a region with no recent history of negotiations, let alone success in that area.

There is no reason at all to expect a rupture in the U.S.-Japan security relationship anytime in the foreseeable future, or even beyond, but we should bear in mind that an alliance formed under very different international conditions, even if it adapts to change, as the U.S.-Japan alliance has done quite successfully, is bound at some point to outlive its usefulness. There can be no harm, only benefit in "thinking outside the alliance" to better prepare ourselves intellectually for unknowable future contingencies. The growth of Chinese military power and global influence, the emergence of a nuclear North Korea, and America's preoccupation elsewhere are particularly significant.[16] It is in this context that it is worth considering the rise of Japanese nationalism and Tokyo's inclination to play a more assertive role in both regional and global politics.

Signs of rising Japanese nationalism abound. It seems increasingly likely that, within the next decade, Japan will revise the anti-war Article 9 of the 1947 constitution, an artifact of the U.S. occupation, and reassert Japan's sovereign right to maintain the armed forces that, of course, it already possesses. Yet, the symbolic value of Article 9 ensures a stiff domestic political fight ahead.[17] Less than two months after becoming prime minister in September 2006, Shinzo Abe reiterated his intention to pursue constitutional revision in order to "protect Japan, and . . . make a global contribution (to security)."[18] On May 14, 2007, the Diet passed a law authorizing a national referendum on the issue, the first step in a long process of constitutional revision.[19] If Article 9 is eventually modified or deleted, it is a sure bet that the PRC will strenuously object, although the Chinese would obviously never adopt a constitution that denied them the right to possess and employ their own armed forces for national defense. In December 2006, the Diet passed a law requiring compulsory education in patriotism.[20] This is part of a renewed effort in Japan to instill pride of country after decades of national self-abnegation and constant calls for the current generation of Japanese to apologize for the crimes of their grandfathers. The generational change in Japanese leadership from leaders who personally experienced World War II to postwar generations for whom the war is history—a history unfortunately as much obscured as clarified by textbooks—means that Japanese leaders and the public at large are increasingly resistant to the history card that their Chinese counterparts shuffle into the deck. This trend transcends the administration of any particular prime minister.[21]

The Japanese push toward enhancing their military capabilities and expanding their freedom of action in the realm of security policy will continue to take place, at least in the near to mid-term, within, rather than outside, the framework of the U.S.-Japan alliance, and will be justified, in part, as a way to augment Japan's contributions to the alliance. By so doing, Japan can reassure Washington, while seeking to minimize the negative impact on its relations with China, which would be more upset by an independent Japanese defense initiative.[22]

In his insightful new book, *Japan Rising*, Kenneth Pyle observes, with respect to China: "The interests of Japan and the United States, the two great status-quo powers of the region, will be the ones most challenged by this emergent new power. How they manage the imminent great power transition—singly or together—will tell much of the story of the international relations of the coming decades. . . . Triangular relations among China, Japan, and the United States will largely determine the new order in East Asia."[23]

This triangular relationship has to take into account not simply geostrategic interests, but also the profound differences in the political character of the United States and Japan, seriously flawed, but nonetheless real democracies, on one side, and the PRC, a kind of vestigial regime, extremely tenacious and adaptable, but still a throwback to the not so distant days when numerous specimens of *Leninosauraus tyranniensis* roamed the earth. The strategy of engaging China that, for the most part, both the United States and Japan have thus far pursued, reaches its limits in the realm of politics and political values where the supposed Second Coming of Chinese democracy—the first being in 1912 at the dawn of the new republic—is a matter of hope and faith rather than empiricism. Japan has pursued a more realistic or, one might say, amoral and nonideological policy toward China from the beginning of the cold war and continuing to the present, based on calculations of economic and political interest, initially deeply bowing, and later merely nodding, in the direction of Washington, and far less impacted by domestic politics than Washington's China policy. Yet, during his brief tenure, Prime Minister Abe spoke of his determination to engage in strategic dialogues with Asian democracies "with a view to widening the circle of free societies in Asia as well as in the rest of the world."[24] Japanese foreign policy and security initiatives vis-à-vis India, Association of Southeast Asian Nations (ASEAN), and Australia, inter alia, are the practical expression of this policy. The notion of a concert of democracies in Asia can only be read in Beijing as an implicit challenge to the PRC. It should be noted, however, that Tokyo does not entertain the illusions that Washington often has articulated, namely, that engaging China will transform China's political system.

If the "Nixon shocks" of 1971 provided an occasion for Japan to take the initiative in normalizing its relations with China the following year, the "Bush blunders," combined with the natural generational evolution of Japanese politics, open the door to a more autonomous and assertive Japanese policy in East Asia over the mid- to long-term, one that initially steers by minutes rather than degrees away from Washington, but the cumulative effect of which, over time, may amount to a change of course.[25] It seems very likely that whoever follows "Little Bush"—to borrow the flippant Chinese term—to the White House will be cleaning up the toxic domestic and foreign policy wreckage of his failed presidency for years to come.

In the triangular relationship, the greatest challenge, perhaps, is faced by the United States, which, since its rise to global power status, has never been in an alliance of roughly equal powers. As the more powerful senior partner, it has always expected compliance from its junior partners, who are supposed to subordinate their own judgments and preferences to that of Washington in case of disagreement. Witness the American choler at the impudence of a General De Gaulle or a President Chirac. (Nor was this simply an expression of anti-Gallic sentiment.) Thus, the United States is ill prepared, by experience or inclination, to enter into an entente of equals, let alone an alliance of equals. Takeshi Matsuda caustically observes that "Americans seem to deal with problems only when they feel they have an overpowering military and economic advantage. They negotiate with foreigners splendidly so long as their counterparts remain conspicuously inferior to them in power and influence. When Americans see relations of power and influence tipping in a foreign country's favor, they feel less confident and less patient—that is, they begin to feel anxious and threatened and are easily irritated. Then they often behave awkwardly, high-handedly, and even abnormally."[26] The historical experience of China and Japan are equally discouraging in this respect.

America's laundry list of trade and other frictions with China is likely to lengthen, and U.S. anger and frustration to mount, particularly when China's luster dims after the Summer 2008 Olympics.[27] The reflexive American position of bolstering its cold war era alliances in Asia, primarily that with Japan, will become both more attractive and more problematic, depending on how Washington responds to issues of prime importance to Japan, including such current issues as North Korea's abduction of Japanese citizens and, much more important, the question of North Korea as a nuclear weapons state. China might prove more useful to Japan than the United States in addressing these issues.

From the perspective of Japanese leaders going back more than fifty years, the main strategic rationale for the U.S.-Japan alliance was the extended nuclear deterrence the United States provided Japan. At some considerable price in national pride, it obviated Tokyo's inclination to acquire such a capability on its own. It also allowed Japanese leaders, including those who would have preferred to have their own nuclear weapons, to engage in the hypocritical but domestically soothing pretense that they shared the so-called national allergy (read revulsion) toward nuclear weapons. North Korea's development of a limited nuclear capacity reopens the backroom debate in Japan that has only been suspended, never terminated, since the 1950s. The initial response of Japan to the enhanced threat from North Korea was to move closer to the United States, but the longer term response may be to acquire its own "nuclear umbrella" as Japanese confidence in American assurances wavers. I would not expect this to happen within the coming decade, however. The initial post-World War II Japanese overseas troop deployments (to Iraq) occurred within the framework of U.S.-led "coalition" warfare, but once taboos are broken, it is very difficult, if not impossible, to restore them.

Kenneth Pyle bemoans Japan's lack of political principles, a phenomenon he identifies as one of the pillars of its politics.[28] What this may indicate, however, is that Japan is the first truly postmodern state, one whose policies are not fixed, but infinitely flexible and opportunistic, adaptable and unconstrained by rigid principles or transcendent truths other than the bedrock of national interest defined as state power. If that is so, the political landscape of East Asia could further change in ways that scholars who are embedded in the contemporary minutiae of great power interactions may have trouble envisioning.

Imagining the Future

Emboldened by the knowledge that international relations are in constant flux, let us attempt to conceive of the inconceivable, namely, an end to the U.S.-Japan Security Alliance and a thoroughgoing reconfiguration of the Asia-Pacific balance of power. It is precisely the near- and mid-term improbability of such events occurring that, perhaps paradoxically, make them worth considering. No reliable early warning system exists to alert scholars or practitioners to coming international political tsunamis. The question I pose is: how might Japan fare in a future international power transition from a U.S.-dominated to a China-dominated international system and what role might it play in the process of such a transition? The bilateral Sino-American dimension of such a hypothetical power transition is broached in a recent monograph by Zhu Zhiqun.[29] Zhu builds upon a body of International Relations (IR) theory he traces back to A. F. K. Organski, and that includes work by Robert Gilpin, Torbjorn Knutsen, and many others who posit a hierarchical, rather than anarchic, international system in which the transition from one hegemonic power to another is usually, though not always, catalyzed by war.[30] Zhu cogently criticizes this work as simplistic, but his own expanded version of power transition theory includes so many variables affecting whether a power transition will occur peacefully or not that one is tempted to abandon policy studies entirely and take refuge in the sanctuary of history. In any case, by denying that China, which he sees as a status quo power that benefits from the existing international system, has or will ever develop any interest in unhorsing the United States, Zhu inexplicably destroys the premise of his own inquiry. Nevertheless, the question he initially poses is still worth contemplating.[31]

No international regime lasts forever, an axiom whose repetition is unlikely to win one many dinner invitations in Washington, DC. In the arc of history, hegemony is a time-share contract, not a property deed. Although it is impossible to predict when the American age will end or whether China will be the successor hegemon, if nothing else, it may be a useful intellectual exercise to contemplate the possibility.[32] My own conjecture in this regard is limited only to what Japan's role might be.[33]

Let us posit three stages of a possible power transition from the United States to China occurring, say, over the next thirty years, a period I have picked after consulting the actuarial tables for American men in their mid-sixties to ensure my own immunity from long-term criticism.[34] Borrowing from entomology, a field generally neglected by students of International Relations, let us label these the *larval*, *pupal*, and *adult* stages of China's emergence as a possible hegemonic power.

In the initial or larval stage, which, arguably, we are now witnessing, China explicitly and repeatedly denies that it has any intention of challenging the United States. Rather than confront the United States, China follows a policy of reassurance, cooperation, and circumvention, pursuing its interests around the world and expanding its influence through a combination of hard and soft power.

At this stage, Japan, allied to the United States, but tied to China positively by trade and investment, and negatively by geography and history, has no need or reason to choose between them. Strengthening the U.S.-Japan alliance, explicitly in the interests of regional and global security, tacitly as a hedge against growing Chinese power, would not be, and in fact is not, incompatible with the enhancement of Sino-Japanese relations. The approximate parity of power between

China and Japan in this first stage, all things considered, makes such an approach reasonable from the perspective of both Tokyo and Beijing, and creates an incentive on both sides to restrain the ardor of their own hypernationalists. In an environment where the outcome of an incipient power contest between the United States and China is unknowable, Japan is advantageously positioned to benefit from the perpetuation of the U.S.-dominated international system, while carefully observing global trends to gauge whether a power transition to China is underway and enhancing its own international posture through a shift to proactive diplomacy. The United States would be satisfied with Japan's affirmation of its commitment to a strengthened U.S.-Japan security alliance, manifested, perhaps, by the deployment of a theater missile defense force, which Beijing could grudgingly accept, provided its own relations with Japan were otherwise in good order.

In the second, or pupal, stage, let us assume that the United States has entered a period of gradual, but accelerating, relative decline. The signs include a weakening economy, a devalued dollar, a slowdown in technological innovation, a health system in crisis, a mediocre educational system, diminished confidence in the future, and an eroded international reputation due to militarism, unilateralism, and a disinclination to cooperate seriously on pressing international issues such as global climate change. Meanwhile, China, having secured its energy supplies, successfully contained its domestic problems, and on course toward, though still some considerable distance from, rough military parity with the United States, has achieved an unasserted, yet widely recognized, position of *primus inter pares* among the major powers in Asia, including the United States, Japan, India, and Russia. American alliances with Japan and Australia are still intact, but have become hollowed out, as its alliance partners increasingly perceive China as the hegemonic heir apparent. A reunified Korea is pursuing an independent foreign policy. There is little stomach in the United States, focused on domestic problems, to engage in a unilateral attempt to hinder China's upward trajectory.

Parenthetically, it strikes me as highly unlikely that Japan itself would challenge American hegemony by seeking to organize Asia as it did once before with disastrous results. The lessons of the Pacific War will not soon be forgotten, even when Japanese history books become more nationalistic. Incidentally, the concept of Japan as an "Asian Gateway" serving as a bridge between Asia and the world, that then Prime Minister Abe articulated in 2007, reminds one that Japan still rejects an Asian identity, an identity it consciously discarded during the Meiji era. Given Japan's past history, its weakness in soft power (apart from manga and anime), cultural insularity, and dearth of positive international leadership experience, Japan is more likely to be a bridge to nowhere than a mediator between Asia and the world. As noted above, Abe's expressed desire to strengthen partnerships "with countries that share the fundamental values of freedom, democracy, basic human rights, and rule of law" could be read as a challenge to China, which is indiscriminate in its choice of foreign partners and, therefore, better suited to attract camp followers.[35] Yet, given the geopolitics of Asia, such values-based partnerships, even though out of keeping with Japan's amoral diplomacy, make strategic sense as long as China itself remains an authoritarian state.

Faced with a declining American partner on one side and an ascending China on the other, Japan, which, as Kenneth Pyle reminds us, has always closely followed international trends, will likely recalibrate its foreign policy by distancing itself from the United States and strengthening its ties with China, while preserving its own independence. At this stage, Japan would accelerate its own defense buildup and, if it had not already done so earlier, develop its own nuclear deterrent.

In the third, or adult, stage of China's putative transformation into global hegemon of a new international system, Japan would further adjust to this new reality by finally terminating its by now vestigial security treaty with the United States while avoiding any formal bilateral security agreement with China, although a loose multilateral arrangement in East Asia that tacitly acknowledged China's hegemony might be established. Just as it stayed at the margins of the old imperial Chinese world order, Japan would maximize its autonomy in this imagined new Chinese hegemonic system, which would not, however, preclude extensive trade, investment, and other forms of international intercourse. In other words, Japan would be able to exercise greater freedom of action and suffer less subordination and status deprivation in a China-dominated international system than it has in the post–World War II U.S.-dominated world, provided that it at least tacitly acknowledged China's superior position.[36]

Could or would Japan play the role of facilitator in a power transition from the United States to China? There would seem to be no reason to do so. Japan's interests would probably best be served by staying on the sidelines, including in the event of a conflict between the United States and the PRC over Taiwan. The core characteristics of its foreign policy that Pyle defines, including, inter alia, attentiveness to power, pragmatism and the weakness of transcendent or universal ideals, adaptation and accommodation, and autonomy, suggest that Japan could fare equally well in a China-dominated international system as in an American one, particularly since a China-dominated system would be grounded in realism, not ideology, i.e., it would lack the universalistic and messianic pretensions that have characterized the exercise of American global power.[37]

In conclusion, let us turn from our typology borrowed from entomology to country music, an American genre that is popular in China and Japan as well as in the United States. In the event of a United States to China power transition, Japan would accept and accommodate the new reality with little difficulty, while the United States, in the words of country diva Barbara Mandrell, would be left "Sleeping single in a double bed, Tossing, turning, trying to forget."

NOTES

1. Richard Armitage, a former Deputy Secretary of State in the George W. Bush administration, excoriated his former colleagues in that administration for "ignoring Asia totally." *The Australian*, September 3, 2007.
2. For an insightful analysis of U.S.-Japan relations during the administration of President George H. W. Bush, see the memoir by the U.S. ambassador to Japan from 1989 to 1993, Michael H. Armacost, *Friends or Rivals: The Insider's Account of U.S.-Japan Relations* (New York: Columbia University Press, 1996).
3. For a balanced and generally positive Chinese view of Japanese foreign policy and its prospects in the post–cold war era, see Zhou Jihua, "Japan's Foreign Policy Choices for the Twenty-first Century: A Chinese Perspective," in *Japan in the Post-Hegemonic World, ed.* Tsuneo Akaha and Frank Langdon (Boulder and London: Lynne Rienner Publishers, 1993), 185–99. For a somewhat more skeptical, if still balanced, view of this transitional period, see Hwei-ling Huo, "Japan and China: Collaborators or Rivals," in *Japan's Quest: The Search for International Role, Recognition, and Respect*, ed. Warren Hunsberger (Armonk, NY and London: M. E. Sharpe, 1997), 150–66.
4. *International Herald Tribune*, March 14, 2007. Then Prime Minister Howard denied that the agreement was directed at containing China.
5. For Abe's visit to Beijing, see *Japan Times*, October 12, 2006; *New York Times*, October 4, 2006, p. A3.
6. Lecture by retired Japanese diplomat Yukio Okamoto in Missoula, Montana, October 3, 2007. Upon the announcement of Abe's resignation, China's Foreign Ministry praised Abe for his "active and constructive role in developing China-Japan ties." *The Straits Times* (Singapore), September 13, 2007.
7. Cited in *East-West Center Observer*10, no. 4 (Fall 2006–Winter 2007): 3.

8. Cited in Peter Y. Sato, "The View from Tokyo: Melting Ice and Building Bridges," The Jamestown Foundation, *China Brief* 7, no. 9 (May 2, 2007): 3.
9. Horizon Research Consultancy, *Eyes on the World, Future in Hand: The World in Chinese Mind*, 8. December 14, 2006. http://www.mansfieldfnd.org/polls/poll-06-19-.htm.
10. Ibid., 25–26.
11. See Susan Shirk, *China Fragile Superpower* (New York: Oxford University Press, 2007), 141–45. For an authoritative treatment of Sino-Japanese relations in the 1970s and 1980s, see Allen S. Whiting, *China Eyes Japan* (Berkeley and Los Angeles: University of California Press, 1989).
12. Jamestown Foundation, *China Brief* VII, 9 (May 2, 2007): 3.
13. Ian Buruma refers to these in his review article, "Why They Hate Japan" *The New York Review*, September 21, 2006, 79. I have perused the *manga* "Introduction to China" that he references, and can confirm that it is filled with vile, insulting, sexist, and racist images and text. See also Tsuneo Watanabe, "Changing Japanese Views of China: A New Generation Moves toward Realism and Nationalism," in *The Rise of China in Asia: Security Implications*, ed. Carolyn W. Pumphrey (Carlisle, PA: Strategic Studies Institute, 2002), 165.
14. Cited in Kenneth B. Pyle, *Japan Rising* (New York: Public Affairs, 2007), 3.
15. "And now to trilateralism," *Japan Times*, May 10, 2007.
16. At the time of writing, the process begun by an internationally negotiated agreement to roll back North Korea's status as a nuclear weapons state is unfolding, but success in this endeavor is still far from assured. Even if the final aim of ridding North Korea of its nuclear arsenal is achieved, that North Korea was able to become a nuclear weapons state is a fact whose significance cannot be forgotten.
17. The public outcry has already begun. See *The Independent* (London), May 4, 2007.
18. *Japan Times*, November 1, 2006.
19. "Japan to Vote on Modifying Pacific Charter Written by U.S.," *The New York Times*, May 15, 2007.
20. http://news.bbc.co.uk/go/pr/fr/-/2-hi/asia-pacific/6669061.stm.
21. See Tsuneo Watanbe, *Op. cit.*, 165, 176.
22. Then Prime Minister Abe said as much in his graduation speech to the National Defense Academy on March 18, 2007. *Japan Times*, March 19, 2007.
23. Pyle, *Japan Rising*, 311.
24. Policy speech by Prime Minister Shinzo Abe to the 165th Session of the Diet, September 29, 2006, 9.
25. *Japan Rising*, 320; with reference to the "Nixon shocks," Pyle writes: "Painful memories of the U.S. administration's decision to leave the Japanese in the dark still reverberate in Tokyo."

26. Takeshi Matsuda, *Soft Power and Its Perils: U.S. Cultural Policy in Early Postwar Japan and Permanent Dependency* (Woodrow Wilson Center Press and Stanford University Press, 2007), 254. Commenting on Sino-American-Japanese relations following Nixon's opening to China in 1972, Pyle discerns an "implicit entente of the three powers . . . the United States enjoyed close ties with both Japan and China and did not have to choose between them" (*Japan Rising*, 323). However, Washington was clearly the dominant power in both relationships, although the Chinese gave the Americans a much harder time than did the Japanese when it came to negotiations; see Robert S. Ross, *Negotiating Cooperation* (Stanford: Stanford University Press), 1995.
27. See, for example, Robert J. Samuelson, "China's Trade Bomb," *Washington Post*, May 9, 2007, p. A17, which accuses China of pursuing a mercantilist trade policy that is "designed to benefit China even if it harms its trading partners."
28. Pyle, *Japan Rising*, 269.
29. Zhu Zhiqun, *U.S.-China Relations in the 21st Century: Power Transition and Peace* (London and New York, Routledge, 2006).
30. A. F. K. Organski, *World Politics* (New York: Alfred A. Knopf, 1958); Robert Gilpin, *War and Change in World Politics* (New York: Cambridge University Press, 1981); T. L. Knutsen, *The Rise and Fall of World Orders* (Manchester: Manchester University Press, 1999).
31. I do not here enter into the question of whether the PRC is inherently fragile and likely to implode or, alternatively, that its current economic and military growth will proceed in a straight line. I do generally subscribe to what Jim Mann in his recent polemic against China Watchers refers to as "The Third Scenario," namely, that an increasingly powerful China will likely remain a repressive and authoritarian state; Jim Man, *The China Fantasy* (New York: Viking Press, 2007), 1–27.
32. Kurt Campbell, "Hegemonic Prophecy and Modern Asia: Lessons for Dealing with the Rise of China," in Carolyn Pumphrey, ed. *Op. cit.*, 49–62. In a short but pithy essay, Kurt Campbell reminds us of the pitfalls of predicting that one or another currently rising power will attain hegemony.
33. *Ibid.*, 60. Kurt Campbell notes that China's rise "will affect us in what we might call a psychic and philosophic way. Long before it affects us, however, it will affect our friends in Japan and in a much more direct and significant fashion."
34. *Ibid.*, 53. Kurt Campbell further observes: "When you think and talk about hegemonic transitions, it is generally not good to think in such short periods of time. When we look back at the predictions made during the last 25 years, what is most striking is just how wrong many of the pundits and thinkers were when making judgments and assessments of great power." Is it wrong to aspire to join this distinguished fraternity of near-sighted visionaries?

35. "Japanese Prime Minister Shinzo Abe Delivered Policy Speech to the Diet," Cabinet Secretariat, Government of Japan, http://www.prnewswire.co.uk/cgi/news/release?id=189038.
36. Shirk, *China Fragile Superpower*, 180. Shirk writes: "A cosmopolitan young Ph.D. in finance predicted with alarming confidence that Chinese-Japanese relations were bound to improve as China grows stronger. 'Right now there is close competition between China and Japan for leadership in Asia. When China is clearly number one then Japan will accept the situation and relations will be better.'"
37. Pyle, *Japan Rising*, 41–65. On the United States, see Michael H. Hunt, *The American Ascendancy* (Chapel Hill: University of North Carolina Press, 2007).

Chapter 6

The Russian Factor in U.S.–China Relations

Christopher Marsh and Lowell Dittmer

Who has not taken the time to calculate one's sign according to the Chinese zodiac? While waiting for a meal at a Chinese restaurant, there is perhaps no better way to pass the time and partake of Chinese culture at the same time. Although we have probably all done this, and are familiar with many of the signs such as dog, pig, and horse, most would be surprised to learn that there is also "the year of Russia" in China. During 2006, each month was filled with Russian cultural events throughout China, including ice sculptures, traveling ballet troupes, and photo exhibits. The leading Russian news service, *RIA-Novosti*, even used the occasion to launch a Chinese-language Web site. Several academic and business conferences aimed at improving mutual understanding and promoting trade were also held. Of course, there were also high-level diplomatic meetings about strengthening mutual aid and collaboration.[1] The event proved so popular among many that some did not want it to end. Russia is now reciprocating, with the year 2007 being marked as the "year of China" in Russia.[2] The promotion of this event was taken so seriously in Russia that its organizing committee was chaired by then-First Deputy Prime Minister Dmitry Medvedev, Putin's close confidant who shortly thereafter succeeded him as president.

Are these events simply cultural events or vacuous diplomatic maneuvers of little geostrategic significance? Perhaps not. While the year of one's birth, according to the Chinese zodiac, may not say much about one's actually personality, the pronouncements of reciprocal years of Russia and China may say something significant about the future course of Sino-Russian relations and, by implication, about the future of relations among China, Russia, and the United States. Bilateral relations between powers do not take place in a vacuum. Beside the many factors that are central to Sino-U.S. relations, the relations of the United States and China with other countries in the international system themselves impact the course and tenor of the latter. Perhaps no other country plays such an important role in this regard than Russia. Former cold war rival to the United States, and former Communist "big brother" (*laodage*) to China, Russia's relations with each impact Sino-U.S. relations in significant and determinative ways.

In the new millennium, several geostrategic shifts have occurred indicating that a Sino-Russian partnership may, in fact, be emerging. The U.S.-Russian post–cold war marriage is over, and relations between the two have become so soured that Washington and Moscow are beginning to talk of a new cold war. Meanwhile, Sino-U.S. relations remain complicated by the expansion of China's military, U.S. military operations across the globe, and the future status of Taiwan. In such a climate, China and Russia are reaching unprecedented levels of cooperation, on issues ranging from trade and military affairs to cooperation in Central Asia. As a new, post–cold war era takes shape, China and Russia are warming up to each other in ways seldom seen in their histories.

Changing Patterns in Trilateral Relations

Since Russia and China first encountered each other in military and diplomatic spheres, their bilateral relations have ranged from enemy to comrade and every point in between.[3] Just in the twentieth century alone, Russia went from supporting China's fledgling Communist movement, while simultaneously supporting the Guomindang, to becoming "comrades with a special relationship," and then moving to the brink of war over disputed territories along the Amur. Their diplomatic exchanges range from the 1689 Treaty of Nerchinsk, which followed upon Russian incursions into China's borderlands in the seventeenth century, to the 2001 Treaty of Good Neighborly Friendship and Cooperation. Throughout this relationship, no lasting pattern has really ever emerged, and their bilateral relations have always been based on the need for mutual coexistence, the necessity to protect one's rear flank, and the threat of other states in the international system and their ambitions on the Eurasian landmass. What is perhaps clear from this record is that events that occur at the domestic and international levels heavily impact how Russia and China will relate to each other at any given moment.

While relations with Russia were troubled during the initial period of Communist reform in both countries, dating back to the tension surrounding the cross-border skirmishes of 1969 and only exacerbated by the Soviet invasion of Afghanistan a decade later, relations between the Soviet Union and China began to improve under Gorbachev,[4] who was slow to condemn the Tiananmen Square incident, a portion of which he witnessed firsthand. While U.S.–China relations stalled in the aftermath of Tiananmen, Russia emerged from the collapse of the Soviet Union and made dramatic leaps in its attempt to democratize and develop a market economy in the 1990s—developments which paved the way for greatly improved relations with the West, particularly the United States.

This pattern continued more or less throughout the 1990s,[5] although the marriage showed signs of trouble already by 1999, particularly over the North Atlantic Treaty Organization's (NATO) bombing of Serbia. With new blood in the Kremlin and the White House, things began to improve dramatically between 2000 and 2002. These warm relations were at least partly due to President Bush's relationship with Putin, with whom he seemed to develop a rapport early on in his presidency, and also partly based on the pragmatic need to address the mutual threat of terrorism.

In commenting on U.S.-Russia relations in the context of China's bilateral relations with Russia, Chien-peng Chung concluded that China was well aware of the "new and improved relationship between the United States and Russia" that was unfolding during this period, through such agreements as the U.S.-Russia Treaty on Reductions of Strategic Offensive Weapons, the Joint Declaration on a New Strategic Partnership between the United States and Russia, and Russia's partnership status with NATO through the Russia-NATO Joint Council.[6] Others agreed with this assessment, such as Weede, who, in writing on "the rise and decline" of China and Russia, observed that "if relations between America and Russia continue to improve, as they did since September 11, 2001 . . . China will feel encircled."[7]

A lot has happened since 9/11, however, and now relations between the United States and Russia are at a new low, with some in Washington touting America's first-strike capability against Russia. As Robert Legvold has phrased it,

> Gone is the talk of "strategic partnership," not to mention the fanciful vision of a genuine Russo-American alliance held by some . . . not so long ago. Gone is the aura of camaraderie created by Russia's instant support for the United States after September 11 and then the joint effort in winning the Afghan war. Gone are the benevolent winds stirred by Russia's mild response to the U.S. abrogation of the ABM agreement, tolerance of U.S. bases in Central Asia, offer of energy partnership, acceptance of a new Russia-NATO Council, and enthusiastic talk of U.S.-Russian cooperation at the May 2002 Moscow summit.[8]

For their part, Russians are also aware of souring relations between Washington and Beijing. In a joint situation analysis by the journal *Russia in Global Affairs* and the Council on Foreign and Defense Policy in December 2005, a group of more than one dozen Russian experts on China and international affairs, including Timofei Bordachev, Alexander Lukin, and Vladimir Portyakov, pointed to the "growing rivalry between Beijing and Washington" as the "main obstacle" standing in the way of peaceful political and economic affairs in the Asia-Pacific.[9]

The souring in relations between the United States and Russia was certainly unforeseen by most, but by the late 1990s, signs were already beginning to appear. Did the United States think it could engage in such geostrategic initiatives as NATO expansion, the stationing of troops in the Russian "near abroad," and launch a plan to deploy a comprehensive missile defense system along Russia's western flank, and not engender a Russian response? As Legvold argues, it is certainly an unwelcome development that will hopefully be corrected. But what Weede and others have perhaps been missing is that China and Russia have been warming up to each other for quite a while. One of the first signs was the seriousness with which China took the collapse of the Soviet Union and how some in Russia looked to China as a potential model for its own reform.[10] Another early sign was Yeltsin's pronouncement in Beijing during his visit in the fall of 1999 that Russia was a nuclear power. This pronouncement was seemingly directed toward the United States, which had recently completed its military operations in Kosovo and was becoming increasingly critical of Russia's renewed fighting in Chechnya.

It is this turn of events that has probably most significantly affected the course of Sino-Russian relations in the new millennium. Whereas Weede argues that parity between states is dangerous, and that the power transition between Russia and China might lead to a confrontation, in fact, the two are being pushed together by America's hard- and soft-power preponderance, diplomatic language, and military posture worldwide. Both Russia and China feel threatened to some degree by American unilateralism, leading to voices in both countries calling for an alliance to balance against the United States While there are certainly limits to this rapprochement, as Legvold observes, "China [is] a natural soulmate on many critical foreign policy issues [that] render Russia strong."[11] It is in this context that one must analyze cultural pronouncements, diplomatic exchanges, and joint military operations. In short, if one wishes to understand relations between the United States and China and Russia, he or she must take into account Sino-Russian relations and the involvement of each in Central Asia.

Russian Foreign Policy through Chinese Eyes

The sea change that has occurred in U.S.-Sino-Russian relations adds new significance to the Sino-Russian relationship, as each looks to the other as a way of balancing off the United States. Behind this, there has occurred a growth in both countries in terms of positive views of the other. Few in China and Russia care much about whether the other is a democracy or Communist state. Rather, their bilateral relations are based on solid diplomacy, signs of respect, and what is perceived as proper role playing.

Chinese analysts divide post-Soviet Russian foreign policy into three phases.[12] The first phase was the first Yeltsin administration, when foreign policy was dominated by Andrei Kozyrev and the "Euro-Atlantic" faction. Here, the Chinese believe that Russia opened itself too quickly to the West, and was easily "fooled" into giving up too much ground in order to obtain illusory Western aid. The belief that Russia would be rapidly integrated into Euro-Atlantic structures proved to be wishful thinking. Instead, Russia's economy collapsed and the groundwork was laid for NATO expansion right up to Russia's own borders. In other words, the idealistic hopes that Russia would be quickly integrated into the West were used to the detriment of Russia's own national interests.

The Chinese believe that the second phase—when policy was being guided by Yevgeny Primakov—was equally unrealistic. Primakov's view of a multipolar world was amenable to the Chinese, but they believed that Russia still suffered from the illusion that it in fact remained a great power. From the Chinese perspective, the Russians should have reevaluated their policies in light of the overwhelming decline in Russia's economic and military potential and concentrated on internal efforts to strengthen the state, rather than attempt to play a role in the international arena for which it was ill suited.[13]

Overall, the Chinese assess the Yeltsin administration as a period when Russia lost status, where the attempts to cooperate with the United States and foster close relations during the 1990s only further reduced Russian influence by forcing the Russians to make concessions to the United States in exchange for empty or partially fulfilled promises of aid and support. The Chinese leadership has paid close attention to Russian-American relations since the collapse of the Soviet Union, and concluded that a pro-U.S. foreign policy does not pay the dividends it might promise—that a close embrace of Washington may not enhance one's economic position or sense of security. This, in turn, has influenced their post 9/11 behavior—offering guarded support for the war against terrorism, but not moving to cement closer ties with Washington.[14]

Chinese commentators have been much more approving of the foreign policy line implemented by Vladimir Putin and Sergei Ivanov, believing that Russian policy is now guided by *realpolitik*. A realistic, pragmatic policy emanating from the Kremlin is welcomed by Beijing, although Russia's early assessment that a closer strategic partnership with the United States served Moscow's interests led to increased American penetration of the former Soviet space and further compromises on Russia's part, including additional NATO expansion, the demise of the ABM Treaty, and the stationing of U.S. troops inside the former Soviet Union. The Chinese doubted early on whether Putin's decision to align more closely with Washington would bring Russia concrete economic and strategic dividends.

By the early years of the new millennium, Chinese scholars were already identifying Russia's adoption of an extremely pro-U.S. foreign policy as a mistake, as it only facilitated Russia's loss of power and influence. Additionally, by the time Russia realized that its "pro-Western strategy" was not going to work, it was heavily in debt, NATO had expanded, and U.S. troops were based in Russia's "near abroad." Given what he had to work with, however, the Chinese think that, overall, Putin did a decent job of defending Russian interests.

During the cold war, China referred to Russia as its "big brother." Though China does not now see itself as the older sibling, it does want to be treated on an equal footing with Russia. China does not want to see Russia become too powerful or too weak, but rather, "take its proper place in the international system"—not acting as a junior partner to Washington, but as a realistic actor able to maintain some distance from the United States. Additionally, China wants to see a Russia that bases its foreign policy decisions upon realism, instead of trusting the West to support Russian interests.

While the Soviet Union stood shoulder to shoulder with the United States throughout the cold war, today, Russia is a mere shadow of its former self, and its international stature has greatly diminished. For example, an author writing under a pseudonym in the pages of *Nanfang Zhoumo* has argued that Russia needs to find its rightful place in international affairs. As a declined superpower, it cannot play the role of a pole in a multipolar world and it should find a proper role to play, with the author suggesting that Russia might find a place in the world as a mediator between other powers, perhaps even balancing various powers, rather than taking on the role of a great power itself.[15] Such a role would keep Russia in the spotlight and maintain Russia's role in key global issues, but such a role would also be more fitting for a state with diminished economic and military resources.

Chinese perceptions of Russian foreign policy, in general, range from bad to worse, but perhaps all are in agreement that Russia is a declined superpower that maintains illusions of great power status, a theme similar to that voiced in *Nanfang Zhoumo*. The more optimistic assessments consider that Russia was duped by the West's strategy of peaceful evolution (*heping yanbian*) and attempted complete Westernization, including abandoning its ties with its formerly Communist allies and attempting to align itself with the West. Chinese scholars consider this to have been a "fond illusion," for although Russia was promised quite a bit, less has actually arrived, and in the process, the country became bogged down in foreign debt. Other Chinese analysts point to the collapse of the Warsaw Pact, NATO expansion, and the presence of U.S. troops on CIS soil as evidence of the fact that Russia has basically been relegated to the position of a peripheral state in the international system.[16]

As a rising regional power that already feels "encroached upon,"[17] Chinese analysts have concluded that China's own interests are best served by a stronger Russia that is capable of maintaining some degree of distance from the United States. Such a conclusion is not only offered by many Chinese commentators on the subject, but is also apparent by its actions. While it is premature to conclude that Beijing wishes to create some sort of alliance with Moscow against Washington, Beijing would prefer that Russia (and Europe) be able to counter American influence to some degree.

Russia Looks East (or the Limits of a Sino-Russian Alliance)

Some in Russia, however, are explicitly calling for such an alliance. Andrei Devyatov, a former Soviet defense intelligence officer, sees China's rise to global dominance as an opportunity not a threat. His *Krasnyi Drakon: Kitai i Rossiya v Dvadtsat' Pervom Veke* (*The Red Dragon: China and Russia in the 20th Century*), focuses on the geopolitical implications of China's economic success and human capital.[18] Devyatov calls upon Russia to join with China in establishing a multipolar world and balancing American influence.

Throughout the 1990s, leading Russian Sinologist Alexander Yakovlev continually lectured and published on the positive dimensions of the Sino-Russian relationship, and blamed the United States for attempting to promote an anti-Chinese sentiment among post-Soviet Russia's new ruling elite.[19] Yakovlev argued that all states seek to protect their national interests, and that China was not a threat as long as it was not provoked. The scenario that Washington was offering—that China would come to pursue aggressive policies against all of its neighbors—was rejected by Yakovlev in favor of a policy of engagement.[20] It is worthwhile to note that this is an opinion almost universally held by his colleagues at the Institute of the Far East at the Russian Academy of Sciences, which generally holds a favorable view of China and its accomplishments.

It is certainly premature to conclude that Russia would be willing to partner with China against the United States, however, as bad as relations between Moscow and Washington may get. Even during periods of warm relations between the two, Moscow has always remained guarded in its commitment to Beijing, with Stalin's unsuccessful attempt to manipulate Mao during the Korean crisis only the most well-known example.[21] In fact, China's rise probably evokes more fear in Russia than admiration. Many in Russia are fearful of China and see the country as being overrun with Chinese. This is particularly true in the Russian Far East, where Chinese traders are coming across the border by the thousands every day, raising fears of a Chinese takeover of the region.[22]

As early as 2000, Russian writers were coming out with warnings about the threat posed by China. Igor Malevich's *Vnimanie, Kitai* (*Attention, China*), primarily aims to inform readers of the former Soviet Union about China's dramatic rise to a position of influence in the world.[23] Malevich, a former Soviet astronaut, structures his work around the question of whether China represents Russia's future or its past, only to conclude that it is, in some ways, both. Essentially, however, Malevich wants to warn his readers of the potential dangers of a successful and powerful China.[24]

In May 2004, Russian investigative journalist Yelena Masyuk completed a four-part documentary entitled "The Character of Friendship," which was subsequently aired on many stations throughout Russia, despite an order from many local government agencies that it not be aired (an order that was not followed in even a single region). The documentary "exposed" the dangers of China's rise, and the double standards of China's "friendship" with Russia. In an interview by the Russian daily *Sobesednik*, Masyuk further elaborated on her fears of China: "Chinese nationals become Russian citizens, subsequently buying land and turning into full-fledged proprietors. One can see entire Chinese districts even in the Khabarovsk territory; such districts comprise private mansions acquired with the help of agents. This process will escalate, unless it's stopped. Chinese nationals are feeling they are masters."[25] Masyuk's observations reached far beyond investigative reporting, and expressed a deep disagreement with the Putin Administration and its policies toward China: "I can't understand the position of Russia's Foreign Ministry, which doesn't react to the fact that China prints maps showing all regions between Vladivostok and the Urals as Chinese territory. We are keeping mum on this score. Naturally enough, this won't yield any positive results because China, as well as any Asian country, respects force alone."[26] In case her position was not clear enough, Masyuk followed up her comments with a very telling reference: "U.S.-based RAND political science center claims that a Russian-Chinese war seems inevitable by 2020. We are heading in that direction, you know."[27]

While there are certainly voices in Russia speaking out against China,[28] Putin did not seem very affected by them, and he, along with his foreign ministry, continue to pursue a policy of warm relations with China. In the early post-Soviet years, Russia's policy toward China was reflexive, i.e., not systematic or well thought-out, but rather based upon specific issues at any given time. Since this period, a more purposeful strategy has emerged, what Luzyanin has labeled a "systemic realization of a pragmatic policy conditioned by strategic needs."[29] Overall, Putin's policy toward China has been one of involving Russia in Asian affairs and working with China in all forms of cooperation. The limits to this partnership, however, remain unknown and even undetermined.

Luzyanin correctly argues that Putin's China policy is connected to two interconnected policy areas, or "vectors," as they are called in

Russian. The first is the larger context of Russia's relations with Asia, which is institutionalized through Russia's involvement in the Asia-Pacific Economic Cooperation (APEC). While only ten million Russians reside on the Asian continent, Russia does boast the longest coastline along the Pacific, and much of its vast energy resources are situated in Asia, with much of it finding its way to foreign markets via Asian ports, rail lines, and pipelines. In regards to the Asia-Pacific region as a whole, Russia's involvement remains primarily economic, however, and shows little likelihood of extending into other spheres.

When it comes to the second vector, however—that of Russia's involvement with Eurasia—there appears to be a different story. While cooperation in this area, too, began primarily in the economic realm, it is showing signs expanding and deepening, and much of this development is occurring under the aegis of the Shanghai Cooperation Organization (SCO). It is important to understand, however, that to Putin, these three vectors were all interconnected. Putin's "Eastern policy" was based upon the desire to cooperate in military technology and hardware, mutual trade of consumer goods, and the exporting of energy resources. China appears to be the lynchpin to Putin's "Eastern policy," moreover, particularly in regards to the development of a strategic partnership.[30] Luzyanin refers to this policy as a "strategy based upon pragmatic considerations," and agrees that such a policy makes sense given the complementarities that exist between the two countries.

The Central Asia Vector

The recent creation of the Shanghai Cooperation Organization, seeking to strengthen and integrate nearly all the Central Asian States—bracketed (and led) by two very large and previously threatening Eurasian powers, China and Russia—seemed a scant source of solace to Western geopoliticians.

The current era of Sino-Russian cooperation in Central Asia dates from the beginning of the post-Soviet era, when the three newly independent republics sharing borders with China (Kazakhstan, Kyrgyzstan, and Tajikistan) joined with Russia in a team arrangement to negotiate their borders with China, meeting semi-annually in Beijing and Moscow from 1992–96. This culminated in a summit meeting in April 1996 among the five states to ratify and consolidate their shared borders, and then resulted in an Agreement on Mutual Reduction of Military Forces in the Border Region at a second summit the following year in Moscow. A central factor leading to China's renewed interest in Central Asia was the emergence of a separatist movement in the country's westernmost province of Xinjiang.

A historical precedent for an independent state in the region can be traced to the Hui uprising from 1867 to 1877 under the leadership of Muslim leader Yaqub Beg and by the actual establishment of the Turkish Islamic Republic of East Turkistan in November 1933, which lasted less than six months. Again in November 1945, an Eastern Turkestan Republic was set up in Yining, but this lasted only about half a year. A separatist insurgency revived in the region following the Soviet defeat in Afghanistan, with many radicalized Uyghurs returning from fighting alongside the mujahadeen. As early as 1990, there was a Uyghur uprising in Akto County in Xinjiang, which led to the death of more than fifty people in a battle with People's Liberation Army (PLA) troops, and there were a series of bomb attacks in Beijing in 1997 and again in 2002. According to Chinese sources, from 1990 to 2001 there were some two hundred "terrorist acts" in Xinjiang, killing 162 people and injuring 440.[31]

This separatist agitation was facilitated by the demonstration effect of the Soviet Union's Central Asian republics gaining independence in the wake of the collapse of the USSR, and was only exacerbated by border agreements that permitted freer flow of populations between Central Asia and China. All the Central Asian states have Uyghur minorities—Kyrgyzstan has some fifty thousand, and in June 2002, a Chinese consul was killed in Bishkek, while in March 2003 in a bus bombing, twenty-one Chinese were killed, apparently by Uyghur migrants from China.[32] Thus, in November 2003, Kyrgyzstan accordingly banned several groups, including the Islamic Movement of Uzbekistan (IMU), the Eastern Turkestan Islamic Party, and the Eastern Turkistan Liberation Organization. Other separatist organizations, such as the Uyghurstan Liberation Organization and the United Revolution Front of East Turkistan, are apparently headquartered in Kazakhstan.

After independence, Kazakh leaders adopted the slogan "return to your homeland," passing legislation to ease ethnic emigration. While China did not object, the resulting reverse flow of Uyghurs seeking China's higher living standards also resulted in the infiltration of terrorists back into China. Thus, Xinjiang became the first of China's provinces to organize an antiterror corps. Shortly after 9/11, Beijing set up a National Anti-Terrorism Coordination Group (NATCG), with a secretariat led by Hu Jintao, to lead a campaign against the "three evil forces"—national separatism, religious extremism, and international terrorism (*kongbuzhuyi, fenlizhuyi yu jiduanzhuyi*).

Simultaneously, it began to solicit cooperation from neighboring governments to control their ethnic minorities more effectively. There is a distinction, of course, between separatism and terrorism, one seldom acknowledged by the Chinese. Although some separatists do employ violence, a conspiratorial connection between East Turkistan separatists and al Qaeda is difficult to support empirically.[33]

The People's Republic of China (PRC) abhors these separatist and terrorist groups not only because they are intrinsically threatening, but because their activities have prompted the arrival of American forces deployed against a global war on terrorism (GWOT), who, in the wake of 9/11, were permitted with surprising promptness to establish basing facilities in Uzbekistan and Kyrgyzstan (the latter, at Manas International Airport north of Bishkek, hosts three thousand USAF personnel within two hundred miles of the Chinese border) and to enjoy overflight rights in all but one of the other republics (resulting in prompt increases in U.S. aid to the host countries).

Since the NATO "humanitarian intervention" into what was then Yugoslavia in 1999 to prevent ethnic cleansing in Kosovo, the Chinese have harbored the nightmare of some sort of Western incursion into Chinese minority regions on the pretext of support for oppressed minorities.[34] This has led some Chinese strategists to speculate that NATO had shifted focus from Eastern Europe to Central Asia. Though initially welcomed by the republics themselves and then endorsed by Putin, U.S. bases in Central Asia (bracketing China with bases both east and west) were viewed with some reservation in China. Xinjiang is central to Chinese strategic interests, including the nuclear testing range in Lop Nor and the basing area of much of China's Intercontinental Ballistic Missile (ICBM) deterrent force. The buildup of the Kyrgyz base (at a time when operations in Afghanistan had already concluded) could be used for radar reconnaissance against PRC missile launches (according to some reports, missiles launched from Xinjiang or Tibet are beyond the range of U.S. ABM defenses as currently configured). The Americans have, in response, attempted to reassure the Chinese the bases are only temporary, presumably until Operation Enduring Freedom is concluded.

Whereas the Chinese response to ethnic violence in Xinjiang (and by Uyghur confederates beyond) coincided with U.S. interests after 9/11, and while the Chinese did not explicitly object to the establishment of Central Asian bases, this was not viewed as the ideal solution to the terrorist threat in either Beijing or Moscow, and both undertook unprecedented multilateral organizational efforts as more appropriate countermeasures. For Russia, this took the form of the Collective

Security Treaty, formed in the context of establishing the Commonwealth of Independent States upon the dissolution of the USSR in 1991 and was revitalized in 2000, including the establishment of a 1,500-man rapid deployment force (known by its Russian acronym, KSBR), a secretariat, and an Antiterrorist Center in Bishkek; in 2003, Moscow added an air base in support of the KSBR in Kant, north of Bishkek, near the U.S. base. But the Central Asian republics were sufficiently unimpressed by its performance to welcome China's initiative to inaugurate the Shanghai Cooperation Organization in June 2001 in Beijing. This was a direct descendant of the former Soviet border negotiating team—dubbed the Shanghai Five in 1999 and then the Shanghai Forum in July 2000—being retitled, yet again, to the SCO upon the admission of Uzbekistan, a nonborder state of considerable industrial and military power.

Over the past several years, the SCO has seen a shift from a focus on border pacification to antiterrorism and other security concerns. Although China took the leading role in inaugurating this organization, since 2004, it has functioned as an official international organization (but not a military alliance), and is governed by membership consensus, meaning that a single veto can block action. By 2004, the SCO had a secretariat, a $3.5 million budget, a regional antiterrorist structure (RATS) located in Tashkent, and even a festival. This is the first international organization to which China has formally pledged to commit forces beyond its border (in the event of a terrorist threat), and accordingly, in August 2003, participated in a multilateral SCO exercise in Kazakhstan and Xinjiang, and in 2005 (together with Russian forces), simulated an amphibious invasion in Shandong in "Peace Mission 2005" (with obvious reference to Taiwan as a "separatist" target).

Although China has been very cautious in supplying military aid, reserving to Russia its military preeminence in the region, it has provided emergency military equipment to Uzbekistan and Kyrgyzstan and police facilities to Kazakhstan. At the July 2005 Heads of State summit in Astana, the SCO issued a declaration that coalition forces leave Central Asia within six months, and indeed the bulk of U.S. forces departed by November 2005, though they renegotiated their lease in Kyrgyzstan (at a higher price). This signals not only consensual skepticism about the term of the "temporary" bases but a cooling of U.S.-Uzbek relations since early 2005, when Washington took a harsh view of the crackdown at Andijian and called for the international "isolation" of Tashkent.

At the tenth anniversary SCO meeting in June 2006, India, Pakistan, Mongolia, and Iran were invited to participate as observers; the latter three (not India) have since applied for full membership. Sensing the SCO was gaining traction, Washington sought observer status at this meeting, but was turned down. Following a policy review, the new Washington strategy seems to be to try to integrate Central Asia with South Asia, anchored in favorable Indo-U.S. relations (thus, the State Department's South Asian Bureau has been expanded to include Afghanistan and the Central Asian republics).

While the primary Chinese concern with regard to Central Asia has been security, China has also expressed a lively economic interest in the region, partly as a western counterpart to the lucrative opening of the east coast to foreign trade, but mainly as an expression of China's avid pursuit of sources of energy. As the world's second largest consumer (and third largest importer) of energy since 2003, dependent for about half its current imports on the Middle East (which must be imported through straits whose security is assured by the U.S. Navy), China wants to diversify, particularly in Kazakhstan and Uzbekistan. China and Kazakhstan are building a jointly owned pipeline from Atyrau through Kenkiyak, Kumkol, and Atasau to Alashankou on the Xinjiang border, two stretches of which were operational by 2005. The China National Petroleum Corporation (CNPC), China's largest state petroleum corporation, owns a controlling interest in Aktobemunaigaz, a production company in western Kazakhstan. But China also has bigger ambitions: a 2003 bid by China National Offshore Oil (CNOOC) and China Petroleum and Chemical Corporation (Sinopec) to buy British Petroleum shares of Kazakhstan's massive offshore Kashagan deposit was blocked by consortia partners, limiting the bid to half. CNPC did manage to acquire the smaller North Buzachi field and, in 2005, purchased the assets of Petrakazakhstan, giving them the assets of the Kumkol field and shared control of Shymkent Refinery (with Kazmunaigaz). The Chinese are also negotiating with Turkmenistan to purchase oil and gas. From Kyrgyzstan, they have arranged to purchase hydroelectric power, while in Tajikistan, a Chinese telecom station has contracted to reconstruct all the telephone exchanges in Dushanbe.

According to Chinese statistics, trade with the Central Asian states is growing fast, from US$463 million in 1992 to US$872 million in 1997; by 2002, trade with Kazakhstan alone had reached US$3 billion. Yet, this should all be kept in perspective. Chinese energy imports from Central Asia still do not constitute a significant percentage of the total (less than 1 percent of total energy imports). The Central Asian republics are wary of exploitive deals (demanding, for example, that Chinese investment deals reserve 70 percent of the jobs to domestic labor rather than bringing in Chinese work crews), and the Russians, to whom most of the Central Asian pipelines are routed, have been monitoring developments closely. Chinese purchases in Central Asia are designed in part to diversify their stake in Russian oil (currently about 11 percent of total imports), in view of the difficulty the Chinese have had purchasing Russian oil companies or making binding agreements for pipeline routes.[35]

Is the combination of China and Central Asia threatening? This is a complex question, requiring not only a "yes" or "no" answer, but one of "more or less." China's access to Central Asia has the definite potential to strengthen China's economy, particularly by dint of its abundant energy supply. Yet, Western oil companies remain a player in the pursuit of oil; in fact, most of the good fields have been locked up by Western consortia, even in Central Asia. With regard to security, China, in its pursuit of a "peaceful rise," has been even more solicitous of Russian sensitivities than of American: there is no question that Russia remains the dominant military and political power in Central Asia for the foreseeable future. The Americans, in the early years of the new millennium, had a fleeting opportunity to challenge Moscow's hegemonic position, but the liberal U.S. ideological stance (not to mention its failed counterterrorist strategy in Iraq) seems to have nullified its perceived value as an antiterrorist deterrent and useful counterbalance to Russia's dominant position in the region.

In the process of their deepening relations and exchanges with China, both in the Central Asian region and more generally, Moscow is not only sending a message to Washington, they are also facilitating China's rise, both economically and militarily. Did Putin and his foreign policy team not recognize the potential threat that China will pose in the longer-range future, despite whatever sincerity rests behind their current motivations? It is certainly in both Moscow's and Beijing's interests to secure their rear flanks and provide for stability in Central Asia. From the vantage points of both the Kremlin and Zhongnanhai, the greatest threat to peace and the international status quo seems to be emanating from Washington. In such an international environment, Russia's and China's actions make good strategic sense.

Another reason both China and Russia are so willing to cooperate on Central Asia is that neither has realistic territorial ambitions in the region. China itself has no illusions about furthering its reach into Central Asia; its only goals vis-à-vis Central Asia are to keep Xinjiang in, Islamist militants out, and the oil flowing. While Russia may still harbor dreams of someday reclaiming the prize of the "Great Game," China is keenly aware of Russia's impotency in dealing with the Caucasus and Central Asia—not only did it fail in its decade-long war with Afghanistan, its record in keeping separatist Chechnya in the federation illustrates to both Beijing and Moscow that any attempt to move into Central Asia would be disastrous.

Possibly, the most legitimate concern is that the SCO will indeed become what it is sometimes referred to in China—as the NATO of the East—and the only security-oriented intergovernmental organization (IGO) in the world of which the United States is not a member (or even an observer). That is, indeed, the possible outcome of the combination of Chinese and Russian geographic advantages and a series of American missteps. Yet if so, this is not so much a "loss" as an opportunity cost, for the United States, unlike the British Empire of the nineteenth-century "Great Game," was never a player. Only through the fortuitous circumstances attending its Afghan intervention did Washington acquire stakes in the game, but it has not thereafter played its hand very shrewdly.

Riding Russia's Coattails: A Different Take on the Rise and Decline of Two Nations

Today, few would argue that Russia will rise again to rival the United States as the global hegemon, or that China will not threaten U.S. action in the Asia-Pacific—if not across the globe—in the years to come. There not only has been a shift in the relative power capabilities of Russia and China,[36] but also in terms of their relationship vis-à-vis the United States. This shift is not unlike that which took place at the end of World War II. Like the United Kingdom before it, Russia demands recognition of its great power status, despite the fact that its relative power capabilities have declined dramatically. Unlike the United Kingdom, however, it has not been given such recognition by the West.

Even while the sun never set on the British Empire, the United States was being weaned for its future role of hegemon as part of its alliance with England. And once the United States emerged as the leader of the Western world after Word War II, Washington looked to London for guidance and nods of approval. This was a natural handing of the baton, as the United Kingdom was the wise player, had the statesmen, and though its military was good and its economy strong, the country's status had certainly been relegated to a lesser tier. The

United Kingdom continues to enjoy such a role today, as the United States continues to seek its blessing on issues, and if it receives it, it will sometimes count that as enough to move forward on "multilateral" actions. In many ways, they remain our big brother, despite the preponderance of U.S. power.

The Sino-Russian relationship may be moving in a similar direction. Of course, Russia still has a will to *derzhava* (great power status), but really no pretensions to superpower status. Russia wishes to remain a major player in world affairs and have its seat at the table. Much of its actions—from Kosovo to North Korea—can be seen through such a lens. Russia, of course, does not want to be displaced by China. Again, this sounds very similar to the British position after World War II, when U.S. military and technoindustrial superiority did not mean that the British were going to relinquish the moral high ground to the Americans. The same is likely to be true for relations between China and Russia.

This relationship is evolving based on mutual respect, but there is certainly some kowtowing by China to Russia. For example, when Jiang Zemin visited Moscow, he would often speak in Russian (and even sing Russian songs) as a sign of respect for Russian culture and, more than that, for Russia's role throughout most of the twentieth century as the only rival to the United States.[37] China recognizes that Russia's power and stature has drastically declined, but it gives Russia the status it craves and demands as a great power and former superpower. As with the way the United States dealt with its ascension to the role of superpower after World War II, the United States did not just tell the United Kingdom to sit down. Instead, Washington recognized that Britain had a lot to teach us and deserved our respect and a seat at the table.

As for China itself, it is the rising power, and perhaps no other great power is willing to work with it quite the way Russia is. China certainly has global ambitions, but that is not to say that China's foreign affairs as a great power—or even hegemon—will resemble those of the United States or the United Kingdom during their hegemonies, nor that it will ever come to pass. But it is an implicit ambition, despite the fact that most of the pronouncements that come out of Beijing speak of a multipolar world and China's "peaceful rise."[38] This is, of course, the necessary first step, but probably not the ultimate goal in the longer-term future.

China also understands that they have many things working in their favor, including a culture that values hard work and education, a large population, natural resource endowments, and a growing industrial base. Of course, there are problems with each of these, but one must take seriously a country with such a huge landmass, long coastline, defensible interior, and a population that comprises one-sixth of the planet. A partnership with Russia only strengthens that position, as it further guards their rear flank, provides necessary military equipment and technology, and eases their energy requirements, which will only continue to increase in the years to come.

When viewing the contemporary world from such a vantage point, things seem to look quite different from the images of a fallen Soviet superpower and an aggressive, Communist China that are popular in some corners of the Federal Triangle and Foggy Bottom. Rather, U.S. military operations in multiple theaters of operation are seen as the only major aggression by a great power after the end of the cold war, and Russia and China consider themselves on the defensive. The United States must be careful with its dealings with both Russia and China, as its actions will continue to affect the course of the Sino-Russian relationship in the years to come. As Legvold points out, "the considerable parallelism in Russian and Chinese foreign policy will surely continue, but a full-blown alliance directed against the United States, impossible today—because, even if Moscow wanted it, which it does not, the Chinese have the final say—will remain so, unless the United States brings it about through a reckless policy toward China."[39] Such wisdom warns against Washington pushing Moscow and Beijing too hard, for, in so doing, it may push them even closer together and into an alliance against the United States.

NOTES

1. A complete list of events related to "The Year of Russia" in China is maintained by the Russian Academy of Science's Institute of the Far East, "Programma Meropriyatii goda Rossii v Kitae," http://www.ifes-ras.ru/orkd/year.
2. "'God Kitaya' v Rossii—Ukreplenie sotrudnichestvo pri nepreryvnom yglublenii vzaimoponimaniya," http://www.china.org.cn/russian/281184.htm.
3. It is important to point out that, in the popular Russian mindset, Russia's first encounter with China dates back to the Mongol invasion and subsequent overlordship of Russia for nearly two centuries. The name for China in Russian (*Kitai*), in fact, dates back to this period, and is derived from the Russian name for a Mongol tribe (Cathay).
4. Lowell Dittmer, *Sino-Soviet Normalization and its International Implications, 1945–1990* (Seattle: University of Washington Press, 1992).

5. Jeanne L. Wilson, *Strategic Partners: Russian-Chinese Relations in the Post-Soviet Era* (Armonk, NY: M. E. Sharpe, 2004).
6. Chien-peng Chung, "The Shanghai Cooperation Organization: China's Changing Influence in Central Asia," *The China Quarterly* (December 2004), 1006.
7. Erich Weede, "China and Russia: On the Rise and Decline of Two Nations," *International Interactions* 29 (2003): 357.
8. Robert Legvold, "U.S.-Russian Relations: An American Perspective," *Russia in Global Affairs* 4 (October–December 2006).
9. Timofei Bordachev, "Asia's Future and Russia's Policy," *Russia in Global Affairs* 3 (July–September 2006).
10. Christopher Marsh, *Unparalleled Reforms: China's Rise, Russia's Fall, and the Interdependence of Reform* (Lanham, MD: Lexington Books, 2006).
11. Legvold, "US-Russian Relations."
12. Christopher Marsh, "America, China, and Russia: The Trilateral Relationship," *Nixon Center Program Brief* 9, no. 8 (March 10, 2003).
13. See, for example, Xu Zhixin, "Eluosi duiwai zhengce de jiaoxun," *Dongou Zhongya Yanjiu* no. 2 (2002): 54–58.
14. Pei Yuanying, "A Multi-Dimensional View of Russian Diplomatic Strategy," *Foreign Affairs Journal* (Beijing) 65 (September 2002): 55–59.
15. Rong Liang, "Elousi de 'Xinzhuang,'" *Nanfang Zhoumo*, September 30, 2002.
16. See, for example, Xu, "Eluosi duiwai zhengce de jiaoxun," and Pei, "A Multi-Dimensional View of Russian Diplomatic Strategy."
17. June Teufel Dreyer, "Encroaching on the Middle Kingdom? China's View of its Place in the World," in *U.S.-China Relations in the Twentieth-Century: Possibilities, Prospects, and Policies*, ed. Christopher Marsh and June Teufel Dreyer (Lanham, MD: Lexington Books, 2004), 85–103.
18. Andrei Devyatov, *Krasnyi Drakon: Kitai i Rossiya v Dvadtsat'pervom veke* (Moscow: Algoritm, 2002).
19. A. G. Yakovlev, *Rossiya, Kitai, i Mir* (Moscow: Institut Dal'nego Vostoka, 2002).
20. A. G. Yakovlev, "Kitaiskaya Ugroza Rossii: Mif ili Realnost,'" in Yakovlev, *Rossiya, Kitai, i Mir*, 147–62.
21. Richard C. Thornton, *Odd Man Out: Truman, Stalin, Mao and the Origins of Korean War* (Potomac Books, 2000).
22. See Mikhail Alexeev, "Economic Valuations and Interethnic Fears: Perceptions of Chinese Migration in the Russian Far East," *Journal of Peace Research* 40, no. 1 (January 2003): 89–106; Mikhail Alexeev, "Desecuritizing Sovereignty: Economic Interest and Responses to Political Challenges of Chinese Migration in the Russian Far East," in *Sovereignty under Challenge: How Governments Respond*, ed. John D. Montgomery and Nathan Glazer (New Brunswick, NJ: Transaction Publishers, 2002),

261–89; and Mikhail Alexeev, "Socioeconomic and Security Implications of Chinese Migration in the Russian Far East," *Post-Soviet Geography and Economics* 42, no. 2 (2001): 95–114.

23. Igor Malevich, *Vnimanie, Kitai* (Minsk: Kharvest, 2000).
24. Ibid., see esp. 79–81.
25. "Russian Journalist Warns about Chinese Threat," *Sobesednik*, June 16, 2004; *RIA Novosti, Digest of the Russian Press.* Transcript by Olga Saburova.
26. Ibid.
27. Ibid.
28. See also Marsh, *Unparalleled Reforms*, and Vladimir Shlapentokh, "China in the Russian Mind Today: Ambivalence and Defeatism," *Europe-Asia Studies* 59, no. 1 (January 2007): 1–21.
29. S. G. Luzyanin, *Vostochnaya Politika Vladimira Putina: Vozvrashchenie Rossii na Bol'shoi Vostoka, 2004–2008* (Moscow: AST, Vostok-Zapad, 2007), 320.
30. Ibid., 314–45.
31. Xing Guangcheng, "China's Foreign Policy toward Kazakhstan," in *Thinking Strategically: The Major Powers, Kazakhstan, and the Central Asian Nexus*, ed. Robert Legvold (Cambridge, MA: MIT Press, 2003), 107–39.
32. As of 1995, there were 200,000 Uyghurs in Kazakhstan, Uzbekistan, and Kyrgyzstan; see Xing, "China's Foreign Policy toward Kazakhstan."
33. Kevin Sheives, "China Turns West: Beijing's Contemporary Strategy towards Central Asia," *Pacific Affairs* 79, no. 2 (Summer 2006): 205–25.
34. Christopher Marsh and Nikolas Gvosdev, "China's Yugoslav Nightmare," *The National Interest* 84 (Summer 2006): 102–8.
35. Kang Wu, "China's Energy Interests and Quest for Energy Security," in *Islam, Oil, and Geopolitics*, ed. Elizabeth Van Wie Davis and Rouben Azizian (Lanham, MD: Rowman and Littlefield, 2007), 123–44; Martin C. Spechler and Dina R. Spechler, "Conflict and Cooperation in Central Asia after 9/11," in *Eurasia in Balance: The US and the Regional Power Shift, ed.* Arial Cohen (Burlington, VT: Ashgate, 2005), 9–43; Gaye Christoffersen, "Sino-Russian Relations," paper presented at the symposium, "China in Transition," Soka University of America, Los Angeles, CA, May 12, 2007.
36. Wayne Merry, *Russia and China in Asia: Changing Great Power Roles* (Washington, DC: American Foreign Policy Council, 2002).
37. The significance of this fact was not lost on the Russians—not only was it often mentioned in the media, it is also discussed in Luzyanin, *Vostochnaya Politika Vladimira Putina*, 321.
38. *Peaceful Rise: China's New Road to Development* (Beijing: Central Party School Publishing House, 2005).
39. Legvold, "U.S.-Russian Relations."

CHAPTER 7

THE NORTH KOREA NUCLEAR CRISIS AND U.S.–CHINA COOPERATION

Bonnie S. Glaser and Liang Wang

"This whole Six-Party process has done more to bring the United States and China together than any other process I'm aware of," stated Christopher Hill, the U.S. Assistant Secretary of State and the top negotiator at the Six-Party Talks, in a media interview after agreement was reached on the Initial Actions for the Implementation of the Joint Statement in Beijing on February 13, 2007.[1] This remark, along with countless accolades praising Beijing for its cooperation on the North Korea nuclear issue, is a telling indication of the positive impact that the Six-Party Talks have had on the bilateral relationship between the United States and China.[2] Analysts may rightfully note that expressions of appreciation for Chinese cooperation from the United States have been partly intended to press Beijing to do more. Yet, there is little question that successful cooperation on the North Korea nuclear crisis has provided a boost to the U.S.–China bilateral relationship.

The threat posed by North Korea's nuclear programs presented a rare strategic opportunity for close U.S.–China cooperation that would prove to be the first successful comprehensive collaboration on an international security issue of critical importance to both countries since the collapse of the Soviet Union.[3] Determined that the North Korea nuclear issue should be addressed multilaterally rather than bilaterally, the Bush administration sought to involve China from the inception of the crisis in the fall of 2002.

At the outset of the crisis, China preferred to remain uninvolved. Beijing did not view the situation as presenting an opportunity to strengthen ties with the United States or enhance its role in Northeast Asia. Worried by the unraveling of the Agreed Framework, an agreement that Washington and Pyongyang had reached in October 1994 to prevent North Korea from developing nuclear weapons, the Chinese urged the United States to resolve the tense situation through bilateral dialogue with North Korea. Nevertheless, due to domestic and foreign policy concerns in China and external pressure from the United States, Beijing agreed to host multilateral talks.

Over time, China's role evolved from a passive onlooker, to a reticent host, and finally to a "chief mediator" and "honest broker."[4] Today, even though the crisis is far from resolved, and it remains uncertain whether the pronounced goal of denuclearization will be realized, an examination of the process from the beginning of the crisis in 2002 to the February 13 Agreement in 2007 offers a useful framework to examine U.S.–China cooperation on a critical security issue and its impact on the broader bilateral relationship.

This chapter attempts to analyze the influence of cooperation between Washington and Beijing on the North Korea nuclear issue, on the broader bilateral U.S.–China relationship, and on the United States' policy toward China. It begins with an overview of Sino-American ties in the early years of the first presidential term of George W. Bush to provide a backdrop for subsequent bilateral cooperation on the North Korea nuclear challenge. The chapter then traces the initiation and evolution of U.S.–China coordination to respond to Pyongyang's provocations. Next, it explains how the two countries were able to effectively cooperate, despite sharply differing perspectives on North Korea and divergences in their preferred approaches to persuade Pyongyang to abandon its pursuit of a nuclear deterrent.

The chapter then examines whether and how U.S.–China cooperation on North Korea influenced U.S. policy decisions on other issues, including Taiwan. Finally, it explores lessons that can be drawn from U.S.–China cooperation on the North Korea nuclear crisis that might be applicable to other instances of potential Sino-American cooperation.

U.S.–China Relations in the Early Years of the Bush Administration

Cooperation between Washington and Beijing on the North Korea nuclear issue must be examined in the context of the broader development of U.S.–China relations. Essentially, cooperation on North

Korea has been influenced by the general trajectory of U.S.–China relations as much as it has contributed to overall bilateral ties.

Sino-U.S. relations got off to a rocky start when President George W. Bush assumed office in January 2001. In his campaign platform, Bush termed China "a strategic competitor of the U.S, not a strategic partner." Bush's National Security Adviser Condoleezza Rice wrote in *Foreign Affairs* that "the challenges of China and North Korea require coordination and cooperation with Japan and South Korea" and implicitly urged forging closer ties with India to counterbalance China.[5] Mutual suspicion intensified further in April when a Chinese fighter jet collided with a U.S. reconnaissance EP-3 plane over the South China Sea. China lost its fighter jet and a pilot and detained the U.S. aircrew for eleven days. The handling of the incident created negative feelings and stoked nationalist sentiment in both countries.[6]

President Bush's decisions to approve a robust package of arms sales for Taiwan and to grant an unprecedented three-day transit in New York in the spring of 2001 for Taiwan President Chen Shuibian—who rejected Beijing's "one China" principle and was from the Democratic Progressive Party (DPP), which had, for many years, advocated Taiwan independence—touched the most sensitive nerve of an already perplexed Beijing, and added to the strain in bilateral ties.[7] President Bush's comment that the United States would do "whatever it took" to help Taiwan defend itself prompted China's foreign ministry spokesman to warn that the United States "has drifted further on a dangerous road" and generally deepened Beijing's suspicion of the U.S. agenda.[8]

The EP-3 incident provided a sobering lesson to Washington and Beijing about the perils of an antagonistic U.S.–China relationship. In the immediate aftermath of the crisis, both governments agreed to intensify exchanges to ease residual tension. Although mutual irritation lingered and suspicion persisted, the relationship nevertheless took a dramatic leap toward a new and closer chapter of Sino-U.S. cooperation in the wake of the September 11 terrorist attacks.[9] The tragedy offered an exceptional opportunity for China to improve its relationship with the United States, and Beijing acted promptly to grasp it by elevating the antiterrorism agenda in its foreign policy. In the subsequent U.S.-led global war on terror, China "bandwagoned" with Washington. Although China's concerns about terrorism within its borders greatly exceeded its worries about terrorism internationally, it nevertheless stepped up intelligence sharing, law enforcement cooperation, and joint efforts to curb terrorist financial activities.

Faced with terrorism as the most immediate and dangerous security challenge to the United States, the Bush administration relegated its concerns about potential threats from China to the backburner. The administration abandoned its skeptical, and sometimes critical, rhetoric about China and instead embraced an approach that more closely resembled that of its predecessors. In the 2002 *National Security Strategy*, the president welcomed "the emergence of a strong, peaceful, and prosperous China" and declared that the United States would pursue "a constructive relationship with a changing China."[10] According to a senior State Department official, by the fall of 2001,the upward trajectory of the U.S.–China relationship was firmly in place.[11]

Despite the boost to bilateral ties provided by the war on terror, distrust and suspicion persisted in both countries. Skeptics in the United States argued that, due to enduring sources of tension rooted in "ideological differences and shifting of power relations," the convergence of American and Chinese interests and policies on counterterrorism was only temporary.[12] Similarly, Chinese strategists continued to view the Bush administration as resolved to impede China's rise to great power status and portrayed U.S. military operations on China's periphery as part of a broader strategy of "containment" or "encirclement."[13] Some experts even charged that U.S. military activities in Central Asia and the islands of Southeast Asia were purposefully taking advantage of counterterrorism to enhance U.S. military power and presence at China's expense.[14] It was in this complex atmosphere of strengthened official cooperation against a backdrop of continuing mutual suspicion that the North Korea nuclear crisis unfolded.

Getting China Involved: Trilateral Talks and the Six-Party Talks

In the summer of 2002, U.S. intelligence uncovered evidence that North Korea was procuring equipment that demonstrated an intention to create a covert nuclear program based on uranium enrichment. Then U.S. Assistant Secretary of State James Kelly visited Pyongyang in October of that year to confront North Korean officials with the U.S. findings and simultaneously offer a vague "bold approach" to ameliorating U.S.-North Korea relations, under the precondition that North Korea come into full compliance with the Agreed Framework and the 1991 Joint Declaration on the Denuclearization of the Korean Peninsula between North and South Korea. According to Kelly, after initial denials, North Korean Vice Foreign Minister Kang Sok-ju confirmed the veracity of the U.S. charge.[15]

Soon after the nuclear crisis erupted, the Bush administration resolved to adopt a different approach to deal with North Korea than its predecessor had relied on. Judging that the United States lacked sufficient leverage bilaterally to compel North Korea to abandon its nuclear programs, Washington opted for a multilateral strategy that would enable regional actors with a stake in realizing a denuclearized Korean peninsula to pool their sticks and carrots. A multilateral approach especially appealed to Condoleezza Rice, who had a personal interest in promoting the establishment of multilateral security institutions in Asia.[16] The U.S. decision to deal with the North Korea nuclear challenge multilaterally provided another exceptional opportunity for China to further bolster ties with the United States. One analyst later contended that the North Korea nuclear crisis was "a gift from Kim Jong Il" to advance U.S.–China cooperation.[17]

Initially, however, Beijing was reluctant to join in a multilateral effort to persuade North Korea to give up its nuclear ambitions for several reasons. First, China was uncertain about North Korea's nuclear capabilities and intentions. The revelation of North Korea's covert uranium enrichment program took China by surprise, and it had no way of verifying whether Washington's accusations were valid. Second, it was widely believed in China that North Korea was simply trying to position itself for negotiations with the United States and would use its nuclear programs as a bargaining chip to obtain concessions. Therefore, the Chinese believed, the best solution was for the United States to negotiate bilaterally with Pyongyang.[18] Third, Beijing was unsure about U.S. intentions toward North Korea. Even though regime change was not explicitly included in any official U.S. policy statement, the Bush administration's disdain towards Pyongyang and Kim Jong Il led many Chinese officials and analysts to suspect that the Bush administration's main objective was to depose Kim by any means, including using military force.[19] If this were true, Beijing did not want to rally behind the United States publicly in putting pressure on Pyongyang—a long-standing Chinese ally. Finally, China was leery of assuming an active diplomatic role, which was contrary to Deng Xiaoping's guideline to assume a low profile in the international arena—a tenet increasingly subject to debate, but still largely observed by Beijing. Taking up the role of mediator between Washington and Pyongyang, two nations that were implacable foes, was deemed too risky.

The North Korean nuclear issue was at the top of the agenda when President Bush received Chinese President Jiang Zemin at his Crawford ranch in October 2002. According to a former U.S. official, President Bush pressed Jiang to use his country's leverage over North Korea to further the goal of denuclearization of the Korean peninsula, but Jiang demurred. The Chinese president stated "China does not associate itself with North Korea's nuclear weapons program," but nevertheless insisted that the problem was a bilateral issue between the United States and North Korea.[20] Common ground was reached, however, on the goal of achieving a denuclearized Korean Peninsula through peaceful means. At a joint press conference following the Crawford summit, Bush declared: "We agreed that peace and stability in Northeast Asia must be maintained. Both sides will continue to work towards a nuclear-weapons-free Korean Peninsula and a peaceful resolution of this issue." [21] According to a former senior National Security Council official, this agreement was later often referred to by President Bush as the "Crawford Understanding"—the starting point for cooperation between the United States and China on the North Korea nuclear issue.[22]

Yet, the "Crawford Understanding" did not map out specific actions the two countries would take to attain their shared goal. President Jiang Zemin only cautiously pledged to "continue to consult on this issue and work together to ensure a peaceful resolution of the problem." Meanwhile, President Bush's goal to involve China seemed clearer and more assertive: "This is a chance for the United States and China to work very closely together to achieve that vision of a nuclear free nuclear-weapons-free peninsula."[23]

China's attitude toward becoming enmeshed in the North Korea nuclear issues remained lukewarm in late 2002 and early 2003. Reflecting the view of some Chinese officials and possibly the leadership, Chinese analysts blamed Washington's hard-line policy toward Pyongyang for causing the crisis.[24] When a senior U.S. delegation headed by former Secretary of Defense William Perry visited Beijing in November 2002, President Jiang Zemin told the group that the "tense relationship between the United States and North Korea was caused by the United States and the crisis should be resolved by direct bilateral talks between those two countries."[25]

Developments in the North Korea nuclear issue, along with persistent U.S. pressure, began to alter Beijing's strategic calculus in early 2003, however. North Korea's provocative actions—reactivation of its 5 Mwe nuclear reactor in Yongbyon, withdrawal from the Non-Proliferation Treaty (NPT) and expulsion of the International Atomic Energy Agency (IAEA) inspectors—made Beijing worried and discomfited. As the U.S. stance became tougher, Beijing judged that the North Korea nuclear issue was turning into a crisis.[26] It became increasingly clear that the gap between the United States and North Korea was too great to be bridged without the involvement of external actors. Pyongyang repeatedly called for direct dialogue with Washington and refused to "internationalize" the crisis. Washington rebuffed Pyongyang's requests and insisted on a multilateral framework to resolve the standoff. Due primarily to U.S. unwillingness to compromise, Beijing saw its original plan—promoting direct talks between the United States and North Korea—failing.

Fear of U.S. military action against North Korea also played a role in China's strategic rethinking. In September 2002, the United States had issued *The National Security Strategy of the United States of America*, which outlined a doctrine of military preemption, unilateral action, and a commitment to promoting democracy. In the absence of diplomatic progress to shut down North Korea's nuclear facilities, the Chinese worried that the United States might launch a preemptive strike on the nuclear complex at Yongbyon, triggering anarchy in North Korea and resulting in a flood of refugees into northeast China. Beijing's concerns mounted in February 2003, as the United States amassed 100 thousand troops in Kuwait in preparation for the invasion of Iraq to topple Saddam Hussein. China predicted that the U.S. military operation would be successful and concluded quickly. A speedy success in Iraq could then strengthen the hand of those in the Bush administration who advocated use of force against North Korea.

In early March, President Bush explicitly raised, for the first time, the possibility of using military means against North Korea, calling it a "last choice" if diplomatic moves failed to halt Pyongyang's nuclear weapons program.[27] Steps to beef up U.S. military forces in the Pacific, including the deployment of twenty-four B-1 and B-52 bombers to Guam further rattled Beijing.[28] Chinese experts warned that the possibility of an outbreak of a local war and armed conflict on the Korean Peninsula had "markedly grown."[29] In addition to the likelihood that instability in North Korea would spill over into China, a U.S. military strike on North Korea would put Beijing in a dilemma. China hopes to avoid getting dragged into another Korean conflict at all cost, but under the 1961 Sino-North Korean Treaty of Friendship, Cooperation, and Mutual Assistance, Beijing remains obliged to defend North Korea against unprovoked aggression. To avoid having to choose between two undesirable options, some Chinese analysts suggested Beijing propose to North Korea that the mutual assistance clause be excised from the treaty.[30]

Desire to avoid a setback in U.S.–China relations also factored into Beijing's reassessment. Preserving stable ties with Washington was a top priority. Improvement in relations with the Bush administration had been hard won and to some extent remained tenuous since exchanges between the United States and Chinese militaries were still frozen and U.S. intentions toward Taiwan remained unclear. Beijing had carefully averted a confrontation with the United States in the UN Security Council over the Iraq War, and hoped to avoid a downturn in relations over divergent approaches to resolving the North Korea nuclear issue.

Signs of a pending shift in China's position were evident in mid-January. At the press briefing on January 14, Chinese Foreign Ministry Spokeswoman Zhang Qiyue stated: "China has no problem in hosting talks in Beijing if concerned parties are willing to consider such an option."[31] At that juncture, however, China was, as yet, unwilling to commit firmly to multilateral talks and, more importantly, was not prepared to persuade North Korea to attend.

The critical change in China's stance came when U.S. Secretary of State Colin Powell visited Beijing in late February 2003. Secretary Powell delivered a strong message during his meeting with Chinese President Jiang Zemin: "If we are going to solve the North Korea nuclear crisis diplomatically, we have to do it multilaterally." According to a former Bush administration official, Jiang laughed and insisted that Washington and Pyongyang should resolve the North Korea nuclear issue bilaterally. The two men restated their respective positions several times. It finally became clear that Powell would not relent and was representing a determined President Bush. Jiang assumed a dour facial expression and said, "OK, I understand."[32]

After Powell's visit, Beijing quietly dispatched former Vice Premier Qian Qichen as a special envoy to Pyongyang in an effort to persuade Kim Jong Il to participate in multilateral talks. In a move seen by many as an attempt to force North Korea to the negotiating table, China shut down its pipeline from the Daqing oilfield in northeastern China to North Korea for three days in early March, ostensibly for "technical maintenance," shortly after Pyongyang test-fired a missile into waters between the Korean Peninsula and Japan.

Pressure tactics produced positive results in April 2003, when North Korea agreed to hold a trilateral meeting with the United States and China in Beijing. U.S. officials spoke highly of China's conduct at the trilateral discussions. Following the talks, President Bush personally expressed his appreciation for China's positive efforts in a phone call to Chinese President Hu.[33] The trilateral talks did not produce anything substantial, but it marked the beginning of arduous negotiations that would require frequent consultations and coordination between Beijing and Washington. In July, China's executive vice minister of foreign affairs, Dai Bingguo, was welcomed by President Bush in the Oval Office, held a two-and-a-half hour meeting with Secretary Powell, and also had meetings with Defense Secretary Donald Rumsfeld, Vice President Cheney, and National Security Council (NSC) Adviser Condoleezza Rice.

As the trilateral talks later expanded into Six-Party Talks, joined by Japan, South Korea and Russia in August 2003, China continued to play an intermediary role and convinced North Korea to stay in the negotiation process through its shuttle diplomacy and timely promises of economic assistance. After the first round of Six-Party Talks, the U.S. delegation, headed by James Kelly, voiced appreciation for China's efforts as the host. According to a U.S. official, Beijing was particularly helpful in arranging two informal bilateral sessions between the United States and North Korean delegations "in a way that was not awkward" for either side.[34]

In early September, Secretary of State Powell, in a speech at George Washington University, described U.S.–China relations as "the best they have been since President Nixon's first visit" to China in 1972. Powell welcomed the emergence of a "strong, peaceful and prosperous China," and expressed U.S. interest in a "constructive relationship with that China." Citing the Korean Peninsula as an example of where American and Chinese interests overlap, he maintained that the United States had transformed "our common interests with China into solid and productive cooperation over the challenges posed by North Korea." Once again, Powell conveyed U.S. appreciation for "the leadership role that the Chinese have played in trying to find a solution to this problem."[35]

From September 2003 to July 2005, the six parties held the next three rounds of talks, but made little progress. The gap was not narrowed between U.S. insistence on complete, verifiable, irreversible dismantlement of all nuclear activity in North Korea as a precondition for the provision of rewards to Pyongyang and North Korea's demand for a deal that front-loaded economic aid and security guarantees.

During this period, China walked a fine line as an intermediary among the relevant parties, especially the United States and North Korea. Beijing repeatedly prodded Washington to adopt a "more flexible and practical attitude" and offer more concessions in the negotiations. China's frustration with U.S. intransigence was occasionally aired publicly, as when Vice Foreign Minister Wang Yi, head of the

Chinese negotiating team, publicly labeled U.S. policy the "main obstacle" to reaching a breakthrough in negotiations.[36] Beijing also openly expressed skepticism about the purported U.S. evidence that North Korea was pursuing a uranium enrichment program, which had sparked the nuclear crisis.[37] At the same time, however, China remained firmly committed to the goal of removing nuclear weapons from the Korean Peninsula, and through various channels, conveyed to the North Koreans "the benefits and possible costs of different policies" so they could "realize what they should do and need to do."[38]

The Bush administration, while grateful for China's helpful role, became impatient with the lack of progress and urged Beijing to apply greater pressure on North Korea. Internal deliberations focused on how to "incentivize" China to use its leverage, but progress was stalled by divisions at high levels in the administration on policy toward North Korea, as well as by the deterioration of the situation in Iraq, which was witnessing increased insurgent activity.[39] With no good alternatives, the United States continued to rely largely on Beijing to manage the North Korea nuclear issue and cooperation between the United States and China predominated over friction.

In Beijing, pressure started to build for tangible progress in the Six-Party Talks, lest the process backslide or even collapse. As early as the end of the second round talks, Chinese analysts cautioned that the negotiations could not proceed for long in the absence of concrete results.[40] China realized that it had a major stake in the negotiations and began to worry that if the Six-Party Talks failed its reputation could be tarnished. Convening the Six-Party Talks had been lauded domestically and internationally as a "big achievement [*yousuo zuowei* or *dayou zuowei*]" in China's foreign affairs.[41] Failure would reduce people's confidence in Beijing's capability and harm China's international prestige. Moreover, a breakdown in negotiations would likely result in a U.S. push for more coercive measures to squeeze North Korea, including activities under the Proliferation Security Initiative and a resolution condemning North Korea's behavior in the UN Security Council, steps that China hoped to forestall.[42] From late 2004 to mid-2005, CCP Central Party School Professor Zhang Liangui wrote a series of articles counseling urgency in pushing the Six-Party Talks forward and producing concrete outcomes before the mechanism became irrelevant. Zhang proposed that since Pyongyang and Washington rejected each other's proposals, Beijing should develop a practical action plan based on the reasonable requests from both sides and persuade the two sides to move in the direction of an agreement.[43]

When the fourth round of talks convened in September 2005, China assumed a more assertive role in forging a compromise between the United States and North Korea. After consultations with all the delegations, Beijing drafted a carefully worded agreement that took into account the bottom line concerns of Washington and Pyongyang. Then, the Chinese side presented the completed draft as a fait accompli. "Take it or leave it," said Wu Dawei, head of the Chinese negotiating team.[44] According to a Chinese foreign ministry official involved in the negotiations: "We realized that any wording changes would open up a Pandora's box. If we accepted a U.S. change, then the North Koreans would insist on at least another one or two changes.[45] The Chinese made clear that if the United States refused to sign, Washington would have to assume responsibility for a breakdown in the talks. Chinese officials even threatened to inform the press that the United States had sank the accord.[46]

In the end, the United States yielded and a joint statement was released in which North Korea agreed to abandon all nuclear weapons and existing nuclear programs; the United States affirmed that it had no intention to attack or invade North Korea with nuclear or conventional weapons; Russia, Japan, China, the ROK, and the United States agreed to provide energy assistance to Pyongyang; the United States and Japan agreed to take steps to normalize relations with North Korea; and all parties agreed to discuss the provision of light-water reactors to North Korea at "an appropriate time."[47] Even though the agreement lacked specificity, and Washington and Pyongyang soon seized upon its ambiguity to start another round of disagreement, the joint statement was the first of its kind reached at the Six-Party Talks and laid the foundation for the later February 13 accord. On a brief one-day visit to Beijing in November after attending the APEC summit in Busan, South Korea, President Bush publicly thanked China for "taking the lead" in the negotiations with North Korea.[48] He later told the press that the United States had a "good, vibrant, strong" and "important" relationship with China and underscored: "The fact that China and the United States can work on this [North Korea nuclear] issue as equal partners is important for the stability of this region and the world."[49]

The Six-Party Talks process stalled for the remainder of 2005 and 2006 due to Pyongyang's objection to the U.S. Department of the Treasury's designation of Banco Delta Asia in Macau as a "primary money laundering concern" under Section 311 of the U.S. PATRIOT Act, which froze some $24 million in North Korean funds. Although no diplomatic progress was achieved on the multilateral front, Beijing's efforts to prod Kim Jong Il to refrain from further provocative actions and pursue economic reforms at home continued, as did cooperation between Beijing and Washington. President Hu visited Pyongyang in late 2005, and received Kim Jong Il in January 2006 in Beijing after Kim spent a week touring China's booming high-tech southeast. North Korea was a key topic at the Hu-Bush summit in April 2006. After the presidents' tête-à-tête, State Councilor Tang Jiaxuan was hastily dispatched to Pyongyang in an attempt to inject new momentum into the Six-Party Talks.

The two countries stood even closer after North Korea escalated the crisis by testing a round of missiles on July 4, 2006, and especially after its test of a nuclear device on October 9 of that same year. North Korea's defiance in conducting the nuclear test caught China by surprise, and it responded angrily. China's foreign ministry issued an unusually strongly worded statement demonstrating its displeasure, stating that Pyongyang had "defied the universal opposition of international society and flagrantly conducted the nuclear test."[50] Hu Jintao apparently personally proposed use of the term "flagrantly," previously employed to signal a high degree of Chinese anger after the 1999 accidental bombing of the Chinese embassy in Belgrade and Japanese Prime Minister Koizumi's visits to the Yasukuni Shrine.[51] Presidents Bush and Hu Jintao conferred by phone on how to respond to North Korea's nuclear test, and within days, Beijing sent Tang Jiaxuan to Washington for further consultations. China also joined the United States and other members of the Security Council in voting to condemn North Korea's actions under UN Security Council Resolutions 1695 and 1718. In the latter resolution, China, for the first time, voted with the other United Nations Security Council (UNSC) members to impose limited trade and travel sanctions on North Korea.

The next big leap forward for the Six-Party Talks came at the third phase of the fifth round of talks in Beijing. The evident failure of U.S. policy enabled Christopher Hill to successfully press for approval to engage North Korea directly.[52] After a closed-door talk between Christopher Hill and his North Korean counterpart, Kim Kye-gwan, in Berlin in mid-January, the six parties reconvened in Beijing in February 2007. The meeting eventually produced the February 13 agreement, which detailed an action plan to fulfill the September 2005 Joint Statement. According to Christopher Hill, Chinese Vice Foreign Minister Wu Dawei was once again instrumental in bridging differences between Washington and Pyongyang to enable agreement on the action plan.[53]

Finding Common Ground Amid Divergent Perspectives

Cooperation between the United States and China on the North Korea nuclear issue was not inevitable. In fact, the two countries' perspectives on North Korea, and their preferred responses to Pyongyang's pursuit of a nuclear deterrent, diverged substantially from the onset of the crisis. Even before evidence emerged of Pyongyang's suspected uranium enrichment program, President Bush made no attempt to conceal his antipathy for North Korea's leader Kim Jong Il. In his January 2002 State of the Union Address, Bush included North Korea as a member of the "axis of evil," and portrayed the regime as "arming with missiles and weapons of mass destruction, while starving its citizens."[54] In an interview with *Washington Post* reporter Bob Woodward, Bush declared, "I loathe Kim Jong Il," and revealed that his advisors had dissuaded him from adopting a policy aimed at toppling Kim. He attributed his "visceral reaction" to Kim to his belief in freedom and his worry about the human condition.[55]

Once the judgment was reached that North Korea's illicit procurement activity pointed to a determined effort to produce highly enriched uranium, the administration quickly rejected bilateral negotiations. From the Bush administration's perspective, direct dealings with Pyongyang under the Clinton administration had produced an agreement that enabled North Korea to obtain fuel oil, food aid, and a commitment to build two nuclear reactors that posed less of a proliferation threat, while simultaneously pursuing a clandestine nuclear weapons program. Bush refused to replicate a failed policy that might simply result in another deal that North Korea could violate with impunity.

Another reason that the United States eschewed the bilateral approach was that it perceived that Washington had little direct leverage over North Korea. North Korea's inclusion on the U.S. State Department's list of state sponsors of terrorism prohibits any American economic or commercial activities in that country. And while the United States remained one of the largest donors of official food aid to North Korea, Washington had long followed a policy of not employing humanitarian aid as a political tool. Recognizing that China and South Korea had greater potential leverage over North Korea, and viewing a multilateral approach that included all of Pyongyang's neighbors as indispensable to convince Kim Jong Il to give up his nuclear ambitions, the United States instead focused on building a coalition to apply pressure on North Korea.

Squeezing North Korea was central to the Bush administration's strategy. Depriving Pyongyang of badly needed oil would leave the regime with fewer options and create circumstances in which Kim might conclude that heading down the nuclear path was a dead end. Some Bush administration officials, including the president himself, may have even hoped that sanctions would dislodge Kim from power. To inflict pain on North Korea, cooperation from China—the source of as much as 90 percent of North Korea's oil supplies—was obviously essential.

Although some in the Bush administration may have argued in favor of a military strike on North Korea, there are numerous reasons that such a policy option would likely have been rejected. First, an air strike would probably not destroy all of North Korea's nuclear programs. U.S. intelligence has no idea where, among North Korea's numerous caves, it had hidden the gas centrifuges and artillery tubes acquired through A. Q. Khan's nuclear supplier network. Second, North Korea could easily wreak havoc on the South Korean economy simply by shelling Seoul, the capital of South Korea, which is within easy striking distance. Third, there is no constituency anywhere among U.S. friends and allies in East Asia for another Korean war.

From 2002 to 2003, as the Bush administration crafted a strategy to respond to the North Korea nuclear challenge, tolerating North Korea's development of nuclear weapons was rejected as against American interests. The regime already possessed missiles that threatened America's allies Japan and South Korea, and was working on developing missiles that could deliver a deadly payload to the United States. The possibility that Pyongyang might sell its plutonium to a country hostile to the United States or to a terrorist group such as Al Qaeda posed an even greater danger.

China's view of North Korea and the threat posed by its nuclear weapons program differed from Washington's perspective. China and North Korea have been allies for more than half a century. Beijing has supported Pyongyang since Chinese fighters surged onto the Korean peninsula to fight for the Communist Democratic People's Republic of Korea (DPRK) in 1950. A few years earlier, Koreans had assisted the Chinese Communist Party (CCP) during the Chinese civil war. Since the Korean War divided the peninsula between the North and South, China has given both political and economic backing to North Korea's leaders: Kim Il Sung, and his son and successor, Kim Jong-Il. Bearing the burden of propping up the North Korean regime has long been considered a small price to pay for ensuring a stable nation on China's northeastern border and a buffer zone between China and democratic South Korea. North Korea's allegiance has also been important for China as a bulwark against U.S. military dominance of the region and the rise of Japan's military. In recent years, China has begun to reap economic gains from its association with North Korea as trade has expanded and growing numbers of Chinese firms are investing in North Korea.

Since Beijing embarked on a policy of economic reform and opening up to the outside world in 1979, Chinese sympathy and ideological identification with North Korea have waned. Pyongyang's failure to implement economic reforms has been a growing source of frustration for China and its, at times, unpredictable foreign policy has been a cause of irritation. Nevertheless, preserving amicable ties with North Korea remains an important Chinese foreign policy objective.

China unquestionably shares the U.S. objective of achieving a nuclear weapons-free Korean peninsula. North Korea's possession of nuclear weapons is not perceived as posing a direct military threat to China's security, however.[56] Rather, the main danger emanates from the possible responses of other powers to Pyongyang's nuclear gambit. As noted above, Beijing calculated in early 2003 that unless a multilateral diplomatic effort got underway to compel North Korea to relinquish its nuclear capabilities, the United States might well employ the military option. A U.S. conventional strike on North Korea would likely create chaos and force large numbers of North Koreans to flee across the border into China, putting in jeopardy social and economic stability in northeastern China. Should North Korea retaliate against South Korea, Beijing would face the dilemma of abandoning its only treaty ally or being drawn into another military confrontation on the Korean Peninsula with the United States.

Almost as frightening would be a chain reaction in which Japan, South Korea, and even Taiwan decide to go nuclear. For the time being, Beijing judges that the U.S. nuclear umbrella over Japan is sufficiently credible to prevent Tokyo from pursuing the nuclear option in the short run, but the Chinese foresee that the Japanese will eventually choose to join the nuclear club. Whereas China could plausibly adapt to a nuclear Japan, the development of nuclear weapons by Taiwan has long been a formal *casus belli* for the Chinese leadership, and thus would pose very high costs to China, including a likely military confrontation with the United States. The Chinese also worry that a nuclear North Korea could be the death knell for the Nuclear Non-Proliferation Treaty, resulting in the uncontrolled spread of nuclear weapons in volatile regions like the Middle East.

Any of the above scenarios would undermine China's peaceful security environment that is necessary for continued economic growth, which is, in turn, imperative for the sustained legitimacy of the Chinese Communist Party. For these reasons, a nuclear North Korea is "not acceptable to China," asserted a senior Chinese foreign ministry official. "For China to continue its economic development and become a power to be reckoned with in Northeast Asia, it will need a secure, peaceful neighborhood and a peaceful world. . . . Anything that threatens our prospects for development is worrisome."[57]

From the outset of the crisis, Beijing made clear that its favored approach to resolving the North Korea nuclear challenge was peaceful diplomacy, preferably between the "relevant parties," i.e., the United States and North Korea. China did not object to applying political pressure on North Korea—and indeed was willing to do so unilaterally, albeit without public fanfare. But it strongly opposed the imposition of economic pressure on North Korea for a number of reasons. First, withholding fuel and food aid could trigger instability, and even regime collapse, in North Korea that could lead to the dreaded flood of refugees into China. Second, economic sanctions would damage the embryonic process of market reform in North Korea and would inflict the most harm on the most vulnerable segment of its population that resides in the rural areas, not the military or the urban elite. Third, squeezing Pyongyang might not produce compliance and capitulation, but instead could cause North Korea to become more aggressive and unpredictable. Fourth, Chinese participation in sanctions would sour Sino-North Korean ties and likely result in the ultimate loss of Chinese leverage over Pyongyang.

As the United States and China appraised the situation in the months following the revelation of North Korea's uranium enrichment program and the breakdown of the Agreed Framework, it became apparent to both countries that cooperation presented the best opportunity for achieving a nuclear weapons-free Korean peninsula. Recognizing that the Bush administration would not reenter bilateral talks with Pyongyang, and intent to avert a U.S. military strike on North Korea, China reluctantly agreed to cooperate with the United States in shaping a multilateral strategy. For the United States, the lack of a viable military option and the rejection of bilateral negotiations made cooperation with Beijing indispensable. Subsequent challenges in postwar reconstruction in Afghanistan and in quelling the insurgency and sectarian violence in Iraq increased U.S. reliance on China to restrain North Korea's provocations and compel it to negotiate.

Skeptics in both the United States and China argued that differing United States and Chinese priorities and interests created insurmountable obstacles for the two countries to work together successfully to persuade North Korea to give up its nuclear weapons.[58] Rebutting the doubters, Secretary Powell noted in his September 2003 speech at George Washington University:

> American and Chinese interests in Korea may not overlap completely, but they do so considerably. Neither side wishes to see nuclear weapons developed and deployed by the North Koreans on the Peninsula. Neither side enjoys the specter of the chronicled debacle that is the North Korean economy. Neither side has any interest in a worsening refugee crisis on China's border. Neither side relishes a North Korean regime that runs drugs and weapons, and that counterfeits currencies, or that engages in the periodic extortion of its neighbors though brinksmanship military conduct. Neither side, to be sure, has any interest in another Korean war.[59]

Both United States and Chinese officials credit good presidential communication in enabling Washington and Beijing to overcome divergences in approaches, mutual suspicions, and surmount problems at various junctures in the Six-Party Talks process. According to a senior Chinese official: "the United States and China have cooperated very closely since the inception of this issue. Faced with North Korea's nuclear issue, we communicated at the highest level. In this case we can claim real strategic cooperation. We were able to do this because our interests overlap."[60] This view was echoed by a senior American official, who maintained, "Presidential communications are critical. . . . If the two presidents are in sync, then the relationship works. If they are not in sync, the relationship can't rise above all the problems that we know so well."[61]

President Bush has utilized the presidential hotline to break logjams in the negotiations and to promote common responses to North Korean moves such as missile tests and its explosion of a nuclear device. From the beginning of the renewed nuclear crisis in 2002 to the February 13, 2007 agreement, the U.S. and Chinese presidents held at least thirteen telephone conversations specifically focusing on the issue of North Korea. The two presidents also met nine times in bilateral summits and on the margins of multilateral meetings during which the North Korean issue was discussed.[62] Several summits were crucial in building mutual confidence between the two presidents. The groundwork for cooperation was laid at the Bush-Jiang summit in October 2002, when the two presidents agreed on the objective of achieving denuclearization of the Korean Peninsula. Soon after the power transition in China was completed, President Bush met with

President Hu on the margins of the G8 Summit in Evian, France in June 2003, and reiterated "his strong desire for a peaceful diplomatic resolution" of the North Korean issue.[63]

The Bush-Hu summit in Washington, DC in April 2006 marked another major step forward in promoting presidential understanding and trust. At a White House lunch, President Bush spontaneously asked the figure skater Michelle Kwan, who was seated between the two presidents, if he could sit next to President Hu, which contravened usual White House protocol. With only translators present, the two presidents had an intimate talk about the future of the Korean Peninsula. A senior official paraphrased Bush's message to Hu as: "I'll deliver peace on the peninsula, but you have to deliver him [Kim Jong Il]. . . . If you can deliver him, then we can talk about a new Northeast Asia." The official characterized the episode as a "breakthrough in trust between the two presidents."[64]

Communication has also been effective at lower levels. From October 2002 to February 2007, the Chinese foreign minister and the U.S. secretary of state reportedly held thirteen meetings and thirty-two phone conversations focusing primarily on North Korea.[65] In addition, the heads of the U.S. and Chinese delegations to the Six-Party Talks frequently shuttled across the Pacific to consult with each other, as well as with their counterparts from other countries involved in the negotiations. Through this process, according to Christopher Hill, head of the U.S. delegation since March 2004, the United States and China "have been able to synchronize goals . . . strategies . . . and in many respects tactics" in the negotiation process.[66]

A QUID PRO QUO?

Following China's assent to host the trilateral talks and then the Six-Party Talks, there was some speculation that to gain China's further cooperation, Washington might be compelled to make concessions to Beijing over Taiwan. In addition to working with the United States to remove the North Korea nuclear threat, China was helping fight the war on terror and had refrained from obstructing America's Iraq policy in the UN Security Council. Senior Taiwan officials worried that the United States might make compromises under pressure from Beijing that would be damaging to Taiwan's interests, and privately complained that advancing democratic values had taken a back seat to protecting American security interests.[67]

Although China undoubtedly expected that its cooperation with the United States on a range of issues of importance to Washington would result in greater U.S. sensitivity to priority Chinese concerns, especially Taiwan, there was no overt attempt by China to demand a quid pro quo. According to a senior Bush administration official, both sides were acutely aware that it would be dangerous to let the Taiwan and North Korea issues "spill into each other." The two issues were frequently discussed in the same meeting, but always distinct from each other. "There was no quid pro quo; no linkage."[68]

A Chinese analyst affiliated with the Chinese Ministry of Foreign Affairs' think tank bluntly rejected the notion that Beijing ever sought to exploit cooperation with Washington on North Korea to gain concessions on Taiwan. "These are two completely different issues. The Chinese side's active efforts to make peace and facilitate talks on the issue of the North Korea nuclear crisis absolutely cannot possibly be traded for U.S. support on the Taiwan issue," the expert stated.[69] Similarly, a senior PLA officer insisted that "trying to get results in the six party talks is not a favor to the United States. . . . It is also not because China expects the return of a favor from others in the future on another issue. We are doing it to protect our own interests as well as the interests of other players."[70]

Unrelated to Sino-American cooperation on North Korea and other issues, U.S. policy toward Taiwan began to shift in mid-2003 in ways that were reassuring to Beijing. President Chen Shui-bian's plans to hold a referendum on sovereignty issues and draft a new constitution for Taiwan threatened to heighten cross-strait tensions, and therefore provoked U.S. warnings. Taipei's refusal to back down culminated in a public rebuke of Taiwan President Chen Shui-bian by President Bush during a joint press conference at the White House with visiting Chinese Premier Wen Jiabao on December 9. After restating the U.S. "one China" policy based on the three U.S.–China communiqués and the Taiwan Relations Act, Bush went on to say "the comments and actions by the leader of Taiwan indicate that he may be willing to make decisions unilaterally to change the status quo, which we oppose."[71] Bush also privately told Hu Jintao that he opposed Taiwan independence. Even though Washington and Beijing continued to disagree over specific U.S. policies, such as continuing arms sales to Taiwan and transits by Chen Shui-bian to the United States, the two leaders recognized their shared interest in avoiding a cross-strait war. The establishment of a degree of mutual confidence on the issue of Taiwan combined with cooperation on the North Korea nuclear issue further strengthened the U.S.–China relationship.

Not surprisingly, after China agreed to join forces with the United States to persuade North Korea to give up its nuclear weapons, U.S.

officials, on occasion, considered the potential impact on Beijing's cooperation on North Korea when deliberating other issues. Again, China did not blatantly put pressure on Washington or threaten to curtail cooperation on North Korea unless the United States took a specified action. U.S. diplomats simply became more mindful of avoiding actions that would irritate Beijing, especially at sensitive junctures in the Six-Party negotiations. For example, in late 2006, Washington opposed the timing of an initiative by Tokyo to create a four-way dialogue among Japan, India, Australia, and the United States, fearing that China might take offense and that this would jeopardize efforts to reconvene the Six-Party talks. "We worried that China could misunderstand the 'quad' concept as containment," admitted a senior U.S. official. According to the same official, ensuring effective cooperation with China on the North Korea nuclear issue also influenced the Bush administration's approach to trade policy. "We don't want to go too far with trade remedies. . . . We tell congress that we don't want an antagonistic relationship with China because we have bigger fish to fry—keeping North Korea in a box."[72]

Concern about affronting China also factored into the deliberations in preparing the May 2007 Joint Statement of the U.S.-Japan Security Consultative Committee, widely known as the "2+2" statement. In contrast to the February 2005 "2+2" statement, in which encouraging peaceful resolution of issues concerning the Taiwan Strait through dialogue had been highlighted among U.S.-Japanese strategic objectives, there was no explicit mention of the cross-strait issue in the new list of shared goals. While it can be argued that a U.S.-Japan consensus on maintaining stability across the Taiwan Strait had already been established and did not require reiteration, it is also likely that Washington and Tokyo wanted to avoid annoying China.

Analyzing the reason for the omission of the Taiwan issue from the 2007 "2+2" statement Kurt Campbell noted: "it is also true that China has put its enormous influence behind the recent momentum in six-party talks with North Korea, and U.S. diplomats are ever mindful of avoiding what can be seen as potential flashpoints in Sino-U.S. relations. The entire U.S. strategy toward North Korea requires continuing pressure from China on Pyongyang in the background and this is well understood at the State Department."[73]

A desire not to aggravate Beijing also resulted in a decision to omit reference to China's antisatellite test conducted a few months earlier. Instead, the document called for improved transparency in its military affairs, and made an oblique reference to the need for China to "maintain consistency between its stated policies and actions."[74]

CONCLUSION: LESSONS FOR FUTURE SINO-U.S. COOPERATION

The North Korea nuclear challenge is the first example of extensive cooperation between the United States and China on an international security issue of critical importance to both countries since the collapse of the Soviet Union. As the crisis has yet to be resolved, it remains to be determined whether this cooperation will successfully achieve the shared American and Chinese objective of denuclearization of the Korean Peninsula. Negotiations are still underway in the Six-Party Talks, and implementation of the agreements reached in September 2005 and February 2007 has only just begun.

Progress achieved thus far toward the denuclearization of the Korean Peninsula is due, in large part, to Sino-American cooperation. Absent Bush administration willingness to negotiate bilaterally with the North Koreans, Beijing's role has been central in bringing the United States and North Korea to the negotiating table and mediating between the two nations at crucial junctures to advance the process. The shift in U.S. policy in the aftermath of North Korea's nuclear test to allow for greater U.S.-North Korea bilateral discussions may reduce the importance of China and Sino-U.S. cooperation in the next phase of the denuclearization process.

China is likely to be a bigger player on regional and global issues in the future, and Sino-U.S. cooperation will be increasingly necessary to address current and emerging security problems. In addition to North Korea, Beijing has already contributed in important ways—both positive and negative—to the conflict in Sudan and the Iranian nuclear challenge. Engaging China in sustained dialogue about the intersection of United States and Chinese interests in the international system will be essential. The Senior Dialogue between the U.S. deputy secretary of state and China's executive vice foreign minister is an important mechanism initiated under the Bush administration that is designed to advance such discussions. Along with its subdialogues on specific regional and functional issues, the Senior Dialogue should be continued by President Bush's successor. In addition, future U.S. presidents will need to attach high priority to establishing effective and frank presidential communication that facilitates mutual trust.

This chapter has attempted to examine the process of U.S.–China cooperation from the beginning of the renewed North Korea nuclear crisis in 2002 to the signing of the February 13, 2007 agreement, and to assess its influence on the broader bilateral U.S.–China relationship and U.S. policy toward China. Several lessons can be drawn from the above analysis that might be applicable to other instances of potential Sino-American cooperation.

First, cooperation between the United States and China on a critical security issue requires a sufficient overlap of interests, but not full convergence of interests. If the two countries can agree on the ends, then there is an increased possibility that they can manage their differences on the means.

Second, for the time being, Beijing remains reluctant to get overly involved in the resolution of regional and international security disputes. It prefers to focus its efforts on domestic economic construction and avoid the risks of excessive entanglement in contentious security problems outside its borders. China will only opt to take action if the issue directly affects its national security interests and the cost of inaction is calculated to be greater than the cost of cooperating.

Third, lack of mutual trust and suspicion of each other's long-term intentions continue to hamper U.S.–China security cooperation. This can be ameliorated to some extent through frequent and frank presidential communication, as well as effective working level coordination that translates leadership understanding into specific actions.

Fourth, increased Chinese confidence in U.S. policy toward Taiwan can facilitate and reinforce cooperation on other issues. China is unlikely to demand a quid pro quo from the United States for its cooperation, but expects that Washington will take its vital security concerns into account, especially regarding Taiwan, and that the United States will avoid inflicting harm on China's core interests. U.S. need for Chinese cooperation on a critical security issue may result in modification of U.S. policies toward Taiwan to avoid unnecessarily irritating Beijing, but only at the margins.

NOTES

1. U.S. Embassy Beijing Public Affairs Office, "Christopher Hill, Assistant Secretary of State for East Asian and Pacific Affairs, Interview with ABC," February 13, 2007, http://www.state.gov/p/eap/rls/rm/2007/80784.htm.
2. In a talk that Christopher Hill gave at the Brookings Institution, Hill underscored the close cooperation between the United States and China at least seven times. See, Christopher Hill, "Update on the Six-Party Talks," Speech at The Brookings Institution, February 22, 2007, http://www.brookings.edu/comm/events/20070222hill.htm.
3. Although the United States and China cooperated in response to the terrorist attacks on the United States on September 11, 2001, it is the view of the authors that bilateral cooperation in the war on terror was limited

and international terrorism was deemed a greater threat by the United States than by China. See Bonnie Glaser and Carola McGiffert, "China: Tactical Bandwagoning, Strategic Balancing," in *America and the World in the Age of Terror: A New Landscape in International Relations*, ed. Daniel Benjaman (Washington, DC: CSIS, 2005), 1–27.

4. Anne Wu, "What China Whispers to North Korea," *The Washington Quarterly* 28, no. 2 (2005): 35.
5. Condoleezza Rice, "Promoting the National Interest," *Foreign Affairs* 79, no. 1 (January/February 2000): 45–62.
6. For a detailed description of the EP-3 incident, see Bonnie Glaser, "U.S.-China Relations: Mid-Air Collision Cripples Sino-U.S. Relations," *Comparative Connections*, Online journal, July 2001; Pacific Forum, Center for Strategic and International Studies, http://www.csis.org/media/csis/pubs/0102q.pdf. See also John Keefe, *Anatomy of the EP-3 Incident* (Alexandria, VA: Center for Naval Analysis, January 2002). For a Chinese perspective on crisis management in the EP-3 incident, see Zhang Tuosheng, "Zhongmei Zhuangji Shijian jiyi Jingyan Jiaoxun" [The mid-air collision and its lessons], *Shijie Jingji yu Zhengzhi* [World economics and politics], no. 3 (2005): 30–36.
7. Fu Mengzi, "Meiguo Duihua Zhengce de Zhanlue Sikao" [Strategic thinking on the U.S. China policy] *Xiandai Guoji Guanxi* [Contemporary international relations], no. 6 (2001): 12–14.
8. Foreign Ministry Briefing, April 26, 2001, http://www.people.com.cn/GB/shizheng/16/20010426/452955.html.
9. Yang Jiemian, "Sino-US and Cross-Strait Relations under the Post-'11 September' Strategic Settings," *Journal of Contemporary China* 11, no. 33 (2002): 656–72.
10. National Security Council, *The National Security Strategy of the United States* (Washington, DC: The White House, 2002), http://www.whitehouse.gov/nsc/nss.html.
11. Interview with senior Bush administration official, April 6, 2007.
12. Aaron, L. Friedberg, "11 September and the Future of Sino-U.S. Relations," *Survival* 44, no. 1 (2002): 33–50.
13. David Shambaugh, "China's Ambivalent Diplomacy," *Far Eastern Economic Review*, November 15, 2001; and Lin Limin, "Guoji Diyuan Zhanlue Xingshi yu Zhongguo de Xuanze" [The global geopolitical situation and China's choices], *Xiandai Guoji Guanxi* [Contemporary international relations], no. 3 (2003): 26–31.
14. Liu Jianfei, "Meiguo Duihua Zhanlue de Zhuanbian Quxiang" [Tendency of change in U.S. China policy], *Shijie Jingji yu Zhengzhi* [World economics and politics], no. 2 (2005): 30–36; and Ya Liping, "Meiguo Chongfan Dongnanya Jiqi dui Yatai Anquan de Yinxiang" [The return of the United States to Southeast Asia and its implications to Asia Pacific security], *Xiandai Guoji Guanxi* [Contemporary international relations], no. 8 (2002): 18–22.

15. James A Kelly, "Ensuring a Korean Peninsula Free of Nuclear Weapons," Remarks to The Research Conference, North Korea: Towards a New International Engagement Framework, Washington, DC, February 13, 2004, http://www.state.gov/p/eap/rls/rm/2004/29396.htm.
16. Interview with former senior Bush administration official, April 4, 2007.
17. Ralph Cossa, *Associated Press*, "China's Actions on North Korea Proving a Pivotal Test for U.S.-China Relations," *International Herald Tribune*, October 12, 2006, http://www.iht.com/articles/ap/2006/10/13/america/NA_GEN_US_China_Relations_Tested.php.
18. Interviews with Chinese officials and analysts in Beijing in February 2003.
19. Ibid. Also see, Zhu Feng, "Bushi Zhengfu de Bandao Zhengce yu Chaoxian Heweiji" [The Bush administration's Korea policy and the North Korea nuclear crisis], *Xiandai Guoji Guanxi* [Contemporary international relations], no. 2 (2003): 3.
20. Interview with former Bush administration official, April 4, 2007.
21. The White House Office of the Press Secretary, "President Bush, Chinese President Jiang Zemin Discuss Iraq, N. Korea," Remarks by the President and Chinese President Jiang Zemin in Press Conference, Bush Ranch, Crawford, Texas, October 25, 2002, http://www.whitehouse.gov/news/releases/2002/10/20021025.html.
22. Interview with senior Bush administration official, April 13, 2007.
23. The White House Office of the Press Secretary, "President Bush, Chinese President Jiang Zemin Discuss Iraq, N. Korea."
24. See, for example, Piao Jianyi, "Chaoxian Hewenti Jiqi Weilai Zouxiang" [The North Korean nuclear issue and its future trend], *Dangdai Yatai* [Contemporary Asia Pacific], no. 3 (2003): 23–26.
25. Zhu Feng, "Zhonguo Chaohe Zhengce he Celue de Bianhua" [Change of China policy and strategy on North Korea nuclear issue], *China Strategy*, no. 3 (July 2004), http://www.sciso.org/Article/Print.asp?ArticleID=611.
26. Zhang Liangui, "Chonghui Tanpanzuo?" [Return to the negotiation table?], *Xinwen Zhoukan* [News weekly], no. 2 (2003): 61.
27. Mark Matthews and David L. Greene, "Bush Says Force Now an Option on N. Korea," *Baltimore Sun*, March 4, 2003.
28. Barbara Starr, "U.S. Orders 24 Long-range Bombers to Guam," *CNN News*, March 5, 2003, http://www.cnn.com/2003/US/03/04/n.korea.bombers/index.html.
29. Zhang Youxia, "The Iraq War: Effects on the International Strategic Situation and the Security Environment of Our Country"; "Yilake Zhanzheng: Dui Guoji Zhanlue Geju ji Woguo Anquan Huanjing de Yingxiang" [The Iraq War: Effects on the international strategic situation and the security environment of our country], *Guoji Zhanwang* [World outlook], no. 14 (2003): 71–73.

30. Shen Jiru, "Weihu Dongbeiya Anquan de Dangwuzhiji—Zhizhi Chaohe Wentishang de Weixian Boyi" [The urgent measures in maintaining Northeast Asia security: To curb the dangerous games on the North Korean nuclear issue], *Shijie Jingji yu Zhengzhi* [World economics and politics], no. 9 (2003): 53–58. According to one Chinese expert, Beijing asked North Korea to revise the treaty, but Pyongyang refused. The treaty can only be modified through mutual agreement. Interview with Chinese scholar, July 2007.
31. Zhang Qiyue, Chinese Foreign Ministry Briefing, January 14, 2003, http://www.fmprc.gov.cn/ce/ceee/chn/dtxw/t106628.htm.
32. Interview with former National Security Council senior official, April 4, 2007.
33. Xinhua, "Hujintao yu Bushi Tongdianhua, Cheng Zhongguo Youxinxin Zhansheng Feidian" [Hu Jintao and Bush talk over phone saying that China is confident in defeating the SARS outbreak], April 26, 2003, http://www.people.com.cn/GB/shizheng/16/20030427/980382.html.
34. Interview with former National Security Council senior official, April 4, 2007.
35. Secretary Colin L. Powell, "Remarks at the Elliott School of International Affairs," September 5, 2003, http://www.state.gov/secretary/former/powell/remarks/2003/23836.htm.
36. Joseph Kahn, "Chinese Aide Says U.S. Is Obstacle in Korean Talks," *New York Times*, September 2, 2003, http://www.nytimes.com/2003/09/02/international/asia/02KORE.html.
37. Chinese Deputy Foreign Minister Zhou Wenzhong told a *New York Times* reporter "So far, the United States has not presented convincing evidence of the uranium program. We don't know whether it exists." Reuters, "China View on Arms in North Korea Puzzles U.S.," *International Herald Tribune*, June 10, 2004.
38. Interview with senior Chinese expert in Beijing, January 8, 2004. According to a Chinese foreign ministry official, "Hu Jintao let Kim Jong Il know that the six party talks must go forward." Interview with MFA official, November 5, 2005.
39. Interview with former Bush administration senior official, April 4, 2007.
40. Zhang Liangui, "Chaohe Liufang Huitan Buneng Kongzhuan" [The Six-Party Talks should not continue with no result], *Xinwen Zhoukan* [News weekly], no. 18 (2004): 39.
41. Shi Yinhong, "Beijing Liufang Huitan yu Zhongguo Waijiao Zuowei" [The Six-Party Talks in Beijing and achievement of China's diplomacy], *Jiaoxue yu Yanjue* [Teaching and research], no. 10 (2003): 20–23.
42. Zhang Liangui, "2005: Chaohe Wenti Guanjiannian" [2005: A key year for the North Korea nuclear issue], *Shijie Zhishi* [World Knowledge], no. 2 (2005): 25.

43. Zhang Liangui, "Jiejue Chaohe Wenti Guanjiannian" [A key year to solve the North Korea nuclear crisis], *Quanqiu Caijing Guancha* [Global financial observer], no. 1 (January 2005), http://www.gfo.cn/ReadNews.asp?NewsID=13426.
44. Michael Hirsh and Melinda Liu, "North Korea Hold 'Em," *Newsweek*, October 3, 2005, http://www.msnbc.msn.com/id/9468700/site/newsweek/.
45. Interview with MFA official, November 5, 2005.
46. Joseph Kahn and David E. Sanger, "U.S.-Korean Deal on Arms Leaves Key Points Open," *New York Times*, September 20, 2005.
47. Joint Statement of the Fourth Round of the Six-Party Talks Beijing, September 19, 2005, http://www.state.gov/r/pa/prs/ps/2005/53490.htm.
48. Joseph Kahn and David E. Sanger, "Bush in Beijing, Faces a Partner Now on the Rise," *New York Times*, November 20, 2005.
49. "President's Remarks to the Travel Pool in China," White House Office of the Press Secretary, November 20, 2005, http://www.whitehouse.gov/news/releases/2005/11/2005//20-9.html.
50. Ministry of Foreign Affairs of China Statement, October 9, 2006, http://news.xinhuanet.com/world/2006-10/09/content_5180207.htm.
51. Interviews in Beijing, January 2007.
52. Christopher Hill's meeting with Kim Kye-gwan in Berlin was regarded by many as a significant shift in the U.S. approach toward North Korea. See Don Oberdorfer, "How the White House Learned to Live With Kim Jong Il," *Newsweek*, March 14, 2007; Andrew Grotto, "Pragmatism Trumps Ideology on North Korea," Think Tank Town, *Washington Post*, February 23, 2007.
53. Christopher Hill, Briefing at Center for Strategic and International Studies, February 23, 2007.
54. The President's State of the Union Address, January 29, 2002, http://www.whitehouse.gov/news/releases/2002/01/20020129-11.html.
55. Bob Woodward, "A Course of 'Confident Action,'" *Washington Post*, November 19, 2002.
56. Interviews in Beijing, January 2007. Only a small minority of experts maintains that North Korea could some day target its nuclear weapons on China. Zhang Liangui argues, for example, "no one can be sure how things may turn out in five or ten years." Zhang Liangui, "Coping with a Nuclear North Korea," *China Security* 2, no. 3 (Autumn 2006): 12.
57. Interview with a senior Chinese foreign ministry official, April 23, 2007.
58. See, for example, John J. Tkacik, Jr., "Getting China to Support a Denuclearized North Korea," Heritage Foundation Backgrounder # 1678, August 25, 2003, http://www.heritage.org/Research/AsiaandthePacific/bg1678.cfm.

59. Secretary Colin L. Powell, "Remarks at the Elliott School of International Affairs."
60. Conversation with a senior Chinese official in Beijing, April 23, 2007.
61. Interview with senior U.S. official, April 13, 2007.
62. Data extracted from Bonnie Glaser, "Chronology of U.S.-China Relations." *Comparative Connections*, 2002–7.
63. White House Office of Press Secretary, "President Bush's Meeting with Chinese President," June 1, 2003, http://www.whitehouse.gov/news/releases/2003/06/20030601-4.html.
64. Interview with senior U.S. official, April 13, 2007.
65. Data extracted from Bonnie Glaser, "Chronology of U.S.-China Relations," *Comparative Connections*, 2002–7.
66. Christopher Hill, "Update on the Six-Party Talks," Speech at the Brookings Institution, February 22, 2007, http://www.brookings.edu/comm/events/20070222hill.htm.
67. Interviews with senior Taiwan officials in Taipei, January 12–15, 2004.
68. Interview with senior Bush administration official, April 13, 2007; interview with former senior Bush administration official April 4, 2007.
69. China Institute of International Studies senior researcher Jin Linbo quoted in Wang Dejun, "Di'erlun Liufang Huitan Zhaokai Zaiji, Zhuanjia Poxi Wuda Xuanji" [The second round of Six Party Talks is beginning, analyst explains five major issues], *Ta King Pao*, February 14, 2004, http://www.china.com.cn/chinese/2004/Feb/497777.htm.
70. Interview with a senior PLA official in Beijing, March 2007.
71. For a recounting of this episode and the shift in U.S. policy toward Taiwan, see David Brown, "Strains Over Cross-Strait Relations," *Comparative Connections* 5, no. 4 (January 2004).
72. Interview with senior Bush administration official, April 13, 2007.
73. Kurt Campbell, "The Silence in the U.S.-Japan 2+2 Statement," *Taipei Times*, May 10, 2007.
74. Office of the Spokesman, "Joint Statement of the U.S.-Japan Security Consultative Committee," May 1, 2007, http://www.state.gov/r/pa/prs/ps/2007/may/84084.htm.

Chapter 8

The Taiwan Factor in U.S.–China Relations

John F. Copper

When George W. Bush campaigned for the presidency in 2000, he and Republican Party leaders promised to treat Taiwan better, citing, among other things, its longstanding friendship with the United States and its geostrategic importance. They also praised its successful democratization and spoke highly of Taiwan's new president, Chen Shui-bian.

Just a few months into the Bush presidency, George W. extended a huge arms package to Taiwan and, as an additional perk to Taipei, ended the annual review of weapons sales to Taiwan, putting the matter on an as-need basis. Bush further declared that any resolution of the Taiwan problem should have the support of Taiwan's citizenry, and warned Beijing about using military force against Taiwan. Taiwan's diplomatic status was upgraded, and restrictions on its officials visiting the United States loosened.

At this point, pundits in both Taiwan and the United States described relations between the two as closer and friendlier than at any time in recent history, perhaps ever. Officials in Taipei were happy and confident about American support and looked forward to it lasting. But things changed. Relations did not remain cordial. By 2003, the Bush administration was overtly showing displeasure and sometimes contempt toward Chen Shui-bian and his government. What happened?

This chapter offers five theories to explain why the Bush administration's policy toward Taiwan declined so dramatically. They are as follows: (1) Bush was not really hostile toward China, or enamored with Taiwan, as it appeared during the campaign and the first few months of his administration; (2) 9/11 brought the change—the United States now needed China; (3) the Bush administration came to see Taiwan's President Chen Shui-bian as a dangerous provocateur that might ignite a U.S. conflict with China; (4) Chen's leadership and policies changed the positive perceptions of him held by U.S. officials and the American public; (5) the Bush administration came to perceive the opposition in Taiwan as likely, or perhaps, more likely, to support U.S. interests than the Chen government.

In the concluding section, the author will make some judgments about which of these are better explanations than the others. Also, an effort will also be made to answer the question: What does this all mean? Plainly, the Bush administration's change of mind about President Chen has impacted U.S., China, and Taiwan relations and even U.S. policies in East Asia. Some aspects of this will, no doubt, be lasting.

Bush Never Hostile Toward China

During the 2000 presidential campaign, Bush and his foreign policy team advocated building a strong military, refurbishing alliances, and dealing with external challenges to the United States. They viewed Asia as being critically important to the United States and the region in the world where the United States faced new dangers. Japan and several other countries in East Asia were seen as strategic partners. Taiwan was portrayed as a friend and an ally to be treated well in a future Bush administration. China was a hostile power and a challenge to the United States.[1]

After Bush assumed the presidency, it appeared that his administration would design an American foreign policy based on these views. The new administration, in fact, immediately began working on building better relations with U.S. allies. China was viewed as a potential threat. Japan was accorded a more pivotal role in America's strategic planning. So was Southeast Asia. Taiwan was viewed as much more important to the United States than it had been under the Clinton Administration.[2]

The Neocons that were said to dominate foreign policy thinking in the Bush administration, meanwhile, expressed their admiration for Taiwan's democracy and made it known they despised China's authoritarian dictatorship. They called for defending Taiwan.[3] The Neocons and other Bush foreign policy advisors took a special liking to Taiwan's President Chen Shui-bian, and considered his election good for the cause of democracy and for the United States. As a result, the United States treated him with much more respect than the Clinton administration had. This included granting him, and members of his government, transit visits to the United States (which Chen made in May and June of 2001).[4]

This pro-Taiwan, anti-China slant in the Bush White House became even more pronounced after the EP-3 Incident in April 2001, precipitated by a U.S. reconnaissance plane (gathering data on China's newly acquired weapons that might threaten Taiwan) colliding with a Chinese jet fighter aircraft in mid-air over the South China Sea, necessitating a forced landing on China's Hainan Island by the U.S. plane. Afterwards, the Chinese military held the plane and the crew, causing the American public and the Bush administration to vent considerable anger toward China.[5]

Bush subsequently approved a huge arms package for Taiwan, including some that were not defensive in nature.[6] That same month, when asked about the United States defending Taiwan, Bush replied he would do "whatever it took." Many observers took this to mean that "strategic ambiguity" in the United States' China–Taiwan policy, intended to keep the two sides from conflict, was now dead, having been replaced by "strategic clarity" that favored Taiwan.[7]

But all of this, it appeared just a few months later, was less than real. The Bush administration had not truly adopted a hostile policy toward China, or an unabashedly friendly one toward Taiwan. Or, if it had, it adopted new policies.

Observers were, in fact, surprised just days after the EP-3 Incident that President Bush issued what some considered an apology, even though it was clear, under international law, that the fault of the crash had been the Chinese pilot.[8] And shortly after that, Colin Powell negotiated with his Chinese counterparts and succeeded, for all intents and purposes, in ending the crisis and the hostility it had caused, putting U.S.–China relations back to a condition of normality.

At that point, some observers opined that Bush's earlier hostile statements about China were simply campaign rhetoric or an expression of anti-Clinton feelings, reflecting the view among Bush people that Bill Clinton had been a disaster in handling foreign policy. Further evidence of this was the fact President Bush appointed many foreign policy advisors from his father's administration or people his father recommended. Bush, Sr., had been very close to Chinese leaders and, by all accounts, he and most of his advisors were pro-China.[9]

There is yet another reason to think Bush was not disposed to be hostile toward China and unduly friendly toward Taiwan. He was supported by the business community before and during the campaign, and had strongly advanced a free trade agenda. Thus, he did not want to treat China as an enemy, for this might precipitate a serious trade feud with China, plying into the hands of Democratic protectionists.[10] Thus, during the campaign, while Bush presented a tough line on China on strategic issues, he did not make China an exception to Republican free trade policy, and this was vitally important to China.

Hence, in truth, Bush wanted good relations with China. He was critical of China mainly to send the message that his foreign policy was going to be different from Clinton's (in large part, a campaign ploy), and to indicate overall needed change in America's external relations. China's leaders did not overreact to Bush's "provocations," perhaps reflecting some prescience on their part about his true views.[11]

Further proof of this view: commercial relations with China continued to flourish, and Bush said little about a fast growing U.S. trade deficit with China. He pursued trade grievances on a case-by-case basis when he encountered criticism from Democrats and certain U.S. businesses. He certainly made no effort to slow China's economic boom, which was the source of its growing global influence and its military expansionism.

In addition, after Bush entered the White House, he never again used the term "strategic competitor" in reference to China. Nor did he say much about China not being democratic; he certainly never said the United States sought regime change in China. Thus, there was a noticeable inconsistency in Bush's interventionist cum democratizing the world policy: he sided with the hawks on Iraq and Middle East policy and frequently sided with the doves on China policy.[12]

Thus, it seems erroneous, especially in retrospect, to think that Bush or important members of his administration were itching for a fight with China, or that they thought of making China an enemy, as some observers assumed to be the case based on campaign statements and the emphasis Bush placed on improving relations with traditional allies during the first few months of his first term. In counterpoint, it is also wrong to think that the Bush administration was seriously pro-Taiwan or really enthralled with President Chen Shui-bian.

THE IMPACT OF 9/11

The September 11, 2001, terrorist bombing of the World Trade Center in New York—the first significant attack on U.S. soil since Pearl Harbor—had a deep impact on President Bush personally, and on his administration. Observers commented that it made Bush a "war president." Certainly, it made the war on terrorism the clarion call of the administration's global strategy.

The attack had an immediate impact on U.S.–China policy. Bush defined the post–9/11 world as one of America treating nations as supporting terrorism, or not. Although China had exported weapons and technology to some anti-American states, Beijing had no real history of supporting terrorism or any alliances with terrorist groups. Furthermore, President Jiang Zemin immediately sent a telegram to President Bush stating China's opposition to terrorism and his support of the U.S. campaign against al Qaeda.

A fortnight later, Foreign Minister Tang Jiaxuan told U.S. business leaders that "international terrorism is a serious threat to world peace and security" and that "China stands ready . . . for cooperation." President Bush said shortly after this: "China responded immediately" and "would stand with the United States."[13]

In fact, the Bush administration felt strongly that it needed China's help in the war on terrorism, and sought to reward Beijing. The United States named the East Turkistan Islamic Movement (operating in China) a terrorist organization. Vice President Cheney spoke of the "amazing relationship" with China. Officials from both countries visited their counterparts in the other. The two sides agreed on law enforcement procedures (and an FBI office was opened in Beijing) and on port security. The Pentagon's Quadrennial Defense Review of 2001 (issued before 9/11) portrayed China as a major security challenge; subsequently, Pentagon reports viewed China very differently.[14]

Meetings President Bush had with top Chinese officials similarly had positive consequences. Bush traveled to China and spoke of U.S.-China cooperation, saying little about human rights, arms proliferation, Tibet, or Taiwan (all previously points of criticism of China).

Pundits expressed the view at this time that, as with President Nixon when he sought a rapprochement with China to get out of Vietnam, the United States had to sacrifice Taiwan to build a better relationship with China. Indeed, the United States avoided confrontation with China over the Taiwan issue. When President Chen Shui-bian announced he wanted to attend the Asia Pacific Economic Cooperation meeting (which China objected to), Bush gave him no support.

Just before Bush's February 2002 trip to Asia, National Security Advisor Condoleezza Rice said U.S., China, and Taiwan policy was founded on the one-China principle (favorable to China).[15]

Over a period of just over twelve months, President Bush and President Jiang held three high-level meetings: two in China, in October 2001 and February 2002, and one in the United States at Bush's home in Crawford, Texas, in October 2002, an invitation Bush seldom extended to anyone. Bush, as a matter of record, became the first U.S. president to meet with Chinese leaders three times in the course of a year.

In ensuing months, U.S. officials continued to speak of "constructive and cooperative" ties (China using these terms also) about their relationship. In September 2003, two years after the World Trade Center buildings were hit, Secretary of State Colin Powell said relations with China "are the best they have been since President Nixon's first visit."[16] The *National Strategy of the United States*, an official U.S. government document published at this time, contained the words "the U.S. welcomes a strong, peaceful, and prosperous China."[17] Two months later, Secretary Powell, in commenting about this, said: "We welcome it. We do not feel threatened by it. We encourage it.[18]

During 2004, Secretary Powell met with Chinese Foreign Minister Li Zhaoxing three times and talked by telephone numerous times. He spoke of the best communications in thirty years, and about progress on resolving issues such as North Korea, Taiwan, Sudan, Haiti, and more. U.S. efforts in trying to resolve the North Korea problem especially seemed to rely on China. Meanwhile, a Republican pollster reported that fewer than 10 percent of Americans named China the number one threat to the United States.[19]

In 2005, Deputy of State Robert Zoellick coined the term "responsible stakeholder" to describe China. The events of 9/11, it appeared, had caused a permanent shift in U.S. policy toward China. Replacing the term "strategic challenge" with one that indicated a long-term policy of regarding China highly, and as a country important to the United States, was just one example. The following year, testifying before the House International Relations Committee, when asked about President Chen pushing independence, Zoellick said brusquely: "Independence means war. And that means American soldiers."[20]

Since then, the United States and China have found common grounds for cooperation on strategic, as well as a number of other, fronts. The United States has viewed China as helpful in dealing with terrorism, nuclear proliferation, maintaining a stable international trading system, and in a number of other "problem areas." In the process, China has become perceived as more of a friend than an enemy. There was, palpably, a very different trend in U.S.-Taiwan relations.

THE CHEN SHUI-BIAN "DANGER"

During the 2000 presidential campaign, Chen Shui-bian played down the fact he supported a legally independent (of China) Taiwan—an issue that had generated some apprehension within the U.S. government. Prior to his inauguration, he promised to set up a group led by Nobel laureate Lee Yuan-tseh to deal with cross-strait relations, and said his inauguration address would please the United States and would not provoke China.[21]

In that speech, President Chen also announced he would not declare independence, change the national title, push for inclusion of the state-to-state concept in the constitution, promote a referendum to change the status quo regarding independence or reunification, and would not abolish the Guidelines for National Unification or the National Unification Council. This became known as Chen's "five noes" pledge. The foreign media and many observers applauded Chen's "reasonableness." So did Bush's foreign policy advisors.

But Chen also sent contrary signals. He called on Peng Ming-min—the "father of Taiwan independence"—to officiate at his inauguration. He used the term "Taiwan" thirty-five times in his address, and "Formosa" twice (an even stronger term supporting independence, since it denies Taiwan's Chinese roots); he used "Republic of China" (the country's official name and the one Beijing liked) nine times. Chen then appointed a number of former president Lee Teng-hui's friends that were pro-Taiwan independence or supported Lee's China policy, which was anathema to Beijing.[22] The U.S. State Department noticed this.

Soon after his inauguration, President Chen said that he accepted one-China with different interpretations by each side, set forth in the 1992 consensus. But, a month later, he said that there was only a "1992 spirit," apparently denying there was a consensus. The Department of State was miffed. Chen also said he did not accept the one-China principle, which the Bush administration, however friendly toward Taiwan, had not repudicated.[23]

Subsequently, Chen sent orders to his administration to extinguish "China" from government publications, logos, and signs, and even from school textbooks. This troubled American foreign policy makers involved with China and Taiwan policy. In February 2002,

President Bush warned there should be no provocation by either side; this seemed aimed at Taiwan. Three months later, Deputy Secretary of Defense Paul Wolfowitz's said that the United States opposes Taiwan's independence (the usual wording being "does not support").[24] The Bush administration was obviously sending hostile signals to Chen.

In July 2002, President Chen asserted that unless Beijing responded to Taiwan's goodwill, Taiwan would have to "go its own way." Chen followed up, saying that if China would abandon its ambition to take Taiwan by force, Taiwan would not change the status quo. The next month, he said in a speech before a Taiwan independence organization that there is "one country on either side of the Taiwan Strait" and that Taiwan is neither a part, nor a province, of another country. The Bush administration viewed this as confrontational.[25]

In ensuing months, the United States grew even more displeased with Chen's "movement toward independence." In private, Department of State officials labeled Chen a "loose cannon," and called his view that the United States would support him no matter what he did "war mongering." Then, Bush publicly "retaliated" in December when he told visiting Chinese Premier Wen Jaibao: "We oppose any unilateral decision . . . to change the status quo." The comment was aimed at Chen.[26]

Washington again showed its ire with President Chen in early 2004 when he proposed writing a new constitution (which would, no doubt, not say that Taiwan was part of China, and thus infuriate Beijing) and putting referendums on the ballot for the 2004 presidential election.[27] The Department of State protested that Chen had pledged not to do this soon after he became president, and the United States had taken him at his word. Many U.S. officials said they could no longer trust Chen. Both the United States and China showed concern that the situation could get out of control.

Following the election, the results of which U.S. officials thought were questionable, President Chen gave an interview with the *Washington Post*, during which he asserted that the election victory had given him a "mandate" to make Taiwan independent.[28] As if ready to act when there was another provocation, Assistant Secretary of State for East Asia, James Kelley, told a Congressional committee there was a "misunderstanding that the United States would protect Taiwan in any circumstances." One analyst called it the most negative statement on U.S.–Taiwan policy ever delivered in public.[29]

Chen kept provoking, and the United States kept reacting. In October, Secretary of State Powell made a statement that literally unglued officials in Taipei. He asserted that Taiwan did not have sovereignty.

Powell later backtracked, but in the process, had sent a strong message to the Chen administration.[30]

After this, the United States reacted quickly and with open hostility when President Chen provoked trouble. Chen, said some State Department officials, was "put on a warning list." Some others said he needed to be leashed, as Chiang Kai-shek was in the 1950s and 1960s. At this time, U.S. official statements were so public and so negative that they impacted the legislative election held the end of 2004, and another election in 2005 in favor of the opposition (as some thought they were intended to).[31]

Chen was cowed, but not for long. In 2006, he said he would terminate the National Unification Council and the National Unification Guidelines. The United States reminded him he had promised not to do this. Some officials called him a liar and a menace to peace in the Taiwan Strait. Ostensibly in reaction, the Bush administration invited the head of the opposition Nationalist Party, Ma Ying-jeou, to Washington and gave him a "king's welcome" while denying President Chen landing rights in the continental United States during a visit to Latin America.

PRESIDENT CHEN'S MISRULE

The Bush administration, Republicans, and most Americans were enthusiastic supporters of President Chen Shui-bian in 2000. They viewed Chen and his party as less corrupt than the previous Nationalist or Kuomintang (KMT) government and more in tune with the people. American scholars and the U.S. media were enamored with Chen, who came from a poor background and had struggled against an authoritarian regime to win the country's highest office. They spoke of him "finalizing" Taiwan's democratization and building a "new Taiwan."

However, within a few months, the idealism about President Chen began to fade. He and his administration became embroiled in bitter, and often petty, partisan disputes with the opposition, and few of his campaign promises became law. This was, in part, the consequence of Chen's weak victory and divided government. The opposition was also guilty.[32] But seemingly, Chen was more at fault.

The problem that the United States noticed most was the Chen government's mishandling of Taiwan's economy. Six months in office, Taiwan experienced recession. In 2001, Taiwan's economy saw negative economic growth of over 2 percent. Chen blamed the opposition for blocking legislation aimed at reversing the downturn and the weak global economy. He was partly right. But many observers in the United States blamed him since he had been in office for a number of months when the bottom fell out of the economy.[33]

In fact, many in Washington believed the opposition leaders when they said they had created Taiwan's "economic miracle" and Chen had destroyed it. Weakening Chen's argument that it was the downturn in the global economy, especially in high tech products, many Bush administration officials recalled that Taiwan was not hurt by the 1997 Asia meltdown when the previous regime was in power.[34]

To stimulate the economy, while also perceiving he needed the financial support of the business community, President Chen lowered taxes. This forced the administration to scrap much of its agenda of helping the poor, disadvantaged, and elderly, and the gap between rich and poor widened. His supporters at home considered Chen's moves a betrayal. The media and the academic community in the United States were dismayed.[35]

Taiwan pulled out of the recession after a year, but economic growth did not return to its past impressive performance. Americans noticed when Chen's opponents continued to criticize him for his bad management of the economy.[36] Worse, "Chen's bad times" persisted in terms of the perceptions of the public and its negative side effects. The suicide rate increased markedly, youth unemployment grew, and crime became a more serious problem.[37] Even the birthrate—low already—fell noticeably.[38]

The American Chamber of Commerce in Taipei put much of the responsibility for a lackluster economy on President Chen personally, citing his inconsistent policies in commercial relations with China. This view permeated the U.S. business community in Taiwan, and got back to the United States. The chamber's critical view of the Chen administration's economic policies, which began not long after Chen became president, escalated in ensuing years.[39]

Chen perceived that to survive and govern in a milieu of divided government, a very hostile opposition and media, and falling opinion poll numbers, he had to play the "ethnic card."[40] He and his administration stoked ethnic ill will by promoting the Taiwanese language (which many Mainland Chinese, Hakka, and aborigines do not speak), pushing local nationalism, and in a variety of other ways. Mainland Chinese were labeled traitors. Ethnic bias became government policy.[41]

The pernicious effects of this were noticed loud and clear when Bush administration officials got reports that many Mainland Chinese pilots in Taiwan's Air Force had resigned, in protest, over the Chen administration's prejudice against them, and many who remained would likely refuse to go into battle if a conflict with China occurred. U.S. intelligence agencies also heard it when a spate of Taiwan's intelligence agents defected to China, seriously undermining Taiwan's intelligence utility to the United States

Chen's "racist" governance became widely talked about in certain circles in the United States when, during the 2001 election campaign, Chen's Democratic Progressive Party produced a campaign advertisement to appeal to Taiwan's youth by citing model people. One (among four) was Adolph Hitler. The aborigines in Taiwan made issue of this, and it got to Jewish communities in other countries. It no doubt dampened the enthusiasm of the Neocons in the Bush administration for the Chen administration.

Bush administration officials saw Chen's policies of ethnic discrimination as linked to his provoking China (and the Chen danger) and his effort to keep him and his party in office at any cost. President Chen used both to rally his base. Also, rather than being a temporary palliative to fix Chen's declining popularity, it did not abate.[42]

Two other bad traits of the Chen administration became known to Americans and to the Bush Administration: the devolution of Taiwan's democratic polity and fast worsening political corruption. Both badly undermined the good feelings both Taiwan and America espoused toward President Chen.

Reversing Taiwan's democratization was mainly the product of President Chen's inability to rule effectively. Chen had to resort to governing, or at least he said this, in the ways of previous governments—using authoritarian means. Hence, Chen could no longer promote consolidating Taiwan's democracy as the hallmark of his government. Based on local expectations of democratization (political reform, good economic performance, cordial ethnic relations, social stability, and effective foreign and security policies) the view proliferated that Taiwan's democracy had not been consolidated, or if it had been, it was a bad thing.

Global organizations that assessed press freedom, transparency, and a number of other indicators confirmed Taiwan's political devolution. For example, the Paris-based organization Reporters Without Borders that publishes a global press freedom index ranked Taiwan number thirty-five among nations of the world in 2002. Two years later, it put Taiwan at number sixty—below Albania, Botswana, and Ghana, and noticeably way below Hong Kong, which, in 1997, had become part of the People's Republic of China.[43] On the Corruption Perception

Index, Taiwan declined from twenty-eight in the world in 2000, when the Chen administration assumed power, to thirty-five in 2004.[44]

The Democratic Progressive Party (DPP) became perceived as corrupt, more corrupt than the KMT just two or three years after it was in office.[45] Before the 2004 presidential election, it was reported that many Chen officials, perceiving Chen would be voted out of office, "cashed in." Corruption then got worse to the degree that, by 2006, most of the population viewed the Chen presidency as woefully corrupt and "unfit" to remain in office.[46]

In short, unflattering information about the Chen administrations governance got to Bush administration officials. Many American scholars, officials, and visitors to Taiwan noted endemic mass pessimism and lack of confidence in the Chen administration. Opinion polls in Taiwan confirmed this.[47] Many concluded Chen was a failed president.

The Shift in Views of the Opposition

When Chen Shui-bian became president in 2000, many U.S. officials and a large portion the so-called policy elite not only perceived that his victory represented the consolidation of Taiwan's democracy but also comported with America's national interest, in the context of a rising and challenging China, in a separate (from China) Taiwan. Washington emphatically espoused a policy of maintaining the status quo, meaning no unification.[48]

The view that the Chen administration best supported U.S. interests changed. Many both in and out of government in the United States came to see President Chen as dangerous and unprincipled. Some even began to think that Taiwan's incorporation by China was more likely under a Chen presidency, not less. After all, under Chen, Taiwan's economy was doing poorly, and as a consequence, was quickly becoming dependent on China. The capabilities of the military and the intelligence community were declining, making Taiwan more vulnerable to Chinese pressures. Finally, China had become more aggressive toward Taiwan because of Chen's provocations, and was successfully isolating Taiwan diplomatically and in other ways.

Meanwhile, many came to believe the Nationalist Party would not pursue reunification if it were returned to power. KMT leaders realized the party had to heed public opinion or lose elections (and public opinion definitely did not currently favor Taiwan unifying with China).[49] Most citizens favored the status quo, which was what the Nationalist Party supported.

The view in Washington that the KMT would not pursue unification became more widespread after Lien Chan and James Soong lost the 2004 election and Taipei Mayor Ma Ying-jeou became party chairman. Ma had to pay lip service to the idea of reunifying China because that was still the dictum of the party. But he was elected chairman of the KMT based on a program of reform. The elder party members had not supported or voted for him to be party head.[50]

Ma also played down the idea of reunification, saying that this was an issue for the next generation. He pledged that he would abide by the wishes of the people on this issue, which obviously did not favor living under Chinese rule. Thus, many Bush administration officials came to believe Ma would keep the status quo if he were elected president. After the 2005 election, when asked if the election victory for his party meant that reunification was more likely, he replied in the negative.[51]

Ma also avoided being trapped by his party's dictum of one-China by saying that one-China meant the Republic of China, denying that it referred to the People's Republic or that Taiwan should become part of the latter. Meanwhile, Ma cited independence as one of Taiwan's options.[52]

Thus, as President Chen Shui-bian came to be seen more and more as dangerous, and his administration flawed and not really supporting U.S. policy, officials in Washington came increasingly to see Ma as a good option.

And they demonstrated this in their actions. In March 2006, Ma was invited to visit the United States, where he received what many described as a royal welcome. He was accorded visits with high U.S. officials in the Department of State, Department of Defense, and elsewhere. One of his meetings was a very visible three-hour session with Deputy Secretary of State Robert Zoellick. This was noteworthy because Department of State officials, as a practice, did not talk to Taiwan officials, and openly snubbed President Chen. It was even reported that Ma might talk to President Bush.[53]

While in the United States, Ma cleverly used his position as mayor of Taipei to visit counterparts in Boston, New York (including former mayor Giuliani), Washington, DC, and Los Angeles. He spoke at Harvard University, his alma mater. Ma said all of the right things to appeal to his American audiences. He mentioned that he was the first Taiwan politician to oppose China's Anti-secession Law and the only one who had consistently criticized China for human rights abuses and the June 4 Tiananmen Massacre.[54] He even said that he had been to a Falun Gong meeting. Ma declared, to contrast himself with Chen Shui-bian, that Taiwan "should be a peacemaker not a troublemaker." [55]

Ma stated pointedly that he wanted to maintain the status quo and help keep stability in the region. He asserted Taiwan wanted to be a "responsible stakeholder."[56]

When in Washington, Ma also conveyed a position on the purchase of U.S. weapons that the Bush administration wanted, even though his party had opposed the transaction on the grounds that Chen would use the weapons to proclaim independence and the public did not favor the purchase. Later, Ma even said that he agreed with President Chen on the matter.[57]

In short, Ma convinced officials in Washington that his views were in consonance with U.S.–Taiwan policy and that he would not provoke China. He thus became a good alternative to Chen Shui-bian.

CONCLUSION

All of the theories advanced above help explain the astounding downturn in U.S.–Taiwan relations during the George W. Bush administration. The salient question is how much weight to give to each? This, of course, is like comparing apples and oranges. Pundits have talked much more about the first three. Some were more obvious factors affecting the Bush administration's change in policy early on toward Taiwan (the first two). Some—four and five—came later. Some reinforced another, some did not.

The argument that Bush was not anti-China, as it appeared during the campaign and the first few months of his administration, was an easy argument to grasp, and scholars and the media made a lot of it. Some said that it should have been expected. After all, every president since World War II switched his position toward China and Taiwan from the days of campaigning for office to the first few months into the presidency. It is nothing out of the ordinary, then, that Bush changed his China and Taiwan policy—it was simply more pronounced.

The fact that 9/11 changed the Bush administration's view of China, and that Bush seemingly had to downgrade relations with Taiwan to get Beijing's help in the war on terrorism, to many, was axiomatic. It was certainly a factor in the Bush administration's souring on President Chen, though it was probably exaggerated in its importance.

It needs to be recalled that China's policy shift toward cooperating with the United States actually came before 9/11, not after. On September 11, China simply restated it in a different context.

Furthermore, China bargained hard with Washington to make compromises on Taiwan, and the United States refused. Colin Powell rejected making any concessions to Beijing on Taiwan. In January 2002, former U.S. ambassador to the United Nations, Richard Holbrooke, wrote an op-ed piece in the *Washington Post* suggesting a "fourth communiqué" with China to fix what ails in U.S.–China relations. The administration nixed this idea. Throwing cold water on the notion China would get something on Taiwan for its cooperation with the United States, Deputy Secretary of State Richard Armitage said: "This won't happen!"[58]

When in Beijing, on one occasion, President Bush spoke approvingly of the Taiwan Relations Act (which is favorable toward Taiwan) and said nothing in public about the three communiqués (that favor China). Soon after, the U.S. Department of State gave a visa to a high defense official from Taiwan to attend a meeting in the United States The head of the American Institute on Taiwan, Richard Bush, visited Taiwan at this time and supported Taipei's rejection of the one-China principle as the basis for talks. China cancelled a U.S. Navy visit to Hong Kong and some other military events as a result.

It thus seems reasonable to believe that while 9/11 affected the Bush administration's perception of whether China was a friend or enemy to the former, it did not immediately have an impact on U.S.-Taiwan policy. China's continued cooperation with Washington on important issues, on the other hand, no doubt did. Thus, it is difficult to discern to what degree it was closer U.S.–China ties or a U.S. change of mind about Taipei that did it. Certainly, it seems accurate to say that as the United States prosecuted the war on terror, it became more evident that China was a player.

The view that President Chen constituted a danger, in that he did not mind inciting a U.S.–China conflict, was one that, early on, affected foreign policy officials (rather than the public or Congress). It grew in momentum. It was a big factor to the Department of State, and department officials spread the idea that Chen was a "loose cannon" to other government agencies, including the White House. In the view of this writer, this had greater impact than was generally realized.

Initially, however, distrust of President Chen was restrained due to the fact that there were very good feelings toward Taiwan in Congress and among the American people. In addition, a separate Taiwan (though not legal independence) was in the interest of the United States, and the United States had a "Taiwan card" that it could play against China and wanted to keep. The concern that Chen was a danger was also dampened by the fact that Chen's replacement, were he to be impeached or step down, was Vice President Annette Lu, who was considered more pro-independence, and thus possibly more dangerous than Chen.[59]

Similarly, the "warts" of the Chen administration gradually impacted decision-making in the United States. Initially, Congress, the press, the general public, and academe all espoused very positive views of the Chen administration. The opponents of Taiwan in the Bush administration, notably the State Department, for a considerable time, were reluctant to say much. But when it reached a critical mass, many came out and spoke very ill of President Chen and his administration.

Though by 2003–4, the evidence was overwhelming and came from many sources, there was still reluctance on the part of the media and academe in the United States to castigate the Chen administration, which they viewed with considerable enthusiasm. It was also U.S. policy not to favor one political party over another in a democratic country.

A new and positive view of the Nationalist Party and Ma Ying-jeou was slow in developing. The opposition made the case early on that President Chen did not have a mandate, was incompetent, did not mind getting the United States and China into a war, and was racist. Even as these charges became irrefutable, the Bush administration did not want to be seen as not supporting Chen's position that he was consolidating Taiwan's democracy by getting rid of the old order. This was late in changing.

In summation, five factors prompted President Bush and his administration to reassess and change U.S. Taiwan policy. And they did it with what appears, in retrospect, as quite amazing speed.

NOTES

1. See, for example, articles written by Condoleezza Rice and Robert Zeollick in *Foreign Affairs*, published during the campaign. Even before this, conservative Republicans issued a public statement to the effect that the United States should come to Taiwan's rescue in the event of a Chinese attack or blockade. See James Mann, *Rise of the Vulcans: The History of Bush's War Cabinet* (New York: Penguin, 2004), 243.
2. See Jean A. Garrison, *Making China Policy: From Nixon to G. W. Bush* (Boulder, CO: Lynn Rienner, 2005), 165.
3. See Project for the New American Century, "Statement on the Defense of Taiwan," August 20, 1999, http://www.newamericancuentury.org/Taiwandefensestatement.htm.

4. See Richard C. Bush, *At Cross Purposes: U.S. Taiwan Relations Since 1942* (Armonk, NY: M. E. Sharpe, 2004), 239.
5. Steven Mufson and Philip P. Pan, "Spy Plane Delays Irk President," *Washington Post*, April 3, 2001, p. A01. It was reported that Bush "sternly demanded" the return of the twenty-four crewmembers. Members of Congress suggested the crewmembers were hostages and that strategic partnership was dead.
6. Submarines, which are not considered defensive weapons, were included in the package. The U.S. law governing arms sales is the Taiwan Relations Act, which promises only defensive weapons. This, however, is not so startling in view of the fact that Robert Dole pledged to sell Taiwan submarines during the 1996 campaign. See Mann, *Rise of the Vulcans*, 232–33. The size of the package was large, but that was, in part, because sales had been postponed during the last years of the Clinton administration.
7. See Nancy Bernkopf Tucker, "Strategic Ambiguity or Strategic Clarity?" in *Dangerous Strait: The U.S.-China-Taiwan Crisis, ed.* Nancy Bernkopf Tucker (New York: Columbia University Press, 2005).
8. President Bush issued a statement of regret that many, both in the United States and China, considered an apology. The United States had pointed out that, under international law, the smaller plane should move to avoid a collision. Also, U.S. officials said the Chinese pilot was known for harassing U.S. planes by flying too close. See "Whose Fault is It?" *Straits Times*, April 15, 2001, p. 14.
9. See James Mann, *About Face: A History of America's Curious Relationship with China, from Nixon to Clinton* (New York: Alfred A. Knopf, 1998), 175.
10. Mann, *Rise of the Vulcans*, 284. It may also be worth noting that Bush's uncle, Prescott Bush, Jr., had had extensive business ties with China. See James Mann, *The China Fantasy: How Our Leaders Explain Away Chinese Repression* (New York: Viking, 2007), 85.
11. See David Shambaugh, "Sino-American Relations since September 11," and Denny Roy, "China and the War on Terrorism," in Liu, ed., *Chinese Foreign Policy in Transition*, 204, 333.
12. See Mann, *The China Fantasy*, 86.
13. See Bates Gill, *Rising Star: China's New Security Diplomacy* (Washington, DC: Brookings Institution, 2007), 129.
14. Nancy Bernkopf Tucker, "Balancing Act: Bush, Beijing and Taipei," in *George W. Bush and East Asia: A First Term Assessment*, ed. Robert M. Hathaway and Wilson Lee (Washington, DC: Woodrow Wilson International Center for Scholars, 2005), 132. The author notes that China provided the United States with intelligence, helped track financial networks, sealed borders, and helped Pakistan fight al Qaeda.
15. "Bush to Focus on Terror, Security, Economy in Asia Trip," transcript of Condoleezza Rice briefing to the press, February 14, 2002, cited in Jean

A. Garrison, *Making China Policy: From Nixon to G. W. Bush* (Boulder, CO: Lynne Rienner, 2005), 184.

16. "Shaping Ties with China," *Straits Times*, December 1, 2003, http://lexis-nexis.com.
17. This document can be found online at http://www.whitehouse.gov/jsc/nss.html.
18. Colin L. Powell "Remarks at Conference on China-U.S. Relations," November 5, 2003, http://www.state.gov/secrfetary/rm/2003/25950.htm.
19. Tucker, "Balancing Act," 133.
20. John J. Tkacik, Jr., "Strategy Deficit: U.S. Security in the Pacific and the Future of Taiwan," in *Reshaping the Taiwan Strait*, ed. John J. Tkacik, Jr. (Washington, DC: The Heritage Foundation, 2007), 15–18.
21. For details, see Ma Ying-jeou, "Cross-Strait Relations at a Crossroad: Impasse or Breakthrough?" in *Breaking the China-Taiwan Impasse*, ed. Zagoria, 41–43.
22. Ching Chong, *Will Taiwan Break Away? (*Singapore: World Scientific, 2000), 79. For an interpretation of the significance of this, see John F. Copper, "Taiwan in Gridlock: Thoughts on the Chen Shui-bian Administration's First Eighteen Months," in *Taiwan in Troubled Times: Essays on the Chen Shui-bian Presidency*, ed. John F. Copper (Singapore: World Scientific, 2002), 24–25.
23. Alan D. Romberg, *Rein In at the Brink of the Precipice: American Policy toward Taiwan and U.S.-PRC Relations* (Washington, DC: Henry L. Simpson Center, 2003), 199.
24. Ibid., 206–7. The author, however, characterizes Wolfowitz's statement as a slip.
25. Clearly, the Bush administration was angry. According to one writer, Republicans at this juncture had become as annoyed with Chen as Democrats. See Richard C. Bush and Michael E. O'Hanlon, *A War Like No Other: The Truth about China's Challenge to America* (Hoboken, NJ: John Wiley and Sons, 2007), 79.
26. Richard C. Bush, *Untying the Knot: Making Peace in the Taiwan Strait* (Washington, DC: Brookings Institution, 2005), 2.
27. See John F. Copper, *Taiwan's 2004 Presidential and Vice Presidential Election: Democracy's Consolidation or Devolution? (*Baltimore: University of Maryland School of Law, 2004), 20–21.
28. For details on the aftermath of the election and the interview, see John F. Copper, *Taiwan's 2004 Legislative Election: Putting it in Perspective* (Baltimore: University of Maryland School of Law, 2004), 22.
29. Bush, *Untying the Knot*, 252.
30. Ching Cheong, "U.S. Needed to Jolt Taipei Awake," *Straits Times*, October 24, 2004. Taiwan's Foreign Minister Mark Chen called it a "severe blow."

31. For details, see John F. Copper, *Taiwan's 2004 Legislative Election: Putting it in Perspective* (Baltimore: University of Maryland School of Law, 2005); and John F. Copper, "A Referendum on President Chen," *Far Eastern Economic Review*, December 2005.
32. Chen won the presidency with less than 40 percent of the vote and his victory came because the opposition split. Thus, he did not have a good mandate. His party controlled only one-third of the seats in the legislature. A serious standoff followed between Chen, who some said did not know how to govern, and the opposition that thought it was still in power or should be. For details, see John F. Copper, "Taiwan in Gridlock," in Copper, ed., *Taiwan in Troubled Times.*
33. See Shelly Rigger, "The Unfinished Business of Taiwan's Democratization," in Tucker, ed., *Dangerous Strait*, 16–20. As in assessing new administrations in the United States, many Americans feel that a new government can blame the preceding one for problems only for the first three months or so.
34. Taiwan was barely affected by the 1997 "Asian meltdown," which hurt many East and Southeast Asian countries. Many attributed this to Taiwan's better banking system and to government policies in force at the time. Many praised the KMT-run government at that time.
35. President Chen advocated more social programs and programs to cut the gap between rich and poor in the past and during the campaign. Most felt that he had not lived up to expectations, or worse.
36. In 2006, it was reported that six years previous, when Chen Shui-bian became president, Taiwan's gross national product was 30 percent of China's. Now it was 18 percent. South Korea's per capita income, two-thirds of Taiwan's less than a decade earlier, had recently passed Taiwan's. When Chen became president, Kaohsiung was the second busiest port in Asia; now it was number seven. See David DeVoss, "Tear Gas and Running Dogs," *Weekly Standard*, December 4, 2006, p. 18–19.
37. For information on the suicide rate, see "Suicide Rate Rises Further," *Taipei Times*, July 2, 2006, p. 3. For unemployment, see "Youth Unemployment at All Time High," International Labor Organization, August 11, 2004, http://ilo.org. The annual yearbooks on Taiwan published by the Government Information Office, controlled by the presidential office, publishes data on these things, but left crime out of the recent issue.
38. It is projected that the number of first graders will decline by one-third in the next five years and, according to polls, 85 percent attribute the reason for not having children to the economy. See "Lowering Birth Rate Reflects Economic Woes," *China Post*, January 11, 2007, p. 2.
39. Recently, the American Chamber of Commerce in Taiwan suggested that the Chen administration change its "China adverse posture," pointing, in particular, to its foreign investment policies. See "The 40% Regulation's Negative Impact," *Topics*, December 2006.

40. Chen looked to the Taiwanese that hailed from Fukien Province to support him. He saw the Mainland Chinese, who came to Taiwan with Chiang Kai-shek, as his "enemies." He sometimes appealed to the Hakka and the aborigines, but since the Fukien Taiwanese were 65 percent of the population, he often favored them alone.
41. See Kathrin Hille, "Taiwan's Ruling Party Promises to Span Political and Ethnic Divide," *Financial Times*, September 27, 2004. The DPP, in this instance, responded to public demonstrations against President Chen's policies of accentuating ethnic divisions.
42. Recently, a pollster asked whether the ethnic situation is a serious problem: 47.3 percent said "yes," and 38.7 percent said "no." The percentage saying it is serious has risen significantly in recent years. See "Nearly Half say Ethnic Problem 'Serious': Poll," *China Post*, February 26, 2007, p. 1. The poll was done by Academic Sinica.
43. This data can be found online at http://www.rsf.org/article.php3?d_article=4116.
44. This data can be found online at http://www.iscgg.org/corruption.cpi 2006 html.
45. *Kissings Contemporary Archives*, a widely used reference source, in mid-2002, cited a poll taken in Taiwan in which more respondents said the DPP was more corrupt than the KMT. In October, six months after the 2004 election, an opinion poll showed that 49 percent of respondents said the DPP was corrupt (more than KMT); 56 percent expressed dissatisfaction with the DPP; and even more said the DPP had lost its core values. See *United Daily News*, October 7, 2004.
46. See John F. Copper, *Taiwan's 2006 Metropolitan Mayoral and City Council Elections and the Politics of Corruption* (Baltimore: University of Maryland School of Law, 2007), 12–34.
47. In early 2007, a well-respected business magazine published the results of a number of surveys it did. According to its polls, 41.6 percent of respondents were pessimistic about the future, compared to less than 10 percent when Chen Shui-bian became president. Most blamed Chen. A startling 70 percent said they did not think education would improve their lives. More than half said the next generation would not have as good a life (compared to 10 percent who said it would be as good). See "2007 State of the Nation Survey," *CommonWealth*, March 28, 2007, http://www.cw.tw/english/.
48. The United States formally supports a one-China policy, but also demands that the "Taiwan issue" be resolved peacefully and that the people of Taiwan decide their future. A one-China policy could be taken to mean that the United States will help bring about unification; but the latter tenets of American China and Taiwan policy contradict that since the population of Taiwan opposes reunification at the present time.

49. See Carol Lee Hamrin and Zhang Wang, "The Floating Island: Change of Paradigm on the Taiwan Question," *Journal of Contemporary China* (May 2004): 346–47.
50. See "Ma Ying-jeou Scores a Landslide," *Politics from Taiwan*, July 16, 2006, http://jujuflop.yule.org/2005/2007/16/ma-ying-jeou-scores-a-landslide.
51. See Ellen Bork, "One China, One Taiwan," *Weekly Standard*, December 15, 2005. *Weekly Standard* is a noted Neocon publication.
52. See Kathrin Hille, "Cultivated Charisma in the Spotlight Ma Ying-jeou," *Financial Times*, March 13, 2007, http://lexus-nexus.com.
53. Lawrence Chung, "KMT Leader to Raise Arms Deal during U.S. Trip," *South China Morning Post*, March 20, 2006, http://lexus-nexus.com.
54. Goh Sui Noi, "KMT Chief to Explain Party Policy to U.S.," *Straits Times*, March 18, 2006, http://lexus-nexus.com.
55. "Cross-strait Issues and a Vision for Taiwan," *Straits Times*, March 18, 2006, http://lexus-nexus.com.
56. Lawrence Chung, "KMT Chief 'has Secured U.S. Backing,'" *South China Morning Post*, March 29, 2006, http://lexus-nexus.com.
57. "Ma 'agrees' with Chen on weapons purchase from U.S.," *China Post*, November 3, 2006, p. 4. Ma's assistants told American officials that when they talked to Ma (since he speaks impeccable English), nothing will be lost in the translation and that Ma was known for keeping his word (two matters that made many U.S. officials dislike President Chen).
58. See Dennis Van Vranken Hickey, "Continuity and Change: The Administration of George W. Bush and U.S. Policy toward Taiwan," *Journal of Contemporary China* (August 2004): 474.
59. This became obvious during 2006 when President Chen was seemingly about to be forced to resign or would step down. See Copper, *Taiwan's 2006 Metropolitan Mayoral and City Council Elections and the Politics of Corruption*, 62.

Index